PISA and Global Education Policy

Comparative and International Education

A DIVERSITY OF VOICES

Series Editors

Allan Pitman (*University of Western Ontario, Canada*)
Miguel A. Pereyra (*University of Granada, Spain*)
Suzanne Majhanovich (*University of Western Ontario, Canada*)

Editorial Board

Ali Abdi (*University of Alberta, Canada*)
Clementina Acedo (*Webster University Geneva, Switzerland*)
Mark Bray (*University of Hong Kong, China*)
Christina Fox (*University of Wollongong, Australia*)
Steven Klees (*University of Maryland, USA*)
Nagwa Megahed (*Ain Shams University, Egypt*)
Crain Soudien (*University of Cape Town, South Africa*)
David Turner (*University of Glamorgan, England*)
Medardo Tapia Uribe (*Universidad Nacional Autónoma de Mexico*)

VOLUME 48

The titles published in this series are listed at *brill.com/caie*

PISA and Global Education Policy

Understanding Finland's Success and Influence

By

Jennifer Chung

BRILL
SENSE

LEIDEN | BOSTON

All chapters in this book have undergone peer review.

The Library of Congress Cataloging-in-Publication Data is available online at http://catalog.loc.gov

Typeface for the Latin, Greek, and Cyrillic scripts: "Brill". See and download: brill.com/brill-typeface.

ISSN 2214-9880
ISBN 978-90-04-40751-0 (paperback)
ISBN 978-90-04-40752-7 (hardback)
ISBN 978-90-04-40753-4 (e-book)

Copyright 2019 by Koninklijke Brill NV, Leiden, The Netherlands.
Koninklijke Brill NV incorporates the imprints Brill, Brill Hes & De Graaf, Brill Nijhoff, Brill Rodopi, Brill Sense, Hotei Publishing, mentis Verlag, Verlag Ferdinand Schöningh and Wilhelm Fink Verlag.
All rights reserved. No part of this publication may be reproduced, translated, stored in a retrieval system, or transmitted in any form or by any means, electronic, mechanical, photocopying, recording or otherwise, without prior written permission from the publisher.
Authorization to photocopy items for internal or personal use is granted by Koninklijke Brill NV provided that the appropriate fees are paid directly to The Copyright Clearance Center, 222 Rosewood Drive, Suite 910, Danvers, MA 01923, USA. Fees are subject to change.

This book is printed on acid-free paper and produced in a sustainable manner.

*To Jan Dizard, David Phillips, and Michael Crossley,
whose inspiration and support have been invaluable to me over the years*

Contents

Foreword XI
    Michael Crossley
Acknowledgements XIII

  Introduction 1

1 **The Global Context of Education Policy-Making** 6
    1 Introduction 6
    2 The Economic Factor 6
    3 International Achievement Studies 10
    4 The Globalisation and Politicisation of Education Policy 11
    5 Global Trends, Policy Convergence, and Transfer 17
    6 Summary 22

2 **The Backdrop for Success: Finland's Context and Configuration** 24
    1 Introduction 24
    2 History of Finland to Independence 24
    3 Independence and War 29
    4 Finland after World War II and the Golden Age of the Welfare State 32
    5 The 1980s, Recession and Recovery to 1990s Neoliberalism 34
    6 What Makes Finland "Finnish"? 36
    7 Summary 47

3 **The Education System of Finland** 49
    1 Introduction 49
    2 History and Development of the Finnish Education System 49
    3 Educational Legislation in Finland 56
    4 The Current Education System of Finland 58
    5 Education Provision for Minority Groups 65
    6 Teacher Education in Finland 67
    7 Summary 74

4 **The Programme for International Student Assessment: The Birth of an Achievement Study that Captured Worldwide Attention** 75
    1 Introduction 75
    2 The OECD 79
    3 PISA 80
    4 Summary 89

5 Issues of Policy Transfer 91
1. Introduction 91
2. Background and Theory 91
3. Examples of Cross-National Attraction 97
4. Finland and Cross-National Attraction 99
5. Negative External Evaluation 101
6. Examples of Policy Borrowing 102
7. Dangers of Policy Borrowing 103
8. Summary 104

6 Strengths of Finnish Education 106
1. Introduction 106
2. Teachers 106
3. Equality 111
4. High Value of Education 114
5. Structure, Organisation, and Characteristics of Finnish Schools 120
6. Summary 128

7 Weaknesses of Finnish Education 130
1. Introduction 130
2. The Downsides of Mixed Ability Teaching 130
3. Decreasing Importance of Education 137
4. Lack of Enjoyment in School 139
5. Budget Cuts 141
6. Structural Weaknesses 143
7. Summary 145

8 Finnish Responses to PISA 147
1. Introduction 147
2. Positive Responses to PISA 147
3. Negative Responses to PISA 158
4. Additional Responses to PISA 168
5. Summary 175

9 Cross-National Attraction and Education Policy Transfer 177
1. Introduction 177
2. Views of Education Ministers 177
3. Views of Head Teachers 179
4. Views of Teachers 180
5. Views of Professors 182
6. Views from the OECD 186

7   National Character   190
8   Summary   192

10 **The Temptation of Uncritical International Transfer: The Politics of Finland's Success in PISA**   194
1   Introduction   194
2   Policy Transfer   194
3   Examples of the Politicisation of PISA   196
4   Major Policy Borrowing from Finland: The Case of the MTL   200
5   Major Policy Borrowing from Finland: The Case of the White Paper   203
6   Education and Education Policy in the 21st Century   206
7   Summary   209

Conclusion   213

Appendix: List of Participants   219
References   222
Index   233

Foreword

The field of comparative education has long been concerned with the processes of education policy transfer but recent decades have seen a resurgence of interest in this core theme and in the comparative field itself. To some extent this has been generated by the intensification of globalisation and, more specifically, by the influence of cross-national surveys of student achievement and related competitive national league tables. This book recognises these contemporary developments and makes a timely contribution to the international literature on education policy transfer in the light of original theoretical and empirical research on the performance of Finland in the OECD's influential, if controversial, PISA studies.

In my recent Presidential Address (Crossley, 2019) for the British Association for International and Comparative Education (BAICE) I have argued that increased attention should be given to new advances in the international theoretical literature on educational policy transfer, and that this should be used and applied to strengthen the critical analysis of proposals for education policy transfer and "borrowing" worldwide. Without this, it is argued that educational policy that is seen to be successful in one context may struggle to be implemented with any degree of success where the external environment and the internal characteristics of educational milieu differ elsewhere. Context does indeed matter, more than many policy makers, and some researchers, realise. While this has long been argued within the field of comparative education, and attention to policy mediation is increasingly recognised, my own work suggests that context sensitivity continues to be underplayed or overlooked in many policy circles worldwide; and, given the powerful influence of global student achievement league tables, the dangers of uncritical educational policy transfer can be seen to be becoming more frequent and problematic. Jennifer Chung's well informed, locally grounded and clearly argued analysis of these processes in operation has both practical and theoretical potential for policy researchers and theorists, for stakeholders at all levels engaged in education in Finland, and for external observers and analysts involved in learning from the successful experience of Finland in the PISA studies.

This is a most welcome and helpful book that pays close attention to context at all levels – from the global to the national and the local. In doing so, the text develops a lively, well informed and critical analysis of the strengths and weaknesses of the Finnish education system, along with an assessment of implications for the international community, for other systems of education and for the future prospects for education in Finland itself.

Reference

Crossley, M. (2019). Policy transfer, sustainable development and the contexts of education. *Compare: A Journal of Comparative and International Education* (in press).

Michael Crossley
Emeritus Professor of Comparative and International Education
Centre for Comparative and International Research in Education
University of Bristol
UK

Acknowledgements

Although only one person penned this book, many others made it possible.

I thank Michael Crossley for seeing the potential in my research and in my academic career. It is an honour.

I also thank David Phillips, my supervisor and mentor throughout my postgraduate career. I was truly lucky to be under his watchful eye, and his gentle, astute, and intuitive guidance is most appreciated.

Many thanks go to my parents, Whan Soon and Moon Ja Chung, who supported wholeheartedly all of my academic endeavours throughout the years. I also wish to thank Joe McDonald who tirelessly proofread so many drafts of my writing.

I express my appreciation to Mark McDonald for his unwavering, steadfast support and encouragement over the years.

An enormous amount of gratitude goes to the kind people who took part in this study. I extend my thanks to those who generously interviewed with me and offered boundless insight and information. Finally, I thank my friends in Finland, especially Jose Ignacio Villegas, Stuart Ravenscroft, and Kaisa-Leena Juvonen, who made so much of this research possible.

Introduction

In 1900, Michael Sadler delivered a speech in Guildford, England, which embodies one of the underlying purposes of the field of comparative education: "The practical value of studying [...] the working of foreign systems of education is that it will result in our being better fitted to study and to understand our own" (Sadler, in Higginson, 1979, p. 50). The field of comparative education, although traceable to the times of Herodotus in Ancient Greece, has recently seen increased global interest in response to the grown of international achievement tests and comparisons (Phillips & Schweisfurth, 2006). While comparing education has existed since antiquity, this book focuses on more recent times, comparative education in the era of international assessments. This contemporary global context for education, with the work of organisations such as the United Nations Educational, Scientific, and Cultural Organisation (UNESCO), the Organisation for Economic Cooperation and Development (OECD), and the International Association for the Evaluation of Educational Achievement (IEA) has generated an era of highly influential educational comparison on an international scale.

Such international achievement surveys have also placed the spotlight on countries with high educational performance. The Programme of International Student Assessment (PISA), administered by the OECD, which began in 2000, has had a huge impact in the educational world. Finland, traditionally not an avid participant in other international assessments, has attracted much attention due to its leading performance in all assessed areas, and this has given the country new status as a global leader in education. Consistency across the PISA surveys for Finland, coupled with its high performance, makes the country even more alluring to those seeking the guidance of educational models, and this has attracted many to the Finnish education system.

Finland, thus, has become a target for potential education policy transfer. As long as Finland maintains this level of performance in PISA, the education system will continue to attract the interest of other countries seeking to understand the reasons behind its success. This attraction to Finland is now a widely recognised phenomenon, although the Finns perceive this interest in their education system with some bemusement:

> The outstanding success of Finnish students in PISA has been a great joy but at the same time a somewhat puzzling experience to all those responsible for and making decisions about education in Finland. At a

single stroke, PISA has transformed our conceptions of the quality of the work done at our comprehensive school and of the foundations it has laid for Finland's future civilisation and development of knowledge. (Välijärvi et al., 2002, p. 3; 2007, p. 3)

Finland traditionally looked towards other countries for educational examples, first Germany, then later, Sweden (Välijärvi et al., 2002, p. 3). Indeed, a Finnish adage says, "In reforming school, Finland makes exactly the same mistakes as Sweden. Only it happens ten years later" (ibid.). The new international attention has made Finland *the* educational example for other countries. Hence, this has prompted the Finns to look inwards and investigate the perceived exemplary characteristics within the home education system.

Moreover, the case of Finland and subsequent international interest in the education system draws further attention to Sadler's argument, that the exploration of foreign systems of education needs to take careful account of the influence of external factors:

> In studying foreign systems of Education we should not forget that the things outside the schools matter even more than the things inside the schools, and govern and interpret the things inside. We cannot wander at pleasure among the educational systems of the world, like a child strolling through a garden, and pick off a flower from one bush and some leaves from another, and expect that if we stick what we have gathered into the soil at home, we shall have a living plant. A national system of Education is a living thing, the outcome of forgotten struggles and difficulties, and 'of battles long ago.' It has in it some of the secret working of national life. (Sadler, in Higginson, 1979, p. 49)

In other words, in addition to the structure and governance of the Finnish education system, the "things outside the school" also influence contemporary performance and achievements. International surveys of student achievement have impacted, not only upon the stakeholders in education and the educational world, but also upon politicians, the press, and the general public. PISA and other cross-national assessments have placed education in a more visible arena, in addition to providing a catalyst for discussion and debate. Throughout the mass media, the successes and failures of education systems have come under close inspection. Survey results also reach and influence education ministers and politicians, both at home and abroad.

International league tables can also prompt haphazard and unrealistic policy decisions. Indeed, educational competition on an international level has led to an increased impetus to borrow education policy in order to increase future educational attainment. Bringing educational ranking to a global realm has resulted in a paradigm shift for education policy making. Policy is now strongly influenced on this global stage and this is reflected in both local and national arenas. Furthermore, educational accountability has now reached an international level, with tests such as PISA and others measuring the quality of education systems. For these reasons, the global context of education policy-making now increases the danger of "quick fix" policy decisions and the potential for uncritical policy transfer for political reasons. This demonstrates the politicisation of international assessment.

International achievement studies such as PISA have essentially created an educational Olympics. Previous to these assessments, most could only speculate about the best features of education systems, and which countries had the most successfully educated citizens. One could argue that PISA has made a significant contribution to education, allowing nation-states to see their educational strengths and weaknesses, and creating a dialogue from which to discuss education on an international level. The advent of these studies has expanded the possibilities for borrowing, and the temptation to transfer education policy stemming from the attraction some countries exhibit towards "enviable" education systems. A relatively recent phenomenon, such international surveys have already changed the future of education.

The case of Finland in PISA and the subsequent interest in the education system require re-examination of Sadler's speech; the exploration of foreign education systems necessitates examination of external influences (Sadler, in Higginson, 1979, p. 49). In other words, in addition to the structure and governance of the Finnish education system, one must delve into the "things outside the school" and find the factors that positively influence the current education system. This book, therefore, uses PISA and the cross-national attraction it has inspired as a catalyst for further investigation into the Finnish education system. It principally focuses on the perceptions of Finnish educational stakeholders of this attraction and the unique characteristics of Finland and of Finnish education, the cause of so much interest. It also delves into the context of Finland, by exploring its history, society, politics, religion, and culture, and looks at how these factors affect the education system that has been so prominently successful in terms of PISA outcomes. Through semi-structured interviews with educational actors in Finland, it investigates the reasons behind Finnish success in PISA and the factors within the Finnish context that have arguably contributed to the outcomes. Throughout the investigation and exploration of the aforementioned topics, this study addresses the following research question and two sub-questions:

- In light of the results of the OECD's PISA surveys, how can we explain the phenomenon of Finland's educational success?
  - What are the perceptions of Finland's education officials, PISA test administrators, heads of schools, and teachers of this success and how do they explain the outcomes?
  - Which external factors, historical, social, political, and cultural, influence the success of Finland in PISA?

Furthermore, this book examines the reasons for Finland's success in PISA; the contemporary, global context of education policy; policy transfer; and the politicisation of international achievement studies.

Chapter 1 focuses on the global context of education policy-making. It investigates how global factors influence education policy, and how they influence surveys such as PISA. The chapter also explores the close, yet tenuous, relationship between economics and education, including the connection between education and a country's global competitiveness. Related to this, the chapter discusses the power that international organisations now hold over education policy and policymaking.

Chapter 2 focuses on the background of Finland. It explores Finnish history from antiquity to the present, in addition to its languages, society, politics, and religion. Finland's relationship with the Nordic countries and the Nordic Council also comes under discussion, as does the Finnish concept of *sisu*, which arguably plays a significant role in Finnish culture and society. Chapter 3 more specifically details the education system of Finland, its structure and history, including education for Swedish-speaking Finns and the nature and quality of teacher education.

Chapter 4, which focuses on the contextual background of the study, investigates the OECD and PISA in further detail. The chapter also explores the literature on school effectiveness, which has now evolved due to PISA, since it is often assumed that high PISA outcomes relate to school effectiveness.

Chapter 5 explores policy transfer in terms of the comparative education literature, as much of the interest in Finland stems from the attempts to improve education in the "home" context. Comparative education as a field has had a resurgence, due to the renewed interest in education policy transfer on both an academic level, and especially within education policy and practice. This renewed interest correlates to the high impact of international achievement studies such as PISA. Because successful performance in PISA has resulted in increased global interest in the Finnish education system, the chapter examines the processes of policy borrowing.

Chapter 6 identifies the strengths of Finnish education, from the perspectives of empirical research gathered from education ministers, professors of education, head teachers, teachers, and OECD officials. Chapter 7 similarly explores the weaknesses of Finnish education also from these diverse perspectives. Chapter 8 takes into account the responses and reactions to PISA as an assessment, and to its impact, from those involved in the Finnish education system as well as OECD officials.

Chapter 9 then contains the views of Finnish Ministers of Education, professors of education, head teachers, and teachers about the attention Finland has received due to PISA and the possibility of education policy transfer, taking into account the beliefs of OECD officials.

Chapter 10 revisits the political and economic influences on education policy, and examines the pressures to borrow Finnish education policy in order to improve performance in international "league tables." This chapter thus explores the temptation to borrow education policy and practice from high-achieving countries such as Finland, and the politicisation of achievement studies such as PISA.

The attention Finland has received due to PISA has unleashed a worldwide fascination with the country and has prompted education policy decisions, often misinformed and haphazard. This book thus aims to uncover the story behind the "Finland Phenomenon," to shed light upon the history, context, intricacies, and nuances that build today's Finnish education system. Therefore, analysts should keep Sadler's comments in mind, even as they view the Finnish education system with high regard and respect.

CHAPTER 1

The Global Context of Education Policy-Making

1   Introduction

Global factors increasingly influence education policy. International assessments and their escalating importance illustrate a standardisation trend within and among education systems (Kamens & McNeely, 2009). International agencies such as IEA, which runs the Trends in Mathematics and Science Survey (TIMSS) and the Progress in Reading Literacy Survey (PIRLS), and the OECD, which generated the Programme for International Student Assessment (PISA), help disseminate the norms, models, and techniques for testing. It has been argued that international organisations such as these have more influence than national conditions in international education reform. International achievement studies increasingly shape education systems, and this intense testing culture comes from a new, modern obsession with education (e.g. Kamens & McNeely, 2009; Pongratz, 2006; Moutsios, 2009, 2010; Takayama, 2008, 2009). This constant need for improvement, combined with the increase in international assessments, sets a new, global context for education policy-making.

2   The Economic Factor

The relationship between education and economics has been firmly established, and this phenomenon only seems to grow in today's continually changing view of education. A country's economic status dictates the perception of its social institutions, especially its education system. A country with a booming economy, therefore, finds much merit in its own education system. Conversely, a country that faces economic problems or an economic decline is quick to blame its education system as a source of its financial problems. For example, the much-envied economy of Japan in the 1980s gathered attention from around the world, and even within the country itself (Tobin et al., 2009). The economy, a source of admiration at that time, gave the education system positive reinforcement, and even credit, for Japan's economic success in that era. However, the economic decline of the Asian economy of the 1990s, which included Japan, "created a climate of pessimism, blame, and recrimination," where parents and teachers blamed one another for the flaws and shortcomings of Japanese children at the time (ibid., p. 228). The praise and self-satisfaction with which

Japan, and the rest of the world, viewed the Japanese education system disappeared. According to Tobin et al., "an economic crisis leads to harsher analyses of social institutions and to an eagerness to blame" (ibid.). The Japanese thus placed some of this blame upon their education system. This example illustrates the close connection and relationship between education and economics, especially when giving credit for success or placing blame for failure.

Similarly, Tobin et al. (2009) cite how over the past two decades, economics has driven change into some social institutions, including education, and use the example of early childhood education to illustrate this. The relationship between education and economics has caused, for example, US politicians to stress the importance of literacy and academic readiness in the early years in order to keep the country economically powerful in the future. Similar initiatives have occurred within the UK, where policy changes have emphasised the professionalisation of early childhood teachers and the importance of early years education on an individual's life and their impact on the country's economy (Palaiologou, 2010).

Thus, the relationship between education and economics deeply influences education policy-making. Waldow (2008) even asserts that education policy making has always relied on the relationship between education and economics, as a general assumption exists that the development of education policy is a reaction to economics. A certain "time lag" occurs between economic occurrences and education policy discourse, as policy makers must note these happenings within the economy before discussion about education policy change can occur. This implies that education policy change generally happens after times of economic difficulty, and perhaps this occurs not only on the nation-state level, but also continentally and globally, depending on the state of the economy within a regional, continental, and global context.

Economics also affects the changing role of education in society. Kamens and McNeely write about the role of education in society in terms of educational ideology. As countries can no longer rely on natural resources for economic stability and growth, "brain power" becomes increasingly important (2009, p. 10). Education, therefore, benefits both the individual and the nation. These benefits also involve economic growth and prosperity. Furthermore, globalisation has made significant changes in world culture, and education now needs to prepare individuals for their role locally, nationally, and internationally, as global citizens. In addition to this, an individual's role locally, nationally, and internationally also involves economics, as education prepares people for future economic attainment. International achievement studies, therefore, hold much importance for countries, for they give an idea of educational achievement, and thus of economic success. Politicians have a vested interest in achieving high rankings in international league tables and have an impetus to steer policy in this direction.

In addition to the economic influences on education policy, Waldow (2008) argues that neo-institutionalism also influences education policy discourse, and then ultimately formation. Modernising societies feel compelled to conform to a world polity based upon western values, and international organisations facilitate this by instigating and disseminating these visions of world polity. One could argue that these organisations coerce nation-states and municipalities into adopting these views and visions, as countries feel the need to conform in order to increase their legitimacy in the world arena. Although PISA is a relatively new phenomenon, its example neatly fits into Waldow's assertions. International organisations, such as the OECD, hand down their values, including educational values as dictated by PISA, onto the world. PISA then produces a set of educational benchmarks and standards, as imagined by the OECD, which then disseminates these globally. The publishing of PISA results, in league table format, forces conformity to these new educational standards, and therefore world polity. This pattern of conformity also applies to education and education policy. Neo-institutionalism's influence on education policy discourse and formation, therefore, can complement the relationship between economics and education, as illustrated by the OECD. The role of the OECD expanded with the implementation of PISA, developing a particularly high reputation internationally for education and educational research and issues. Furthermore, the Organisation, in addition to setting educational standards, strengthens the relationship between economics, education, and education policy. Even its name, the Organisation for Economic Cooperation and Development, again emphasises the relationship between economics and education.

Due to this shift of educational power from the local and national level to the transnational space, education policy transfer has altered (Waldow, 2008). The definition of educational success now becomes quantified according to surveys such as PISA. Because of this, transnational policy now defines the new meaning of educational success, and education policy borrowers and lenders both make policy change and comparison in reference to PISA. The search for supposed "best practice" has come under a new context, as these transnational policies now define new educational aims. For example, international surveys such as PISA can trigger education reform at the school level. Germany's PISA-Shock, as discussed later in this book, is one such example. Despite international organisations such as the OECD disseminating their view of world polity, and setting educational benchmarks and standards, the possibility of education policy transfer, according to Waldow, has been overlooked. Later chapters in this book discuss the issue of policy transfer and its difficulties, along with the transformation that a policy must make in order to be properly implemented. In fact, Waldow astutely states that an analysis of the "concrete processes through which the national and the international discourse on educational policy-making are constructed" would be of most interest (ibid., p. 247).

In addition to this neo-institutionalism, neoliberal economic values also affect education policy (Moutsios, 2009). These values emphasise human capital production, the growth of economies, and global competitiveness, further illustrating the close connection between education, education policy, and economics. The OECD, through PISA, envisions education as a vehicle for economic development. Therefore, in this view, education promotes and contributes to economic productivity. The OECD's measurements of education, such as PISA, are designed to measure human capital. The focus of PISA's assessment does not involve traditional measurements of school curricula; rather, it looks at the application of real life knowledge. The structure of PISA is discussed at length in Chapter 4, but international assessments' transition from a survey of curricula learned to a measurement of human capital further illustrate the increasingly influential relationship between education and economics. Transnational organisations such as the World Bank, the OECD, the International Monetary Fund (IMF), and the World Trade Organisation (WTO) agree that policy, including education policy, needs to cultivate human capital, social capital, and social cohesion of society. It is through this that individuals can better access economic resources. This agreement among these international organisations reinforces Waldow's (2008) world polity view.

Transnational and international organisations arguably define educational aims, as these international institutions view education as a tool to promote a country's economy in terms of global economic competition (Moutsios, 2009). As stated previously, the increasingly close relationship between economics and education, along with globalisation, has moved policy influences from the local and nation-state level to an international realm. Both national and transnational bureaucracies de-democratise the education decision-making process. Thus, stakeholders' influence on potential education policy has decreased, as international organisations have more power and influence in setting educational agendas. In other words, the rise of global business has also influenced the agenda setting in education and education policy. Policies of significance now find influences from the international level, indicating an "asymmetrical" distribution of power; the power lies within the global economy and global competitiveness rather than taking into account national needs (ibid.). Thus, the increasingly economic view of education has therefore changed education policy and policy-making.

3   International Achievement Studies

International achievement studies such as PISA play a large, and increasing, role in the global context of education policy-making. As discussed, education has ascended to a global stage in recent years, as its role in economic development and democracy has been widely documented and accepted (Kamens & McNeely, 2009). Globalisation and the globalisation of economics and education, therefore, have led to a recent explosion of international achievement studies. Earlier, it was argued that international organisations impose world polity with a power shift to the transnational level, which produces asymmetrical policy influences. However, Kamens and McNeely state that benchmarks generated by these assessments allow educational actors to see the strengths and weaknesses within their education systems, recognise supposed "best practice," and plot a trajectory for improvement. The production of these surveys and their now firm existence in the educational world has produced a relationship between international achievement studies, policy change, and education reform.

International assessments have added to the global rise in testing. The growth of standardised testing, especially on the international level, has made assessment an obligation on the national level as well (Kamens & McNeely, 2009). Interestingly, the rise in international testing has led to a corresponding increase in national assessments, especially in the primary and lower secondary sectors. A culture of testing has spread worldwide. The national assessments often mirror the international assessments, meaning they evaluate achievement in the same subjects. This trend could relate to Waldow's and Moutsios' views that the transnational level now shapes policy. In fact, national assessments occur nearly all over the world, are increasingly on the rise, and are, in essence, commonplace in today's educational realm. This signals a new purpose for educational testing. Formerly, educational testing measured students' ability to enter the next stage of education, for example, the 11+ exam in England. Currently, however, educational assessment measures the outcomes of education systems, and the pressure to test is strong. Kamens and McNeely attribute the mass growth in educational testing to three main reasons: world educational ideology, the hegemony of science, and the notion of a "managed" society (2009, p. 9).

Kamens and McNeely (2009) argue the world educational ideology accepts that education is needed to contribute to the labour market, and that education and the economy are intrinsically linked. Therefore, the creation of international assessments helps measure human capital and future economic success. Secondly, they state that the hegemony of science also contributes to the increase in international achievement studies. Viewing the world in a rational, scientific way encourages viewing education as governed by causal laws and relationships. This positivist view encourages measurement of education, not only nationally, but also internationally. Therefore, this scientific perspective allows educational experts to isolate supposed "best practice." The results of surveys such as PISA allow for such measurement. The increase in international achievement studies stems from the belief that the discovery of good methodologies and "best practice" will improve achievement in education systems. When identified, the supposed "best practice" is "distilled" into an easily transferable "tool kit" for practical use (ibid., p. 12). This "distilled" form may travel far from its original context. This book also addresses the importance of educational context in comparative education theory, in terms of the reasons for Finland's success in PISA, and in terms of policy transfer. The "distillation" of "best practice," while useful in the global context of education policy reform, may indicate that uninformed and uncritical policy transfer has occurred. Policy borrowing and uncritical transfer are therefore discussed at length in Chapter 5.

Finally, Kamens and McNeely attribute the increase in international testing to the spreading view that society can be "managed" (2009, p. 13). Successful models of success, as indicated by assessments such as PISA, inspire education policy makers. Finland has become such a source of inspiration. This managerial view of society allows for standardised answers to educational problems, also promoting the need for testing. Assessments and benchmarking facilitate this. A managerial view of education could stem from the importance of economic success attached so closely to education. Thus, the increasingly managerial approach to education calls for a standardised view of the discipline, promoting the need for testing and models of successful systems.

4   The Globalisation and Politicisation of Education Policy

Both champions and sceptics of globalisation acknowledge how the increasing exchange of "goods, ideas, and people" diminishes the uniqueness of culture, and that nation-states increasingly become more similar (Tobin et al., 2009, p. 231). Globalisation in terms of "world systems theory" states that "powerful" countries export their ideas which then prevail over those of less dominant countries (ibid.). Therefore, the world becomes more aligned with one system and its dominant ideologies, including those of education. A "powerful" country could be defined as one with economic prosperity, a large population, or perceived educational success, for example, top scores in PISA. Tobin et al.'s statement relates to Waldow's view of conforming to a world polity and Moutsios' argument of asymmetrical power. Although Tobin et al. do not refer to international organisations or transnational spaces, the domination of certain ideas certainly echoes these views.

Education policy research has recently looked internationally for inspiration for national change (Jakobi, 2009). For example, when looking to make reforms within a nation-state, politicians and policy makers look internationally to find valid and successful education policies. A country with top scores on PISA could provide such an inspiration. Through this, education has become part of a global policy process. This has uncovered a "rescaling" of politics and policy, and "sociological institutionalism" has highlighted the importance of a world society on a national level, illustrating that national and international policy development are intertwined and interrelated (ibid.). Needless to say, these changes to general policy also greatly affect education policy. The growing literature in reference to this, for example, on policy transfer, confirms this internationalisation of education policy. Much of this literature is discussed throughout the book.

Currently, education policy bases itself on objectives and data produced at the international level by international organisations (Moutsios, 2010). International organisations, such as the OECD, have become both "in authority" and "an authority" (ibid.) in terms of education. Therefore, these international agencies "are valued as superior and neutral agencies of policy formation" (ibid., p. 125). Transnational institutions remain neutral by utilising specialised knowledge, such as giving solutions to problems. The use of such data by governments and the mass media shows the authority agencies hold, such as the OECD with its PISA data. However, the interpretation of or use of these data does not indicate that they are used in a neutral manner. In fact, the mass media and government officials use PISA data to put forth certain agendas and reforms. These are discussed at length later in the book.

International influences often affect policy on a national level, using top-down approaches (Jakobi, 2009). However, this does not represent the only way international influences disperse. Policy diffusion can also occur, where countries all over the world adopt specific policies. In other words, policy diffusion happens when the adoption of an idea occurs and spreads to international political systems. For example, one could argue that the 1988 Education Act in England is one such example of policy diffusion. The Global Education Reform Movement, or GERM, discussed more fully later in this book, introduced competition, standardisation, and accountability to the vernacular of education policy-making and reform (Sahlberg, 2011). The increasing importance of and attention to international assessments adds to both of these methods of policy dispersion and diffusion. Both the top-down approach, such as the Master's in Teaching and Learning (MTL) in England, discussed further in Chapter 10, as well as the aforementioned policy diffusion model illustrates a movement towards international goals. These international goals could come from standards set by international organisations, such as the OECD, and their educational surveys, such as PISA. In order to assess the impact of international influences on policy, such as education policy, one must measure the impact of global policies by depth in one country and breadth in the number of countries influenced by the policy. The internationalisation, along with the breadth and depth of policy influence, shows the increasingly common ground of policy (Jakobi, 2009).

Politics does not equal policy making (Moutsios, 2010). Politics questions and challenges a society's laws and institutions, while allowing citizens to form new laws and institutions and to see them through. Education politics, therefore, allows citizens to question teaching and learning, and, if necessary, promote reform. Ideally, stakeholders, the citizens, should have a vested interest in education politics and the ability to influence reforms to benefit them, their children, and their country. Similarly, expertise does not equal political opinion. Policy-making requires knowledge and specialisation; therefore, it should be removed from politics. However, this is not the case. Politics and policy-making have become more closely intertwined with the new global influence on education and education policy. Moutsios cites that, in the twentieth century, bureaucracies such as ministries, inspectorates, and statistical services made up the core of education policy-making. This, much like Kamens and McNeely (2009) stated, implies that policy-making has now become influenced by positivist and scientific views, that the stakeholder has been taken away from the process, and that politics and policy-making are too closely connected.

International organisations also create a forum for a discussion of global public policy (Jakobi, 2009). The ability to allow for this public policy space on a global level allows policy, including education policy, to ascend to a more international role. International organisations have the ability to direct political activity and address political issues with a global impact. Therefore, they set national policy change. They use "coordinative functions," or surveillance and monitoring systems, which assess the progress of countries achieving a common aim (ibid., p. 476). Once again, the case of the OECD and PISA allows for illustration of Jakobi's assertions. For example, the OECD is such an international organisation, and it measures, by surveillance and monitoring, the common aim of educational achievement through PISA. Therefore, transnational organisations influence national policy and internationally-influenced policy change within countries. Organisations such as the OECD can be agenda-setters. Therefore, the emergence of this global policy space, through international organisations such as the OECD and its international surveys, influences policy on a national level.

Moutsios also argues that the OECD allows for "surveillance" of wealthy countries' economic outputs, which thus influences global politics (2009, p. 468). This echoes Jakobi's (2009) view that transnational organisations use surveillance in order to monitor their goal of member countries achieving a common aim, in this case, educational goals and targets. Since the 1990s, the OECD has significantly expanded its already existing role in education policy to the role it holds today as the generator of PISA. Furthermore, the OECD has even expanded its role in global education policy. In 2013, the Organisation released its first Programme for the International Assessment of Adult Competencies (PIAAC), assessing adults aged 16–65 in 24 countries in literacy, numeracy, and problem-solving skills (OECD, 2013a). Much like PISA, PIAAC measures these skills in reference to "real" life. Furthermore, the OECD hopes to carry out a full survey measuring higher education students' skills upon graduation. The Assessment of Higher Education Learning Outcomes (AHELO) was completing its Feasibility Studies in 2013 (OECD, 2014). These new assessments confirm the role of surveillance by transnational organisations, especially the OECD. This further illustrates the OECD's growing role in influencing education policy and change.

Thematic analyses undertaken since this time have allowed the OECD to expand its role in education policy, as well as expand the breadth and depth of its role in education policy, in much more of an international arena. PISA, PIACC, and AHELO signify the OECD's expanded "surveillance," especially into the education realm and in terms of global education policy. For example, PISA has caused political crises, as with German PISA-Shock, discussed in Chapter 10. Education ministers often use PISA as a benchmark when discussing educational reform (Moutsios, 2009). The advent of PISA has created a paradigm shift in education policy-making. It allows for concrete evidence of a country's performance within an international context, and these benchmarks and league table-like results lead to increased global competition within the educational realm. The creation of PIAAC and AHELO, in addition to PISA, only shows that this will grow.

The differences between policy and research, due to international organisations, have become blurred. What was once considered research may now constitute policy, and a difficulty exists in distinguishing the line between policy and research (Moutsios, 2009). The implications, thus, are that "the production and use of specialist knowledge is of crucial importance both as a process and as an instrument of policy making" (ibid., p. 471). The OECD's research agenda, meaning the quantitative data for educational comparison, gives legitimacy to its influence over global education policy. National education policy now comes from decisions made from data stemming from this transnational research. Transnational policy-making, as stated previously, de-democratises the decision-making carried out in the new, global context of education policy.

Therefore, these internationally-influenced reforms have allowed for a standardisation of education, implemented in order to promote this global competitiveness (Moutsios, 2010). Nation-states agree to this, due to the importance of global competitiveness, globalising education policy, and the power of international organisations. These institutions, in essence, ask nation-states to become globally competitive through the measurement of skills and knowledge. Furthermore, the OECD officially states that all education should lead to a rise in productivity. As mentioned previously, the OECD has launched data collection for more education surveys. AHELO will, no doubt, much like PISA, become an attention-grabbing survey, but this time, of higher education. PIAAC managed to make waves within the mass media with its first release in 2013. If PIAAC follows PISA's pattern, the global interest in the survey will grow exponentially over time. The launch of data collection for AHELO and PIAAC perhaps has changed the definition of education. Global productivity now defines education systems, despite the deep roots within each education system's unique context.

Societies and nation-states no longer have abstract goals to which their education systems guide the citizens (Moutsios, 2010). This new view of education stresses that societies should be heading towards goals set by transnational institutions' global policy-making. The OECD is one such notable leader in this process. Progress is now measured in a global context and subject to policy influenced by these transnational institutions. It can be seen as evidence-based policy making, as quantitative measures and benchmarks are produced, as seen with PISA. However, this chapter will later suggest that surveys such as PISA force "policy-based evidence-making" (Yore et al., 2010, p. 597). Nevertheless, education, now regarded as central to a society's and a nation-state's advancement, has become measurable. These measurements, compared internationally, will occur well into the future. A survey such as PISA certainly looks as if it will continue measuring and ranking education systems for years to come, and the addition of PIAAC and AHELO confirms this. Therefore, progress in education now translates into high scores in international assessments and the benchmarks they produce. While this view envisions education as measurable in quantitative terms, it cannot measure true progress:

> There can be no progress, and therefore no measurement, if by education we mean cultivation of the inner self, individual and collective autonomy, freedom of spirit, the search for and creation of personal meaning; in other words, if we mean *paideia*. (Moutsios, 2010, p. 135)

Nevertheless, the paradigm shift of education's purpose in terms of economic survival, and ultimately success, allows it to succumb to measurement (Moutsios, 2010). Transnational education policy has become legitimate. The reasons why involve the evidence-based policy-making by international organisations such as the OECD and its PISA test, and the view that societies progress through production potential and capacity. For this reason, this form of expert-driven policy-making is now valid and dispersed globally. This parallels the earlier discussion of policy dispersion, and the example of the 1988 Education Act in England, and GERM (Sahlberg, 2011). Education around the world, therefore, is moving in the same direction. The "faming" and "shaming" by transnational organisations allow for this acceptance (Moutsios, 2010, p. 136). Therefore, the power in education policy-making has shifted from local actors to the transnational level.

The league tables that PISA has created, in addition to the targets that they set every three years, have led to the increased politicisation of these international achievement studies. This is also discussed at length in Chapter 10. For example, Goldstein asserts that these positivist and quantitative targets are "dysfunctional" and that "any rise in test scores should not be confused with a rise in learning achievement as opposed to test-taking performance" (2004a, p. 10). These numerical targets, even on the international level, have led to "highly dysfunctional consequences" (ibid.). He worries about the "distorting effects that 'high stakes' target setting can lead to, by encouraging individuals to adapt their behaviour in order to maximise perceived awards; viewed as a rational response to external pressures" (ibid., p. 8). In other words, education policy makers can use and do use PISA achievement as a goal from which to tailor education policy. Goldstein warns of the possible politicisation of high-stakes testing, applicable to the influence PISA can have on education, education policy, and politics:

> When learning outcomes are made the focus of targets, those who are affected will change their behaviour so as to maximise their 'results,' even where this is dysfunctional in educational terms. At the international level it would not be surprising if we witnessed similar kinds of behaviour where the curriculum and educational infrastructures were manipulated to maximise performance on the international performance measures, whatever the deleterious side effects that this might produce. (Goldstein, 2004a, p. 11)

He recommends that policy should not concentrate on these aforementioned targets, but should design "delivery, curriculum design, pedagogy, financial incentives, etc. that work best *within each country*. Each educational system can develop different criteria for assessing quality, enrolment, etc. [...] instead of monitoring progress towards an essentially artificial set of targets" (2004a, p. 13). Unfortunately, as Moutsios argued, a country's individual context and specific needs are not addressed in the new world polity and transnational policy space.

Pongratz describes PISA as a "power stabiliser" (2006, pp. 471, 481), for which PISA "functions as a switching point as well as a driving force" (ibid., p. 481). It not only sets standards, but it also sets into motion a "never-ending hunt" for achievement in the survey, as "the push for improved performance never stops" (ibid.). PISA instills an enormous pressure for reform, but pressure in a global sense. It has both an academic and a political agenda, more specifically, the OECD's agenda of reforming education along business and economic principles. This economically competitive view of education colours the perception of PISA, as people view it through this globally-imposed lens. PISA is also not neutral; rather, the OECD has established its own standards of education and education measurement. For example, the notion of "literacy" within the PISA context differs from traditional definitions of the word. This signifies a "commercialisation of knowledge" (ibid., p. 478). Furthermore, PISA does not measure the past, but rather the ability to deal with the future.

5   Global Trends, Policy Convergence, and Transfer

With the appearance of transnational policy-making and the increased importance of international organisations, and with countries striving to achieve the same numerical targets, comes the inevitable risk of policy convergence. The emergence of common education policies has been documented for decades (Grek et al., 2009; Moutsios, 2010). However, the globalisation trends discussed in the previous section illustrate the increasing pace of education policy influences and agenda-setting at the transnational level.

The quantitative educational goals, shift in decision-making power, global policy space, and thus the potential policy convergence, have not only seen their influence in developed, rich countries. They have started impacting education and development in the "south." King illustrates how multi-lateral agencies prescribe development goals for countries in the "south" while not taking into account each individual country's needs and specific contexts:

> In an age when it has become mandatory for donors to stress the importance of the country's ownership of their own education agendas, it would indeed be paradoxical to discover that the allegedly global education

agenda was perceived by many analysts in the south to have been principally developed by multilateral agencies in the north. (2007, p. 378)

Although policy documents such as the Jomtien Framework and the policy document released by the Development Assistance Committee of the OECD "stress the need for a highly context-dependent approach," the commitment to context becomes buried under quantitative goals (King, 2007, p. 382). For example, in the Jomtien Declaration and Framework for Action, the main authors came from multi-lateral agencies. Despite, then, this need for a "highly context-dependent approach," the policies are drafted by multi-lateral agencies, and even the ones that create international achievement studies (ibid., p. 381). The agendas, therefore, of these agencies trickle down into the context-dependent stakeholders. This outcome foreshadows current education policy formation in the advent of PISA. The interest in Finland could lead to uncritical transfer of its education policy. King's illustrations of the power of multi-lateral agencies could easily apply to the influence of PISA in future education policy, where a policy is implemented into a country with no regard for a "highly context-dependent approach."

The influence of international organisations such as the OECD and its PISA survey has also spawned policy spaces and a power shift to the continental level. Grek et al. discuss the notion of a "European Education Policy Space" and its possible relation to international education comparisons (2009, p. 5). This growth in international education data marks a change from national policy to European policy. This European policy space allows for global educational agendas to reach the national policy agendas. Europeanisation has turned the concept of European education from the fuzzy goals of cultural cohesion to a more clearly defined educational competition through cross-national studies such as PISA. Policy makers tend to target outcomes, and with the existence of PISA, a top performance in it. In other words, a supposed "world-best" education system is achieved by success in PISA. Thus, policy makers feel pressured by both European and global influences to succeed in terms of measurement and numerical targets. The OECD, through PISA, while not an educational institution, has strongly established itself as an agency that develops comparative educational data. Furthermore, the OECD now influences the collection of European Union (EU) educational statistics, which, we may infer, will lead to policy convergence and "a global education policy field" (ibid., p. 8). Global forces increasingly influence education worldwide.

However, in more recent years, education policy, as previously discussed, has moved to an international level due to the influence of international organisations. This economically-based view of education has created a "common world educational culture" and a "globally structured educational agenda" (Dale, 2000; Rizvi & Lingard, 2000). The Common World Educational Culture, which views education as a world cultural institution, preceded the pressures of globalisation. However, The Globally Structured Agenda for Education shows the impact of globalisation and economic pressures on education systems, forcing them to adhere to common global agendas (Dale, 2000; Moutsios, 2010; Rizvi & Lindgard, 2000). In other words, economic globalisation has created this transnational education policy space (Moutsios, 2010) and supranational policy flow (Rizvi & Lindgard, 2000). This idea of education and the progress needed to meet its goals gives permission to make policy changes across societies, national borders, and different education systems.

Even in 1995, Halpin and Troyna describe how the "global village," perhaps a nod to globalisation, increased the allure of policy borrowing (p. 304). Borrowing of education policy gave legitimacy to related policies in the home country, as borrowing requires a "synchrony" between the countries involved (ibid.). Even in the mid-1990s, the increasing development of information technology gives enough basis to argue that this, along with the globalisation of economies, influenced the scale and pace of education borrowing, and even policy convergence. Halpin and Troyna also believed that policy borrowing, or at least the possibility of it, helps the analysis of education policy on an international level, and also leads to the universalisation of education reform. Politicians have more interest in a borrowed policy's political power than in the actual implications on the home education system. Therefore, in this view, policies have less significance than the political discourse they generate. Thus, policy borrowing "has more to do with form than content" (Halpin & Troyna, 1995, p. 308), suggesting possible policy convergence would occur due to policy implementation for political influence, rather than educational improvement.

Tobin et al. (2009, p. 231) also discuss the "modernisation/rationalisation" view of globalisation. This follows social Darwinism, suggesting that "over time the most rational, effective educational approaches spread, replacing tradition-bound local approaches," resulting in convergence (ibid.). This includes the convergence of educational policy, theory, and practice. The importance of international achievement studies and the increased influence of economics on education could contribute to this education policy convergence. Furthermore, the previous discussion about policy diffusion (Jakobi, 2009) relates to this. Could the GERM movement, meaning the spread of educational values such as accountability and testing relate to Tobin et al.'s arguments as well? One could argue that the transnational policy space and the politicisation of international achievement studies have led to a convergence of policy, theory, and practice, resulting in the increased power of the transnational policy space over national education policy, and the importance of testing on local, national, and international levels.

However, has this supposed convergence affected education systems as a whole? According to Tobin et al. (2009), the answer is no. Cultural factors play too much of an important role. A detailed discussion of the importance of culture as well as policy borrowing will occur later in this book. For example, "the globalisation of early childhood educational ideas does not flow evenly over time and space" (ibid.). Countries spend time looking outward, but often spend much time looking inward. Tobin et al. use the case of the Reggio Emilia approach, from Italy, as a huge influence in the early childhood sector internationally. They argue, that while the residents of Reggio Emilia have great pride in their preschool system, other citizens of other Italian towns hold the same pride in their own early years schools. "What makes Reggio Emilia's system of childcare and education so special is the same thing that makes Italian wines and cheeses so special – each reflects the locale where it is made" (ibid., p. 233). Therefore, transporting the Reggio Emilia system to the United States, for example, strips it of the ideals of the town itself, not compatible with most American political ideologies. In other words, the Reggio Emilia preschool system is embedded in its socialist principles. The US version of Reggio Emilia has thus been "stripped" of its Italian context, and therefore differs from its original intent. Tobin et al. state that educational policies and practice that move from one country to another, successfully, either have been intentionally designed in a context-free manner, or have been "stripped" of their local context (ibid., pp. 233–234). This echoes the "distillation" process and "toolkit" analogy presented by Kamens and McNeeley (2009) earlier in this chapter.

On a related note, despite all of the attention placed on the success of Japanese education in the 1980s, as discussed previously in this chapter, very little interest has existed in borrowing from their system of early childhood education (Tobin et al., 2009). Tobin et al. suggest this is not down to a lack of literature. They state that "Japanese early childhood education is deeply contextual and resistant to decontextualisation, and therefore, to global circulation" (ibid., p. 239). They argue that such approaches to education can fall into two categories, implicit or self-consciously constructed. This implies that policy convergence does not or cannot occur wholesale and affect entire education systems. A constructed education system often has a pioneering author, such as Maria Montessori, and textbooks and training manuals. The implicit systems, such as Japan's approach to early childhood education, reflect their "deep cultural logic" (ibid.). Furthermore, Japanese preschool aims to make the children Japanese. Tobin et al. imply that this "asymmetric" power and global education policy do not affect all sectors of education.

Yore et al. believe that PISA provides rich opportunities to influence education policy, and they believe the second cycle of PISA, beginning in 2009, allowed for a "sober look" at the first cycle of PISA and its results (2010, p. 594). They do cite, however, that myth can influence policy more than science. They argue that impatient politicians looking for change succumb to myth rather than research. This suggests that the myths generated by PISA have led to policy reform. Therefore, it becomes less likely that research actually informs education policy reform. In fact, policy makers have a tendency to "formulate, announce, and implement policy then encourage research engagement that could retrospectively support the policy" (ibid., p. 597). Here PISA is used as a political tool to justify political actions and policy change. Instead of evidence-based policy change, as Moutsios (2010) suggested earlier in this chapter, it is "policy-based evidence-making" (Yore et al., 2010, p. 597). This dangerous reversal of policy protocol illustrates the lack of informed policy making, and the "phony" and "quick fix" policy decisions made by politicians, discussed later in this book.

Yore et al. cite two cases of policy reform supposedly based on PISA, but where one case illustrates how politicians used PISA for "policy-based evidence making" (2010, p. 597). They contrast Germany's reaction to a mediocre PISA performance, where research influenced policy change, with Denmark's own allegedly PISA-influenced policy reforms. Germany's well-documented PISA-Shock led to policy change, but as Yore et al. argue, it was well-aligned with Germany's context. However, Denmark's policy reactions to PISA have had a more negative impact. While Danish reforms seemed in tune to the release of PISA results in terms of time, they were actually under the influences of the political party in power. Therefore, these reforms did not align with the context of Danish education. Yore et al. thus call for a need to link PISA locally and nationally, to keep PISA relevant to nation-states and their own educational contexts and endeavours. The examples of Germany and Denmark illustrate the politicisation of PISA, and the use of PISA as an education policy tool. PISA's influence on policy and politics has had enormous consequences. Denmark's use of PISA to mask political agendas and related policy reform shows the dangerous nature of retrospective policy justification and dysfunctional importance of numerical targets. Additionally, we see here the importance of context, especially when considering educational reform and policy borrowing. These implications will be discussed at length later in this book.

6   Summary

Education has evolved from a local entity to a global phenomenon, as international factors now deeply influence education policy. Human capital and "brain power" now dominate the idea of education, rather than the more humanistic vision of learning for learning's sake and self-improvement. International organisations help pass these values onto the world, and emphasise the role of economics in education. Education, therefore, has become a tool for global economic competition. The international assessments created by transnational agencies help set the norms for testing and the new standardisation trend in education. Thus, the international realm now has more influence on education than the national arena. Economics, globalisation, and international organisations hold much influence over this new, global education policy.

Economics and education have an established relationship. For example, a good economy acknowledges a successful education system and, conversely, a country with a struggling economy could easily place blame upon a faulty education system. Therefore, education policy and policy change often occur as a reaction to economics and economic instability. Neo-institutionalism influences education policy formation, as international organisations coax nation-states into adopting world polity. Furthermore, economic neoliberalism encourages viewing human capital as connected with the economy and, ultimately, a country's global competitiveness. Education, therefore, is seen as important for economic development. Through the OECD and surveys such as PISA, international agencies now define educational aims and measure educational success in quantifiable terms. Decision-making, due to these organisations, now lies at the transnational and global level.

International achievement studies now hold the role of catalyst for educational change, as they uncover supposed "best practice." Surveys such as PISA have added to the current culture of testing around the world, as they attempt to measure human capital as well as future education success. These have also given rise to a positivist view of education. A new, managerial view of society has taken hold and, with this, a need for testing and benchmarking. This has introduced the idea of standardised answers to educational problems. All of these factors contribute to the global context of education policy making and the increased importance and influence of international achievement studies.

Education policy has now reached a global level. "Powerful" countries, meaning those with economic prosperity and/or educational success, lead to dominant ideologies influencing other countries. This internationalistion trend allows PISA to provide inspiration for education policy and has rescaled politics and policy to incorporate international stimuli. Education policy, thus, has strong influences from the international level and transnational organisations. The top-down approaches and policy diffusion that occur leads to the spread of GERM, with values such as accountability, standardisation, and testing dispersing due to the power shift and rescaling of politics and education policy. The internationalisation of education policy also stems from transnational organisations such as the OECD exerting "surveillance" over economic and educational outputs. This surveillance only increases with the addition of PIACC and AHELO to the OECD's educational testing portfolio. PISA has helped education policy reach into this global realm by becoming a benchmark for educational reform.

International organisations, and the educational surveys they produce, have blurred the lines between policy and research. The research that these agencies create quickly fuels policy targets, rather than noteworthy research outputs. Thus, instead of evidence-based policy making, international achievement studies have led to "policy-based evidence making." The league tables and targets that PISA has spurred, along with the "race" to a top performance in the survey, have allowed educational goals to evolve from the abstract to the quantifiable. This paradigm shift has given rise to the politicisation of international achievement studies.

Thus, these similar goals for an education system have led to a convergence of educational policy, theory, and practice. For example, a European policy space has emerged, which not only adds to the issue of policy convergence, but also allows for global agendas to reach national policy spaces. Furthermore, a "Globally Structured Agenda for Education" has created common agendas for different education systems, and a "universalisation" of education reform. This policy convergence has largely overlooked the importance of a "highly context-dependent approach" to education policy.

All of this educational competition at the regional, national, continental, or global level leads to the question of the possibility of educational policy transfer. Although theorists stress the need for synchrony between the countries borrowing and lending, myth can influence policy more than science, giving rise to policy-based evidence making, rather than evidence-based policy making. This further emphasises the increasing importance of exploring and understanding policy borrowing and transfer at length, as the education policy increasingly looks towards international achievement studies as inspiration. Policy borrowing and transfer will be discussed at length in another chapter.

CHAPTER 2

The Backdrop for Success: Finland's Context and Configuration

1   Introduction

Finland's context plays a strong role in its outcomes in PISA. Following Phillips and Schweisfurth (2006) and Halls' (1970) approaches to comparative education, this chapter explores Finland's historical and social context in order to better understand the country's educational achievements. An education system, as a "living thing," according to Sadler (in Higginson, 1979, p. 49), merits investigation within its context. The Finns need and deserve more than a brief description to explain and clarify their unique qualities. The question, "Who are the Finns?" necessitates a long answer:

> But where does Finland belong? Is it a Baltic state, like Estonia? Is it part of Scandinavia, like Denmark, Norway, and Sweden, with which it is linked and with which it has such close ties? Is it really a part of Russia? Or is it something different from all these? A great part of Finnish history has been devoted to trying to solve this problem. (Bacon, 1970, p. 16)

This chapter strives to clarify the Finnish context, and therefore how this eventually influenced high PISA outcomes in all administrations of the survey. It also explains the Finnish education system after exploration of "things outside the school system" (Sadler, in Higginson, 1979, p. 49). This approach will enlighten the context in which the education system lies.

2   History of Finland to Independence

The Finnish people kept to themselves throughout their early history. "Due partly to the size of the country and their own small numbers, the Finns have striven throughout their history to live their own lives, avoid assimilation with their neighbours and remain aside from the quarrels of the rest of the world" (Juva, 1968, p. 17). The recent attention accorded to Finland has been an interruption to the country's traditionally quiet existence.

The first settlers in Finland emerged as far back as 7000 BC, a people who subsisted mostly on elk hunting and fishing. Archaeologists account for speakers of Finno-Ugric languages in modern Finland from about 4200 to 2200 BC (Chislett, 1996). By the Iron Age of Northern Europe, approximately the 6th Century BC, the beginnings of what we understand today as Finnish culture emerged, especially along the coast. The Finns of that day managed to elude their Indo-European counterparts for centuries. By the Bronze Age in that area, between 1800 and 500 BC, the Scandinavians reached the Southwest coast of Finland. Roman senator and historian Tacitus first mentioned the Fenni in his work *Germania*. Many believe he referred to the Finnish people in this account of 98 AD (Chislett, 1996; Niiniluoto, 1960). Until then, the Finns lived in relative obscurity from the rest of the European world. Tacitus's account described the people as living in extreme poverty, and he did not make clear the difference between the Finns and the Lapps.

No historical accounts of the Finns clearly designate a place of origin. Juva (1968) cites that Blumenbach of Göttingen described Finns as a people from Central Asia. He based this assessment on their non-Indo-European language and the customs that differed from the customary Western ways. Some even have connected the Finns with the Turks. However, most trace their ethnic origin to the language, which has relations, whether close or distant, to Estonian, Hungarian, and Lapp, as well as the languages spoken by ethnic groups in northern Russia. These languages form the Finno-Ugric group. Although most linguists take great interest in the dissimilarity of the Finnish language from other European languages, Finnish can express the same notions as Indo-European languages (Niiniluoto, 1960). Most believe that, perhaps about four thousand years ago, those belonging to the Finno-Ugric language family came from the same geographical area. Although no conclusive data exist, many think they came from Central Asia, but some archaeologists suggest that the origins of the Finns may have been as close as Estonia, where they lived before they crossed the Baltic Sea into Finland (Hall, 1967). However, no historical records, whether oral or written, have accounted for this migratory past. Slavic peoples absorbed some ethnic groups speaking a similar language to the Finns. Only the Finns, Estonians, and Hungarians achieved independence. In the context of world history, these groups led an isolated existence (Niiniluoto, 1960). The Finnish people, often confused with and lumped together with their Scandinavian neighbours, actually possess a completely different language and background from most of their European counterparts, and may understandably feel somewhat different from mainstream Europe.

In order to understand Finland's history, culture, and ties with Scandinavia, one must investigate the country's relationship with Sweden. In fact, the Swedes did inhabit some places in modern Finland, especially around the coast and in the west and southwest. These areas of Finland always possessed a

Swedish-speaking population (Niiniluoto, 1960). Nevertheless, the Finns lived in a separate, isolated peace until the Middle Ages:

> [The Finns] remained for hundreds of years without any coherent political or social organisation to connect their sparse and widely separated settlements, although their western neighbours were already progressing towards a more unified state. Thus, in the Middle Ages, their country could be easily annexed by Sweden, and gradually swallowed, administratively, into the kingdom of Sweden-Finland. (Hall, 1967, p. 14)

Finland was part of Sweden for 600 years. In 1323, a peace treaty assigned Eastern Finland to Novgorod and the Western and Southern parts of Finland to the Kingdom of Sweden. By the middle of the 14th century, Sweden held Finland fully under its control (Chislett, 1996). However, the Swedes "were benevolent overlords, who brought them learning and industry, and married their own political and legal organisation to the native Finnish instinct for social democracy" (Hall, 1967, p. 16). Sweden viewed Finland as a group of provinces, and granted much power to the Bishop of Turku, then the main city in Finland. The Bishop represented Finland at the Royal Council of Sweden. By 1362, the Finns did have a voice in the election of a new King of Sweden, and by the 16th century, Finland had representatives in the Swedish parliament (Chislett, 1996).

The Kingdom of Sweden at that time did not have the power, even if it wanted to do so, to overpower the Finns. "And, separated as the two countries were by the Gulf of Bothnia, the liaison was conducted in twin beds, with a corresponding increase in independence" (Bacon, 1970, p. 52). Therefore, the Finns felt no bitterness towards their rulers, and even appreciated the benefits of Swedish rule. In fact, "Finland gave constantly faithful service to her suzerain power, and on her side Sweden showed a generous appreciation of Finnish loyalty" (Fox, 1926, pp. 8–9). The only source of contention, however, came through the use of language. The Finns held on tightly to their Finnish identity and language, even though they needed the Swedish language in schools, politics, and all aspects of official life. Educational and social advancement required the use of Swedish, but most Finns refused to give up their unique language. At the height of Swedish power, 20% of the population of Finland spoke Swedish, either as a native or adopted tongue (Hall, 1967).

Finland, geographically sandwiched between Sweden and Russia, became the battleground for continuous wars between 1300 and 1800. Sweden enjoyed time as a great power between 1617 and 1721. Its control over the Baltic even expanded the Finnish border further east into Russia. However, from 1714 to 1721, Russia occupied Finland. The Treaty of Uusikaupunki saw Sweden hand over

Inkeri, Estonia, and Livonia to the Russians. This marks the decline of Swedish power and the emergence of Russia as a power in the Baltic (Chislett, 1996).

In 1807, Alexander I of Russia and Napoleon of France signed the Treaty of Tilsit, staking the claim of both France and Russia on the rest of Europe. Russia heightened security from its enemies in the Gulf of Finland. Finland's geographical location worried Russia, since enemies could use the land to facilitate attack. The Russian empire also had long coveted Finnish occupation. Russia took advantage of Sweden's dwindling power at that time and gained control over Finland, a key country in the Baltic due to its strategic geography. Control of Finland would allow better access to Western Europe (Fox, 1926). Therefore, in 1808 Russia invaded Finland (Chislett, 1996). The Finnish war between Sweden and Russia in 1809 ended the 700-year relationship of Finland with the Kingdom of Sweden, and began a new era of Finland as a Grand Duchy of Russia.

Despite its Russian connections, Finnish law still used the influences from Swedish rule. The Finnish national movement, which began under Swedish rule, gained new momentum under Russian rule (Gilmour, 1931). Despite residual historical animosity towards Russia, some of the Czars did much for the future of Finland. For example, Alexander I declared that the Russian empire would not interfere with the rights of self-governance for the Grand Duchy of Finland (Fox, 1926). He promised to maintain the existing structures of Finland in return for the support of the Finnish people (Hall, 1967). This granted autonomy strengthened the groundwork for the future of an independent Finland and also garnered respect for their first Czar (Chislett, 1996).

Finnish autonomy also helped isolate Finland from Sweden. Nevertheless, the Lutheran Church remained the religion of the Finns, and Swedish continued as the official language. Helsinki, much closer to the Russian border than Turku, became the new capital of Finland (Chislett, 1996). The Bank of Finland, founded in 1811, also moved to Helsinki from Turku, and the university followed in 1828. Alexander I helped create a separate government for Finland, by creating the Diet of Four Estates, a parliament with representation from the clergy, nobility, peasants, and middle class. This helped endorse the rights and privileges of all social classes in Finland (Chislett, 1996). During this time, Finland's post office was developed in 1811, and the board of health in 1812. Alexander I also granted back the land, ceded to Finland under the Treaty of Uusikaupunki, which would remain in Finnish hands until the Second World War. Finland's governance allowed for a senate consisting only of Finns. The Grand Duke of Finland, Alexander I, would hold responsibility over the senate. At that time the Finns had control over their own government, legal system, churches, and schools. In addition, their economy remained separate from

Russia, and the rule of Alexander I did not differ much from that of Sweden (Hall, 1967).

Alexander II instituted a system of popular education (Fox, 1926). He also, quite significantly, championed the use of the Finnish language. Even though he allowed Swedish to remain the official language of Finland, he permitted the Finnish language to have the same rights as the Swedish language. History documents that, as late as 1833, Alexander II insisted on the use of the Finnish language in official documents in the Autonomous Grand Duchy. The time of Alexander II also allowed Finland to develop economically, separate from Russia or Sweden (Hall, 1967). Alexander's liberalism began to worry Russia, and its countermovement assassinated Alexander II in 1881. This would allow the future Alexander III to exercise conservatism during his reign.

Russian rule did not prove to be always beneficial for the Finns. A famine from 1867 to 1868 claimed the lives of 100,000 Finns, then 8% of the population (Chislett, 1996). The Finnish Diet passed an act in 1878 that allowed Finland to have its own army. The increasing tenacity of the Finns began to worry the Russians. They felt that this growing self-sufficiency would lead to other groups within the Russian empire also asserting their independence.

If only Alexander I and Alexander II had ruled over the Grand Duchy of Finland, the attitudes of the Finns towards Russia could have been radically different. However, Alexander II, whose rule encouraged Finnish independence and language, preceded the rule of Alexander III, who removed the freedoms bestowed upon Finland by his predecessors. Under his rule, both Finland and Russia suffered (Fox, 1926). The reigns of Alexander III, who ruled from 1881 to 1894, and his successor, Nicholas II, in power from 1894 to 1917, mark a much more conservative era of Russian rule over Finland. This conservatism strangled the autonomy of Finland and began the attempted "Russification" of the Finns (Chislett, 1996, p. 22).

In 1898, General Nikolai Bobrikov took over as the governor-general of Finland, and almost immediately placed all Finnish activity under Russian supervision. "At a single stroke Finland's autonomy was destroyed" (Hall, 1967, p. 102). He also shut down the Finnish newspapers. In 1901, the Finnish military, which had had its own defence forces since 1878, came under Russian command and was forced to speak Russian (Chislett, 1996). This caused an uproar as well as fear among the Finnish people. Some members of the Diet fled abroad, while young men tried evading the draft. More than 500,000 Finns signed a petition against the measure. This caused the Russians to surrender this policy, and disband the Finnish army.

The assassination of Bobrikov in 1904 and the Russian Revolution in 1905 gave the Finns some respite from the Russians. In 1906, the new parliament, or

Eduskunta, replaced the old Diet. This reform gave Finland a single-chamber parliament as well as universal suffrage. Finnish women thus became the first in Europe with the right to vote (Chislett, 1996). With no real army, Finland maintained neutrality during the First World War. However, at that time Finland's people had begun to divide into two groups, the "Whites," consisting mainly of bourgeois, Finnish military officers, and the "Reds," the extreme socialists and the working class (Chislett, 1996; Hall, 1967). The Russians supported the Reds and the Germans supported the Whites.

Elections held in 1916 saw 103 social democrats come to parliament, and in March 1917 Oskari Tokoi became the first democratically elected socialist prime minister in the world (Chislett, 1996). The following November, parliament passed a resolution granting it the power formerly possessed by the Czar of Russia and the Grand Duke of Finland (Hall, 1967). Lenin, a supporter of Finnish autonomy, came to power in November 1917 (Chislett, 1996). The Finns declared their independence on 6 December 1917, and on the "last day of 1917 Lenin's government recognised the new state, and Finland stood alone before the storms that were brewing at home and raging abroad" (Hall, 1967, p. 105).

3 Independence and War

Unfortunately for the Finns, their independence did not come at a peaceful time. Throughout 1917, the class divide began to grow. The harshness of war triggered the decline of the working class, weighed down by unemployment, near-famine, and poverty. The war, however, supplied the middle and upper classes with economic gain (Hall, 1967). The divide between the Reds and the Whites began to grow, and this fissure eventually led to a coup in January 1918 (Chislett, 1996). The Reds had approximately 100,000 people on their side, while the Whites had about 70,000. The Reds received help from now-Soviet Russia, and the Whites, led by General Mannerheim and supported by Germany, ended up with victory. This war, not only a Civil War for Finland, also marked the liberation from Russian rule. It also came at a heavy cost. Nearly 37,000 people died as a result of the Civil War, whether they were killed in battle, executed by the enemy side, died in prison camp, as a result of prison camp, or were missing in action.

In addition to the loss of life, the Finnish Civil War left deep wounds that would remain in the Finnish psyche for the next half century. The war, however, did bring social and political stability, mainly through a programme that allowed tenant farmers to purchase their farms (Chislett, 1996). Post-Civil War Finland sought a monarch for its new, independent land. Sweden, which wanted to maintain neutrality during the war, did not support the victorious

Whites, which therefore ruled out importing a Swedish monarch to occupy a Finnish throne (ibid.; Fox, 1926). For this reason, the Finns looked to Germany to find their ruler. They chose Prince Friedrich Karl of Hessen as their new king. However, in November of 1918, the German monarchy collapsed along with the surrender of Germany, and, under Allied pressure, Prince Friedrich Karl abdicated his throne even before arriving in Finland. Afterwards, Finland soon became a republic (Chislett, 1996).

Instead of a monarch, Finland's constitution now calls for a president elected every six years. The president appoints the prime minister, conducts foreign policy, and has the right to disband parliament and organise new elections. Originally, the president inherited many of the powers possessed by the Grand Duke of Finland, the Russian Czar (Chislett, 1996). The president, unlike his or her counterparts in some other countries, renounces any political party affiliation once in power. Therefore, he or she does not act as the leader of his or her party, rather, as the leader of his or her country. Finnish politics also possesses two other distinguishing features: "The use of qualified majorities for approving legislation (which acts like a built-in stabiliser preventing sudden swings between right and left in government policy); and the protection of private property rights against government intervention. Such measures have helped to establish a consensus system of politics" (ibid., p. 24).

After the Civil War, Finland lived in a time of peace and hope. The country asserted neutrality after independence, and hoped Finnish neutrality would be much like the neutrality in the Scandinavian countries. Twenty years after the Civil War, however, the beginnings of another war began to simmer. "But for the Finns the choice between neutrality and belligerence had been eliminated, though without their knowledge, before the outbreak of the Second World War [...] The great powers – by which Stalin meant the Soviet Union and Germany – had between them already decided Finland's fate" (Hall, 1967, p. 110). In 1939, Germany and the Soviet Union signed a pact secretly consigning Finland to the Soviet "sphere of interest" (Chislett, 1996, p. 24). After Germany defeated Poland in 1939, Finland refused Soviet demands to build a military base on its land. The Finns feared for their independence. In response, Stalin and the Soviets attacked Finland on 30 November. The Winter War, although but a hiccup in the grand scheme of the Second World War, commanded great respect from other countries in the world. The scenario of the Finnish David and the Soviet Goliath prompted Theodore Roosevelt and Winston Churchill to denounce the Soviet attack on Finland and to strongly support the Finnish resistance movement. Roosevelt referred to the Winter War as the "rape of

Finland" and Churchill stated the invasion was "a despicable crime against a noble people" (ibid.).

A peace treaty on 12 March 1940 put an end to the Winter War. Ultimately, Finland ceded 10% of its land to the Soviet Union. The population in the ceded land, more than 400,000 Finns, moved within the new Finnish borders (Chislett, 1996). Finland joined World War II when Germany invaded the Soviet Union in 1941. Finland did not ally itself with Germany; rather, the country fought against the Soviets to regain the land lost during the Winter War. The Continuation War, a bitter battle, ended with the Moscow Armistice. In the end, Finland ceded back to the Soviet Union most of the land originally ceded after the Winter War, in addition to Petsamo, a nickel mine and port on the Arctic Ocean. The Armistice also demanded that the Finns expel the Germans from their territory, which eventually caused the Lapland War. "Finns saw the liberty and independence of Finland as their chief concern [...] Indeed, this was the point they stressed during the Continuation War – that their sole object was to maintain the integrity of Finland. They only wanted to be left alone" (Bacon, 1970, p. 225).

The Lapland War followed the Continuation War, extending from September 1944 to April 1945. The Germans sought the strategic nickel mines in Petsamo, and the Finns tried to protect them while also attempting to expel the Germans from their country (Chung, 2009). The Germans employed a scorched-earth policy, which ended in severe destruction in Northern Finland. The Finns finally banished the Germans in 1945 and drove 200,000 of them out of their country. Finland lost 87,000 of its people during the wars between 1939 and 1945, amounting to 2.3% of the total population (Chislett, 1996). The War also left 60,000 disabled and 4,000 refugees in Finland, in addition to the devastation of the North due to the scorched-earth policy (Eskelinen, 1968).

War and strife ironically united the Finnish people. In the words of US President Franklin Roosevelt, "The Finns have won the moral right to live in everlasting peace and independence in the land they have so bravely defended" (Saari, 1944, p. 37). All the conflict united the Finnish people and their differences of opinion. Hence, the Finns in following generations valued freedom, liberty, and democracy. After the Second World War, Finland "was a nation crippled and exhausted, but Finland survived. This may seem a pitifully unheroic end to a story of so much effort and sacrifice, suffering and blood, but for a small nation, in the iron times of the Second World War, survival was a rare triumph" (Jacobson, 1987, p. 43). Finland also evaded the Soviet Union's grasp. "One theory is that Stalin feared the Finns would take up arms again and mount a ferocious resistance" (Chislett, 1996, p. 26).

4   Finland after World War II and the Golden Age of the Welfare State

After the War, Finland spent time recovering from the battle wounds. The Finnish tenacity during the War continued in its post-War relations. President Paasikivi, successor of the previous President and War hero, Mannerheim, needed to balance Finland's Soviet relations and the country's strong commitment to democracy and independence, and did so successfully. Finland even rejected millions of dollars in Marshall Aid from 1948 to 1952 because of Soviet pressure. The rejection of the aid gained the trust of the Soviet Union (Chislett, 1996).

The resettlement of the Eastern Finns after the border changes actually expanded the rural and agrarian labour force after World War II; Finland was the only OECD country to do so (Chislett, 1996). Finland also recuperated its post-war economy through importing raw materials and semi-finished products, which consisted of 10% of GDP. Finland paid off its war debts, the only country involved in World War II to do so, by 1952, the same year as Helsinki hosted the Olympics. This time signified the end of an era in Finland, a time of unease and apprehension. Problems began to decrease (Hall, 1967). In 1955 Finland joined the United Nations and the Nordic Council.

After the eradication of war debt, Finland and the Soviet Union began new relations. The death of Stalin in 1953 allowed for a better relationship between the two countries (Hall, 1967). The Soviet Union also became Finland's main trading partner. Ironically, the relationship became "like a colonial one in reverse: The Soviet Union, the 'colony,' supplied Finland with raw materials, oil and gas, and Finland, the 'metropolitan power,' exported value-added products" (Chislett, 1996, p. 28).

Politically, post-War Finland underwent tremendous change. After the Communist defeat of 1948, the Social Democrats and the Agrarian party took turns as the dominant political party in Finland. Between 1950 and 1964, Finland had nineteen different cabinets (Chislett, 1996). Urho Kekkonen undertook his presidency in 1956, at the height of the Cold War between the Soviet Union and the United States, but promised to maintain neutrality. "No country felt the Cold War more keenly than Finland – which shares a 1,300 kilometer-long border with Russia and is close to the Kola Peninsula on the Arctic Sea where Moscow had a third of its nuclear arms – and it lived on a knife's edge" (Chislett, 1996, pp. 28–29).

In 1960, the Social Democrats regained power and achieved a national consensus. They initiated an incomes policy and came to terms with the Communist party (Chislett, 1996). The incomes policy led to economic and social reforms, paving the way for the Welfare State. In the 1960s, the Finnish government implemented pension programmes and illness insurance, and a more comprehensive pubic health care system emerged in the 1970s. These came at a similar time as the reforms in the education system. At this time the state identified the importance of education and reformed the education system to improve its quality. The Finns had long realised the importance of strong language skills, which, along with technological skills and strengths in science, led to economic success and social development. Also at this time, the amount of spending for social welfare increased quickly.

The Nordic welfare state, as characterised by Esping-Anderson's (1990) seminal text, follows a socio-democratic regime, adhering to values of equality, generosity, and solidarity, based on universalism (Antikainen, 2010; Hiilamo, 2012; Kuisma, 2007). The Nordic welfare state is often extolled as "exceptional" in academic literature and in the mass media (Kuisma, 2007, p. 10), but has its shortcomings. After the 1960s, when the Nordic countries carved out their identity as a welfare state near-nirvana, the countries kept veering to the right, where social democracy kept losing out to neoliberal values (Lehtonen, 2016, p. 73).

Interestingly, Protestantism, or more specifically, the Lutheran Church, is credited as evolving the church-state relationship so that, eventually, the church bestowed the responsibility for welfare to the state (Hiilamo, 2012). The Christianisation of the entire Nordic region between 900 and 1300, and the ascent of King Gustav Vasa of Sweden in 1523 gave way to the Lutheran Reformation (Kuisma, 2007, p. 15). Lutheranism is credited with instilling work ethic, literacy, and equality as values of the Nordic welfare state (Antikainen, 2010). In fact, the Finnish "proverb *'oppia ikä kaikki'* (all life is learning) was quoted as early as the 1600s, and free education from primary school to university is also a historical feature dating back to the 1800s or the early 1900s" (Antikainen, 2010, p. 532). Lutheransim and its values paved the way for consensus politics and a Nordic welfare model, based on an autonomous civil society, and a respect for education in Finnish society.

These values of solidarity and equality carved a path for the Nordic welfare state. Interestingly, "the first agreement between employers and the unions was signed during the Winter War in January 1940, at the same time as Soviet bombs were falling on Helsinki" (Antikainen, 2010, pp. 532–533). The time of peace that followed from 1950 to the 1980s is considered the golden age of the Finnish welfare state. At this time, Finns viewed the welfare state as a long term, if not permanent, solution to poverty. However, the deep economics crisis of the early 1990s, discussed next in this chapter, suddenly ended this golden age of the welfare state. The austerity measures that followed caused some changes, including a "mixed economy of welfare" and a "more permanent change in the welfare state ethos" (Hiilamo, 2012, p. 411). In the crisis of the 1990s, some even viewed the Nordic welfare state as "outdated" and incapable of facing modern challenges (Kuisma, 2007, p. 18). The economic crisis led to the view the "necessity" of "social democratic accommodation" moving to a "market-oriented neo-liberalism" (ibid.). This change is discussed at length in the next section of this chapter.

5 The 1980s, Recession and Recovery to 1990s Neoliberalism

The 1980s saw Finland expand economically. Finland's growth in the 1980s came at the top of the performance levels of OECD countries, "leading Finns to refer to their country as the Japan of Europe" (Chislett, 1996, p. 32). Finland also managed to diversify its industries. For example, the formerly dominant wood and paper sector decreased from 77% of its exports in 1950 to 39% in 1990. Meanwhile, the exports of metal and engineering products increased from 5 to 43%.

The 1980s also saw Finland assert a more European identity. Finland joined the European Free Trade Association in 1989, despite the pressures from the Soviet Union. At that time Austria and Sweden applied for European Community membership, but Finland felt it would affect its neutrality. The persistence of the Cold War meant that Finland had to tiptoe around such matters (Chislett, 1996). However, the European Commission created the European Economic Area, which gave Finland a loophole. The Finns could have a more European economy without needing to integrate with the other European countries politically.

Also during this time, the Finns still lived in fear of the Soviet Union and its oppressive regime. During the 1980s, this fear manifested itself in Finnish media, especially television and radio (Chislett, 1996). Also at this time, Finnish politics turned more conservative. In 1987, a political turning point occurred when the National Coalition Party won in the elections and formed an alliance with the Social Democratic Party. This trend continued further in 1991 when the Centre Party, formerly known as the Agrarian Party, became the strongest party and formed a union with the National Coalition Party. The Centre Party's turn in power marked a change from past Finnish politics. It looked favorably upon European Community membership, and did not take as seriously the relationship with the former Soviet Union.

The conservative turn of Finnish politics coincided with a coup attempt against Mikhail Gorbachev's disassembling of the communist system. The attempted coup, in 1991, had both favorable and adverse consequences for Finland. Economically, Finland suffered because of the close trade ties with the former Soviet Union. However, the collapse of the Soviet Union benefited Finland politically and opened the door for membership of the European Union. Previously, the close ties with the Soviet Union did not allow for EU membership (Chislett, 1996). The failed coup in the Soviet Union turned over a leaf in Finnish politics. Finland then could coordinate its politics with the rest of Europe and not worry about the relationship with the Eastern neighbours. The Finns subsequently voted in favour of European Union membership, implying a disdain for their erstwhile Soviet neighbors and their stronghold and a hope for the future. "Never would the country be left alone again to face Russia as it was in 1939" (ibid., p. 35). On 1 January 1995, Finland became a member of the European Union, becoming the first new or successor state after the First World War to become a member of the EU. With Finland's membership, the EU extended its borders to Russia and to the Arctic Circle.

After twenty years of steady growth, the Finnish economy took a dive in 1990, the steepest decline of any OECD country (Chislett, 1996). The virtually full rate of employment plummeted to an unemployment rate of 20%. 430,000 jobs were lost during that time. The recession, lasting from 1991 to 1993, so deeply affected Finland that many Finnish economists liken it to the Great Depression of the 1930s. The loss of the Soviet market, a trade relationship that had lasted for more than forty years, profoundly influenced the Finnish economy. The overvalued Finnish Mark and rising debts also added to the deep recession. The Finnish Mark devalued by 12% in 1991, then depreciated a further 20% in 1992. It took until 1996 for Finland's economy to regain the economic level it had attained before the recession, and eventually to fulfill the criteria for the European Monetary Union and transfer the Finnish Mark to the Euro in 1999. The recession made Finland realise the need for economic support. During the recession, Finns queued for food handouts, delivering a blow to a country that had become one of the world's ten richest within thirty years.

After the so-called golden age of the welfare state, Finland tried to position itself as a globally competitive country. For example, in 1992, the lifting of limitations on foreign ownership led to an expansion of non-Finnish companies in the country. Furthermore, Finland's membership in the European Union and European Monetary Union relinquished much of Finnish control over its own markets. Between 1990 and 1996, Finland privatised more of its public sector than any other OECD country in that time. The occurrences of the latter half of the twentieth century in Finland shaped the change from idyllic welfare state to a nation gradually shifting towards the political right: "Hence, neoliberal policies have proceeded as 'little neoliberal adjustments,' which nonetheless have accumulated over time and are gaining ground gradually as the Finnish political field has shifted to the Right since the recession of the early 1990s" (Lehtonen, 2016, p. 73). These new neoliberal values also affected the Finnish comprehensive school in the form of decentralisation. This is discussed further in Chapter 3.

This recession of the early 1990s led to austerity measures, which allowed for economic recovery. Finland recovered, and by 1995 ranked fifth out of 174 countries in the 1995 United Nations Human Development survey. Seven years after the recession, exports doubled, and a smaller labour force managed to produce a large output (Kirby, 2006). The electronics market has become a huge industry for Finland, with a very large amount of exports, rivaling the old export powerhouses such as wood and paper from Finland's forestry industry. A report in 2003 by the OECD praised Finland for high levels of investment in research and development, a strong financial sector, and a post-recession economic growth rate double that of the OECD as a whole. However, a downside to this rapid economic growth exists. Finland has high unemployment, as the export market recovered more rapidly than the domestic demand for labour. These austerity measures remained even after the recession, with the continuation of limited social services (Hiilamo, 2012). In fact, Jensen (2011, p. 125) even refers to an "era of permanent austerity" after the "'Golden Age' of welfare expansion." The subsequent European economic collapse in 2008 changed the Finnish landscape with widening poverty and inequality. More recently, while Finns still do support the Nordic welfare state values, politically, in terms of elected officials, votes are turning to the neoliberal right.

6   What Makes Finland "Finnish"?

This part of the chapter discusses aspects of Finland that make it decidedly "Finnish." Those not particularly familiar with the Nordic countries often categorise Finland as "Scandinavian." The following section reveals features of a unique Finland, focusing on unique language, politics, society, religion of the country, uncovering the concept of *sisu*, and finally discussing Finland's participation in the Nordic Council.

6.1   *Language*

The Finnish language possesses unique characteristics that separate it from other European languages. In fact, the distinctiveness of the language demonstrates the Finns' uniqueness as a people and remains an extraordinary characteristic (Bacon, 1970). The mysterious nature of their origins as well as the nature of their language, in concert with their history under foreign rule, adds to pride in their exceptional language.

The centuries under Swedish rule enhanced the pride in their language, due to the necessity of Swedish in all officialdom, including education (Hall, 1967). The bilingualism of Finland, stemming from Swedish rule, adds a new dimension to the influence of language. In order to better understand Finland one must understand its ties with Sweden and the reasons behind its bilingualism.

During their time under the reign of the Kingdom of Sweden-Finland from the thirteenth century to 1809, the Finns were forced to accommodate the Swedish language. The people of Finland expressed their nationalist feelings in Swedish, as the educated people of Finland used the Swedish language, and Swedish remained the language of instruction in all schools (Bacon, 1970). With the implications of language use in Finland, a feeling of superiority developed in reference to the Swedish language. The advantages for Swedish speakers were significant. Because the educated spoke Swedish and schools used Swedish as the medium of instruction, those wishing to advance in society adopted the Swedish language as their mother tongue. Even workers along the mainly Swedish-speaking coast assumed Swedish as their native language. So powerful did the Swedish language become that a Swedish-born professor in the university in Turku promoted the abolition of the Finnish language and even the prohibition of sauna use, a most unique Finnish custom. Since the dual-language system in Finland hindered complete unity of the Kingdom of Sweden-Finland, the Swedes worked hard to change all language use into Swedish. Churches and schools used Swedish. People even adopted Swedish names to better assimilate into the upper class. This movement would later create social problems that resonated for centuries (Hall, 1967).

Despite, or because of this, a Finnish nationalistic sense emerged, and through this came the fight for the Finnish language. "More correctly they might be called the harbingers, since at first they were less concerned with the possibility of an independent Finland than with the new interest in things Finnish" (Bacon, 1970, p. 73). This nationalism emphasised education for all, and the expansion of the Finnish language to a position equal to Swedish, and the need to have two official languages in Finland (Saari, 1944). At this time, the rebellion against the Swedish language began, quite possibly the only source of tension during Sweden's rule of Finland. The push for the Finnish language came on two levels. The first, more practically, advocated the use of Finnish in terms of government and administration. The other, on a more emotional level, saw Finnish as a unique language, influencing the character of the Finns and most highly valued by them. However, this new push for the Finnish language raised many questions for both the Finnish and Swedish-speaking inhabitants of the country. The sole use of Finnish, so different from European languages, would immediately isolate Finland and its people. Would the abandonment of the Swedish language have adverse effects for Finland? After the annexation by Russia, Swedish curiously remained the language of administration and of schools. Upon closer examination, however, one can understand the reasons. Many feared that the rejection of Swedish would allow for Russian to take its place (Hall, 1967).

Many in Finland championed the cause of the Finnish language. For example, many consider church reformer Mikael Agricola as the father of written Finnish. In the 1540s he produced a Finnish alphabet book (Louhivouri, 1968). Agricola also translated the prayer book and the New Testament into Finnish. Owing to these accomplishments, many call him "the father of Finnish literature" (Hall, 1967, p. 87). Ironically, those who fought most for the rights of the Finnish language came from the Swedish-speaking minority and aristocracy:

> A group of Swedish-speaking Finns took up the unlikely task of advancing the Finnish language at the expense of their own. Foremost among them was J.V. Snellman (1806–81), teacher, editor, and administrator, who devoted himself to a crusade to persuade his compatriots that unity and independence could never be achieved until the whole country spoke and used the Finnish language, and only the Finnish language. A country, he affirmed, in which the bureaucracy and the cultivated class spoke Swedish and the rest Finnish, was a country divided against itself, and one which laid itself open to the imposition by the Russians of their own language. It was therefore the duty of Swedish-speaking Finns to learn and adopt the Finnish language, and so identify themselves with the nation as a whole. (Hall, 1967, p. 92)

The efforts of people like Agricola and Snellman allowed for more acceptance of the Finnish language. A.I. Arvidsson, the Finnish poet, encouraged modernisation and the expansion of education. Finland could achieve these goals, he felt, by removing the language barriers and tensions between Swedish and Finnish: "We are no longer Swedes, we cannot become Russians, let us therefore become Finns in thought, feeling and deed" (Saari, 1944, p. 35). Finnish, formerly the language of peasants, started to infiltrate education. In 1841, the Finnish Lyceum started teaching Finnish, and the university in Finland established a chair of Finnish in 1850. In 1858, the first Finnish secondary school started in Jyväskylä, followed by another school in Helsinki in 1869. Finnish secondary schools followed later in the cities of Kuopio, Joensuu, and Hämeenlinna. By 1860, Finnish-speakers joined the cultured social class (Gilmour, 1931). Through this history, one can more clearly understand the bilingual rights of the dwindling Swedish-speaking minority in Finland. The Constitution of 1919 declared the official bilingualism of Finland. However, the animosity and tension between these two groups does still exist, even to present day. "But the Finnish national conscience, now wide awake, remains unsatisfied, and a new generation of 'Pure Finns' has arisen to demand rights strictly proportional to their numbers" (Gilmour, 1931, p. 22). In addition to these problems, "the battle has been transferred to the scholastic areas where the pure Finns oppose the preferential treatment accorded to Swedish education" (ibid.). Therefore, according to the aforementioned references, one can understand how the tensions surrounding the Finnish and Swedish languages infiltrated all aspects of Finnish culture and even education.

However, this link to Swedish culture and language allows Finland to cooperate in the Nordic community. To the casual observer, Finland belongs to the group of Scandinavian countries by proximity of geography:

> Finland participates as the easternmost of the Nordic countries, or of Fenno-Scandinavia, as the geographer would say. But it would be a mistake to imagine that this cooperation is motivated by purely or even primarily geographic considerations. There is so much else to bring the Nordic countries together. They all have the same cultural background, and a historical fellowship of fate. (Fagerholm, 1960, p. 69)

With the onset of independence in 1917, Finland turned to its Swedish roots for guidance as a new country, despite the time as a Russian Grand Duchy. In the end, Russian influence did not shape Finland as much as Sweden. Upon Finnish independence in 1917, they chose to begin their time as an independent country upon the previous Scandinavian foundations (Fagerholm, 1960). Furthermore, the influence of the Swedish language allows Finland to assume Scandinavian identity. Finland secured its position as part of the North, rather than the East. Despite the differences from its Scandinavian counterparts, modern, independent Finland has formed its unity and identification with them (Hall, 1967).

6.2 *Politics*

Finnish politics has largely enjoyed consensus and coalition governments. Due to a multi-party system, no party has enough power to solely govern the country. The coalition-style politics have given continuity and consistency on many fronts, including economics, education, and foreign policy (Chislett, 1996). For the most part, the Centre Party, formerly the Agrarian Party, and the Social Democrats have been the two leading parties in Finnish politics.

Parliamentary elections come every four years. The 200-member *Eduskunta* has proportional representation. The presidential elections occur every six years, and the president may only serve two consecutive terms (Chislett, 1996). The Finnish constitution necessitated a two-thirds majority for the passing of bills until 1991, where a simple majority vote replaced the old system. Although nineteen different cabinet regimes came between 1950 and 1964, the governments have been more stable since that time.

The 1919 Constitutional Act grants widespread power to the president. The power of the president offsets the potential instability of the parliament (Chislett, 1996). When taking office, the presidents renounce their political party affiliation in order to take precedence over any political skirmishes between the many political parties. As previously stated, the president appoints the ministers, runs foreign policy, forms majority governments if needed, and commands the armed forces. The president originally had limitless jurisdiction to dissolve parliament, but an amendment in 1991 added the requirement of the prime minister's consent.

Finland has a relatively large number of political parties. The main political parties follow, with their 1995 percentages: Social Democratic Party (28.3%), Centre Party (19.8%), National Coalition Party (17.9%), Left Alliances (11.2%), Swedish People's Party (5.1%), Greens (6.5%), Christian League (3.0%), Young Finns (2.8%), Rural Party (1.3%), Liberal Party (0.6%), Ecology Party (0.3%), and Other (3.2%) (Chislett, 1996). In 2011, the percentages became as follows: National Coalition Party (20.4%), Social Democrats (19.1%), True Finns (19%), Centre Party (15.8%), Left Alliance (8.1%), Green League (7.2%), Swedish People's Party (4.3%), Christian Democrats (4%), and Other (1%) (Laine, 2011).

6.3 *Society*

Finnish society has long adhered to an egalitarian philosophy. Before the recession of the 1990s, Finland had achieved almost full employment, and had one of the OECD countries' most developed welfare systems (Chislett, 1996). Welfare spending for Finland makes up more than 40% of the GDP. The government spends money on unemployment benefits, education, pensions, health care, and social services. Although high compared to its OECD counterparts, Finland's spending on social welfare remains on an even level to that of other Nordic countries.

The Finnish Welfare State illustrates a lack of social class divide:

> In examining many aspects of Finnish economic, social and cultural life it is apparent that one unusual feature of modern Finland is the relative absence of those invisible social barriers which inhibit the full development of the human spirit [...] The relative absence of class distinctions in education, in everyday social life and in the protocols of public life forcibly strikes a visitor from Britain who spends any length of time in Finland. (Singleton, 1989, pp. 161–162)

The Welfare State adheres to a philosophy of early intervention in order to preempt more severe or chronic problems later. As early as 1895, workers had compensation rights if injured in accidents. By 1968, these rights had expanded to free disabled medical care, allowances, and disabled pensions (Singleton, 1989). Both local municipalities and the national government have plans to treat widespread diseases and other health problems, including alcoholism. Finland also administers state-funded home loans, a programme started in 1944, interest-free for couples under thirty years of age. The repayment scheme reduced the money owed according to how many children were in the household. Finland also has a very generous maternity programme. Mothers-to-be can choose a cash payment or a package of clothing, bottles, and other accessories for a newborn baby.

Finland has long provided women with excellent rights. Finnish women first earned the right to vote in 1906, the first in Europe, as we have seen, and the high proportion of women in parliament also reflects a society with liberated women (Chislett, 1996). In fact, the first parliament in 1906 had nineteen women (Kirby, 2006). Finland had a female president, Tarja Halonen, from 2000–2012. In the 2000 presidential elections, four of the seven candidates were women. Since World War II, the number of women in the workforce has risen by 50%. Similar to other countries after the war, Finland had lost so many men in the war that women needed to join the labour market. "For a generation after 1945 Finnish women bore a heavier responsibility as bread winners than would have usually been the case" (Singleton, 1989, p. 164).

Downsides of the Welfare State do exist. Finland has a sizeable ageing population, and does not have many immigrants to fill the gaps in the labour market (Kirby, 2006). The OECD expects Finland to have the biggest increase of over sixty-five population in the next two decades, which presents problems for financing the welfare system.

6.4   *Religion*

The Church holds much responsibility for the spread of learning and elementary education. The establishment of an organised church sparked a demand for education and academic training (Suolahti, 1960). The Reformation encouraged the knowledge of Finnish, and a Finnish translation of the New Testament appeared in 1548, with a translation of the entire Bible following in 1642. A body of religious literature, in Finnish, also helped the spread of the Finnish language and literacy through the Church (Juva, 1968). Those who could not read could not take communion, and those who could not read their catechism could not marry (Gilmour, 1931). Secondary school education also owes its roots to the Lutheran Church. Cathedral schools, church schools, and monasteries educated the Finns until state schools emerged in the 1870s. Most Finns, close to 90%, belong to the Lutheran Church, and approximately 1% belongs to the Finnish Orthodox Church (Chislett, 1996).

The Lutheran and Orthodox churches did not always co-exist in harmony. In 1656, the "Russian" Finns and the "Swedish" Finns fought, burning many villages. Eventually, many of the Orthodox fled to Russia. "Five centuries of political and ecclesiastical separation had moulded east and west Finns so differently that they could no longer live together" (Juva, 1968, pp. 24–25). The Lutheran Church has played a major part in Finnish history and politics. Lutheran bishops had enough foresight to encourage education and literacy, and the Russian attempts to end Finnish autonomy only reinforced their will (Eskelinen, 1968). An Ecclesiastical Act by the parliament governs the church, and many church members pay an optional church tax to fund the church. Schools teach religious education, mainly within the Lutheran Church, but those with Orthodox affiliations will learn about their Orthodox faith (Bacon, 1970).

6.5   Sisu

The Finnish word *sisu* often arises when investigating and researching the country, including the people, the history, the society, and the culture. The concept of *sisu* permeates everything from the Finnish attitude during the Second World War to its victory in the Eurovision Song Contest:

> *Sisu* is a key word in Finnish. It means dogged determination, strength of character or just plain guts. Few nations have battled against such a harsh climate and, at times, against such overwhelming odds as successfully as the Finns; they have pulled themselves up by their own bootstraps, and today, their average income per head [...] is among the world's 10 highest. (Chislett, 1996, p. 17)

This concept of inner strength denotes the resolve to persevere, no matter what the odds. Many use the example of Finnish winters to illustrate this point (Thomas, 2006). The concept of *sisu* even emerges when discussing the Finnish education system. Another definition describes it as:

> *Sisu* is a unique Finnish concept. It stands for the philosophy that what must be done will be done, regardless of what it takes. *Sisu* is a special strength and persistent determination and resolve to continue and overcome in the moment of adversity [...] an almost magical quality, a combination of stamina, perseverance, courage, and determination held in reserve for hard times. (Sisu Group, n.d.)

This describes the Finnish struggle against intruders, whether in prehistoric times or during the Second World War. These struggles, by the viewpoint of *sisu*, cultivated inner strength within the Finns. It credits *sisu* for the many musicians, artists, designers, and athletes who have put Finland on the map in relatively recent history.

6.6   The Nordic Council

Finland's ascension to the Nordic Council marks a significant post-war accomplishment for the country and its development as a nation. The Nordic Council, consisting of Denmark, Finland, Iceland, Norway, and Sweden, decided to work together in all realms. The Council, born in 1953, officially outlined the cooperation between the Nordic countries, a practice essentially already in place. This cooperation comes at all levels and disciplines, such as politics, medicine, fashion, and the arts (Hall, 1967). In other words:

> Cooperation on this scale becomes part of the life of the ordinary citizen, rather than a remote governmental policy, and it is undoubtedly to this groundwork of solidarity that Northern cooperation in general owes its success and momentum [...] broadly speaking, [to] its forty examinations, cultural exchanges, inter-availability of social benefits, a common labour market, economic cooperation, the establishment of a single passport zone, and cooperation in the development of communications. (Hall, 1967, pp. 132–133)

The Nordic Council, by the 1960s, saw many of its goals realised. The cooperation between the countries, whose population only reaches approximately 20 million, allows for better efficiency in the execution of projects which benefit all five nations (Hall, 1967). For Finland especially, the Nordic Council has proved beneficial. Their struggles before and after independence with neighbouring Russia followed by the Soviet Union, in addition to its geography, placed Finland in a tenuous position. Finland's determination during the Second World War seemingly deterred the Soviet Union from adding the country to its republics (Chislett, 1996). However, the Nordic Council helped cement Finland's position as a Northern democracy, along with its Scandinavian neighbours. This gave Finland protection from encroaching Communism and security as a part of a Nordic union. "The remarkable development in cooperation has made the Finns feel psychologically, as well as politically, more secure, and more satisfied that they are able to play a part in European affairs" (Hall, 1967, p. 134).

The Finnish identity, while not quite Scandinavian, remains elusive. "The Finns know and understand the Russians, and their imprisonment in history, better than do most Europeans; they have long-standing ties of sympathy with the Poles; they have a kinship, if remote, with the Hungarians; and they are part of the Scandinavian family" (Hall, 1967, p. 137). Even though Finland does have many similarities with the rest of Scandinavia, Finland possesses many attributes that render the country different from the Scandinavian countries. The Finnish political system, for example, has a separate history, setting itself apart from its Scandinavian counterparts. The political structure came to fruition at a very different time in history and in very distinct circumstances from the rest of the Scandinavian countries, and these dissimilarities make Finland unique. Nevertheless, Finland's place in the Nordic Council confirms its place among these countries in the modern world.

The Nordic countries in the twentieth century proved themselves exemplary to the rest of the world, and pioneers in peace. Two men from Scandinavia became Secretaries General of the United Nations, Trygve Lie of Norway, from 1946 to 1952, and Dag Hammarskjöld of Sweden, from 1953 to 1961. The United Nations had two more prominent Nordic men as their agents. Folke Bernadotte of Sweden negotiated the release of prisoners in concentration camps. The United Nations then appointed him to mediate the Arab-Israeli conflicts of 1947–1948. Sakari Tuomioja of Finland also served the UN, first as a mediator in the Cyprus dispute of 1963 and then as the general secretary of the UN Economic Commission from 1957 to 1960. During that time, the Nordic countries proved themselves no longer parochial, but rather an example of fine citizens and nations for the rest of the world. "In the North the rest of the world can see on a small scale many of the things it seeks for itself: order and education, social democracy and a simple way of life" (Hall, 1967, p. 205).

Internationalism for the Nordic countries comes on two levels: both in the context of the whole world and within the framework of Nordic cooperation. The five countries in the Nordic Council consider each other when constructing foreign policy (Hall, 1967). The countries do not necessarily adopt identical policies, but the other Nordic partners tend to better understand the differences in outlook when approached with the policies in advance. The Nordic Council also reinforces the opinions of the Nordic countries, since each country has a small population, but collectively, the countries' opinions carry more weight. "The development of Nordic cooperation is one of the great pragmatic successes of the post-war years, and has demonstrated the ability of the Northern countries to absorb the major political differences between them" (ibid., p. 207).

This relationship of cooperation among the Nordic countries provides an excellent example for their counterparts across the world. This cooperation, functional with a great degree of flexibility, shows an affinity between countries not evident elsewhere (Hall, 1967). The Nordic countries also manage to maintain their individuality while in this union. "They have many individual characteristics which they are anxious to retain; they have also many common characteristics which give them a basic similarity of outlook" (ibid., p. 208).

The Nordic countries all have a relatively similar degree of homogeneity and share a similar religion. All, with the exception of Finland, speak a similar language, but the Finns speak Swedish as a second language, and their Swedish-speaking minority has a Scandinavian language as a mother tongue. The Swedish language allows for better cooperation with its Scandinavian counterparts (Hall, 1967). All of the Nordic countries also share similar social backgrounds and small population size.

Most significantly, all Nordic countries pursue the common ideal of the egalitarian society. This egalitarian goal does not push everyone downwards; rather, it levels everyone upwards:

> The North wants to be an educated middle-class society; it rejects the cheap and shoddy and does not deride such attributes as honesty, conscientiousness, good behaviour, and good speech. These may not be universally achieved, but they are commonly accepted as constituting a desirable standard, and this makes the day-to-day operation of social democracy far easier and more relaxed. (Hall, 1967, p. 209)

All Nordic countries have adopted similar social policies, aiming for a welfare state. Even though the countries have differing levels of welfare and benefits, all countries strive for a high quality of life.

The Nordic Council confirmed Finland's ascent towards being a wealthy, independent nation. For the first few decades of independence, Finland struggled with internal disagreements and war, both within the country and through protecting itself from others. For Finland, the Nordic Council "brings to a close the isolation of the past and stabilises her position in Europe and the world" (Hall, 1967, p. 210). It brings great possibilities for social, economic, and cultural development for Finland, more so than Finland could have accomplished without this union. How much Finland will change due to this cooperation remains a question. Isolation and resistance have heightened the tenacity of the Finns. They clearly differ from their Scandinavian counterparts: "The Finns are, as it were, half-brothers who bring a different genetic inheritance into an environment which is comparable, though modified by the duality of the marchland" (ibid.). Finland's former relationship with Sweden also adds another dimension to its membership in the Nordic Union:

> The centuries of subordinate relationship to Sweden have left the Finns with a still unsatisfied anxiety to prove that Finland can do as well as her more advanced and wealthy neighbour. Over the years, many Swedish developments have reached Finland, with a certain time-lag, and made a considerable contribution to the Finnish advance; but Finland sometimes risks overstraining her resources, or choosing less suitable policies, when emulating the Swedes. (Hall, 1967, p. 210)

This statement by Hall reiterates a well-known statement regarding Finnish education, that Finland makes the same mistakes as Sweden, only ten years later (Välijärvi et al., 2002, p. 3). However, Finland's performance in PISA, as well as the interest of the Scandinavian countries in the Finnish system of education, illustrates a new relationship that has emerged as a result of the success of Finnish education.

The Finns will most likely cling to their uniqueness that differentiates them from their Scandinavian counterparts. Their history will make sure of this for some time:

> As the North influences and is influenced by the rest of Europe, the Finns may acquire some of the superficial features of both Northern and Western standardisation. Beneath the surface, out of an instinctive tenacious reaction, they are likely to cling all the more closely to the traditions, the background, the language and the land which have contributed so much to their individuality. The Finns have above all one of the most individual characteristics – they are among the few peoples of Western Europe who are still in love with the world. If they should lose this zest and optimism they would lose themselves and they would no longer be Finns. (Hall, 1967, p. 211)

This statement from 1967 has upheld its claims. However, this has occurred despite the influence of globalisation. While "globalisation and its consequences define the worldwide political discourse and its ideological underpinnings" (Siikala, 2006, p. 154), Finland has managed to maintain many of its unique characteristics. In fact, the success of Finnish products such as Nokia, Angry Birds, and, of course, education has added to this. In fact, remaining distinctly "Finnish" has allowed the country to achieve high outcomes in PISA. The "Finnish Way" of trust, respect, and equity (Sahlberg, 2011, p. 182) has avoided the worldwide trend of GERM, which infects even the other Nordic countries through its accountability measures, targets, and testing.

7 Summary

In order to understand the system of education in Finland, one must understand the country and its context. This chapter heeded the warnings of Sadler and others by delving deep into the context of Finland, from a historical, political, cultural, religious, linguistic, and societal view. Gilmour (1931) has described the intertwining of the country and its education system, and rightly so. Finland's unique history, its time as part of both Sweden and Russia, and its subsequent struggle for independence have permeated the psyche and constitution of the Finnish people and infiltrated attitudes towards education.

Finland's history, up to and after independence, has illustrated the tenacity of the Finnish people. After independence, the Finns did not have an easy time; rather, they faced their own internal struggles. During the Second World War, in which they bravely fought powerful invaders, the Finns proved their resolve. Recovery from this war, in terms of the economy and of loss of life, took many years. To add to this hardship, the fall of the Soviet Union triggered a harsh recession that once again damaged Finland on so many levels.

Finnish *sisu* proved its strength through recovery from this recession. This time, however, the Finns pulled through and achieved economic prosperity. This "new" Finland found itself on the world map for various reasons, such as the economic success of its companies and its educational success as now illustrated by PISA.

Finland's unique history as part of two powerful kingdoms, as well as its geographically liminal location between East and West, has given the country its own distinctive character. The time as part of the Kingdom of Sweden has given the Finns linguistic, cultural, political, and societal ties with Scandinavia. The ties with Russia and subsequently with the Soviet Union have given Finland eastern connections, as well as placing the country in a delicate situation during the Cold War. Currently, the relationship with Sweden and the rest of Scandinavia has placed Finland in the cooperative context of the Nordic Council. After the fall of the Soviet Union, Finland emerged as a main player in European matters as a member of both the European Union and the European Monetary Union.

This chapter discussed at length the events in Finnish history that influenced their respect for education. When delving deeper into Finnish history and culture, the importance of Finnish society became evident. The following passage illustrates some of the sentiments felt by the Finnish people:

> The respect for learning and the desire to learn, which penetrate deep down into Finnish society, appearing in the old, vanishing culture of the

Swedish families and in the strivings of the sons and daughters of small farmers and factory workers, still strongly persist. These young Finns will want more learning and social education for their children, and it looks as though they will get what they want. (Binham, 1968, p. 167)

The need to learn, pride in the languages, and the struggle out of peasant life, among other factors, became ingrained within the Finnish psyche and seemingly exist to this day. These factors have influenced the Finland of today, endowing the country with both Scandinavian and eastern aspects.

This chapter's in-depth discussion of Finland's context allows for further insight into the country that produced a widely admired education system. When analysing the reasons for Finland's success in PISA, it is apparent that the country's context plays a very important role.

CHAPTER 3

The Education System of Finland

1   Introduction

In order to understand the Finnish educational system and its relationship with high PISA outcomes, we need to examine the people, their culture, languages, society, and history, in addition to the structure of the education system itself. For example, "To understand the Finnish people you must study their educational system" (Gilmour, 1931, p. 63). Therefore, "to be able to understand the young Finn, we must have some idea of the world he lives in. And since his world is largely school, the Finnish educational world is the best place to start" (Binham, 1968, p. 156). This further reiterates the fact that an education system is delicately woven into a web of a country's larger context.

The current system has evolved from a strong foundation of education from Finland's early days, even before it became an independent nation. The historical context illustrates the connections from previous inceptions of the education system to that of today, the object of much policy interest. The current education system of Finland is presented in Figure 3.1.

2   History and Development of the Finnish Education System

The history behind Finland's education system allows us to embed it within the ever-important context, while uncovering the educational values that have existed in Finland over centuries. From an early stage in the country's history, education was consistently a strong point. Unfortunately, very little writing in English exists on Finnish education from that era, but this chapter incorporates some of the available literature. In 1898 Yrjö-Koskinen wrote about Finnish education at the request of Sir Michael Sadler. In 1907, J.S. Thornton from His Majesty's Inspectorate also produced a document on Finnish education. "Both reports described a country, nominally a Grand Duchy of Czarist Russia, which had developed an educational autonomy not to be found in the Baltic States or in Poland" (Whittaker, 1983, p. 31). Many observers noted the excellence of Finnish education. In 1926, Fox wrote, "The educational system of Finland is excellent. There is practically no illiteracy, and every young citizen has a chance of obtaining a University education" (p. 129). Many also document the egalitarian nature of the education system. "There is in Finland very little class distinction

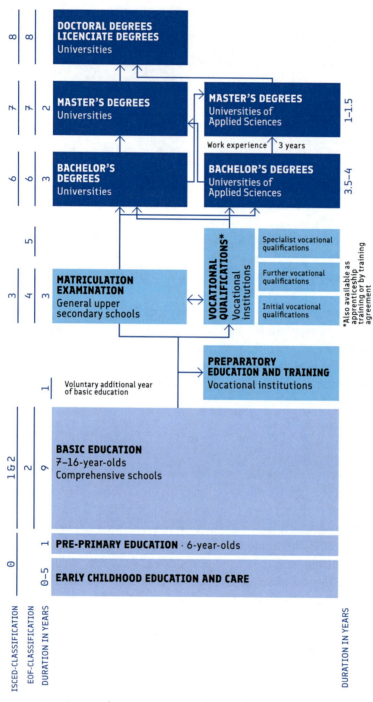

FIGURE 3.1 Current education system in Finland (from Finnish National Agency for Education, reprinted with permission)

in education – at least in the beginning. Most children, both from poor and rich homes, will go to the same kind of school" (Bacon, 1970, p. 210). Furthermore, this excellence and equal access cover the entire span of Finnish education. "Primary school, secondary school, and University education flourish in Finland. The three Universities have yearly increasing numbers of students. The great extent of the international recognition of Finnish scholarship gives proof of the soundness of the country's educational system" (Fox, 1926, p. 132). Contributing to this enthusiasm for education, Finns greatly respect educated people: "There is in Finland a profound respect for an academic education and a profound desire to possess some form of degree" (Bacon, 1970, p. 210).

In order to decipher the beginnings of organised education in Finland, as in most countries, we must look to religion, as discussed at length previously in this chapter. The movement for education and literacy began with the reforms of Mikael Agricola in the sixteenth century. "As early as the seventeenth century the Church set itself the ambitious task of teaching the Finnish nation to read" (Louhivouri, 1968, p. 176). All those wishing to marry needed to have literacy skills. Furthermore, in 1686 the Church also demanded that all should be able to "read and learn by heart a considerable number of religious texts. The penalties for non-compliance were formidable" (Binham, 1968, p. 156). These penalties did not allow Finns to enjoy "civic rights" in addition to the right to marriage. Therefore, the church's influence on education, in addition to educational programmes initiated by the state, allowed for high levels of literacy at an early date. "The first records are for the year 1880, when 97.6 per cent of all inhabitants over ten years old were literate" (Louhivouri, 1968, p. 176).

Despite these movements towards literacy, the Finns did have to fight for their education. "Towards the end of the nineteenth century, the idea of extending folk education beyond religious teaching was first publicly expressed. Progress was hampered by the fact that the Russian tsars did not favour a high standard of folk education" (Binham, 1968, pp. 156–157). In 1863, training began for teachers of non-church education in Jyväskylä, which still has a significant tradition of teacher education. In 1866 the Senate passed a law establishing folk schools. A universal School Attendance Act was passed after Finnish independence in 1917. After independence, the country provided free education for everyone aged seven to sixteen. Furthermore, "a desire for education and knowledge is a natural part of this open, full-stretch society; an equally natural part is a democratic education system which has included neither boarding schools, exclusive or not, nor expensive day schools" (Hall, 1967, p. 65). As a result, state education has reached all populations through its egalitarian philosophy.

Although the growth of Finnish education followed a similar pattern to that of most industrialised countries, this development came later (Antikainen, 1990). For example, compulsory education came later than in other Nordic countries, as well as other European countries. In fact, the Compulsory Education Act did not come into force until 1921 (ibid.; Simola, 2005). Nevertheless, those born in the early twentieth century, although only receiving a primary education, had enthusiasm and respect for education, and "their lifestories contain descriptions of how poverty or their father's decision prevented them from continuing at school" (Antikainen, 1990, p. 76). In other words, the educational situation for past generations formed the respect for education of future generations. We see this play a part in the education system today, as discussed later in this book.

In 1931, Gilmour made an observation of a school in the Helsinki area, the Kaisaniemen Kansakoulu. She documents that all children had medical examinations twice a year (1931, p. 63). She also mentions "the orderliness, the politeness, the independence, the thoroughness, the co-operative spirit, the initiative, the absence of self-consciousness" (ibid.). Furthermore, she writes, "The Finnish elementary school has grown up and developed much along the lines prescribed by Cygnaeus – from the lowest to the highest it seeks 'through labour to labours' to keep a close connection with practical life" (ibid., p. 64). Uno Cygnaeus,[1] a follower of Pestalozzi and often considered the father of the Finnish primary school, remains an important figure in Finnish education to this day. Finland commissioned Cygnaeus in 1858 to draft a plan for the primary school. To do so, he travelled around Finland and studied the curricula in different schools. He even went to Sweden, Denmark, Germany, and Switzerland. Cygnaeus's legacy lives on in Finnish schools, as he believed in crafts and handiwork as a tool for teaching.

Gilmour also remarks how the Finnish school provided a strong foundation for those who continued with study in addition to those would leave the education system sooner than some of their peers. "In the meantime those whose school years are limited find therein practical instruction in matters likely to be useful in after life and an imaginative education that leaves the door open for progress later on" (Gilmour, 1931, p. 64). Even in the 1930s, this practical approach to education, which later was pinpointed by PISA, is seen in the Finnish education system. Furthermore, Binham (1968) notices the strong medical care for the children, which falls under the remarkable welfare available to them through the schools. Free books, meals, medical and dental treatment were provided, even including transport for children living more than five kilometres away from the schools. The practical application of the schools to Finnish life as well as the independent characteristic of Finnish schools was evident even in the early 1900s, with benefits to those who continued with their study and those who left for the labour market. Almost a century later, these values in Finnish education still have a strong influence, and are discussed in later chapters.

In his account of Finnish schools, Bacon also detects this sense of practical and applied education:

> Most Finns will spend a considerable time on modern languages, though they may not learn any classical languages at all. They will study their native language, usually Finnish, first; secondly the other home language, Swedish (or Finnish if they are Swedish-speaking); and thirdly, at least one and probably two foreign languages. (1970, p. 212)

For the Finns, their obscure and not widely spoken language compels them to learn many languages, as Bacon implies. "In a country like Finland, a knowledge of foreign languages is vital. Indeed, one of the most striking aspects of the Finnish secondary school has been the amount of time it devotes to languages" (Binham, 1968, p. 158). Bacon also observes that the entire Finnish system, "though not as rigidly controlled centrally as in many countries, [...] is more centralised than in England" (ibid.). The Finnish education system, through a series of reforms, devolved and decentralised, discussed later in this chapter. Bacon also comments on the curiously small amount of time that Finnish children spend in school. "School begins earlier in Finland than it does in England; usually around eight o'clock. It may finish as early as two o'clock – in winter this is very desirable as it gives the children a chance of seeing the light" (ibid, p. 213). The PISA results also note the comparatively short amount of time Finnish pupils spend in school, especially in comparison to the other high-achieving countries in the survey.

In the nineteenth century, many viewed the education system as biased towards the Swedish-speaking upper class, and not to the needs of Finnish people. "A system of compulsory folk schools began to develop between 1856 and 1866 alongside many private secondary schools, established both to break Church monopoly and to advance the progress of the Finnish-speaking majority" (Whittaker, 1983, p. 32). The creation of these folk schools allowed those without a wealthy background or with Finnish as a mother tongue access to education. At the time of independence in 1917, "the country's system of education [was] seen as a tool for sustaining national identity, basic literacy, and essential political freedom" (ibid.). After World War II, Finland found schooling a bit disjointed owing to the class and language differences; it also had very little possibility of transfer between the tiers of education commenced at age eleven. The post-War system started at seven and had an examination at the age of eleven. Those successful in the examination continued at secondary school. Students could leave school at the earliest at 15 years of age. Those who did not enter secondary school could study more practical subjects, such as forestry (Binham, 1968).

The 1970s brought reforms to the Finnish education system. Since the mid-nineteenth century, educational reform had been at the forefront of Finnish consciousness. This time in Finnish history, as previously mentioned, became a point of transition for many aspects of Finnish life. The government committees proposed to make schools comprehensive and egalitarian, to make general and vocational subjects interrelated, and to standardise schools even in outlying areas. These reforms faced heavy resistance. Opponents to the reforms argued that it was impossible to educate the entire population. The government proposed that these reforms take place in a "rolling" manner, between 1970 and 1985 (Whittaker, 1983). Geography determined the first areas to see reform, as examples of "inadequate education" made way for the new comprehensive system, beginning in the North in 1972 and ending in the Helsinki area in 1977 (ibid., p. 34; Antikainen, 1990, p. 77).

Originally, the education system of Finland was under centralised control. However, in the 1960s a restructuring occurred and the Ministry of Education established a new local education administration. Interestingly, the Finnish ministry found useful models in Sweden and Germany. In the 1980s, the education system undertook a market economy model and underwent decentralisation. Some would see this trend in Finnish education as the influence of a social democracy. This "refers to a general tendency towards equality, in which education is viewed as an agent of social change" (Antikainen, 1990, p. 77). Furthermore, many viewed education as a vehicle for economic growth. The role of education, therefore, had evolved and became more involved with politics and economics.

Decentralisation and market-oriented reforms perhaps best exemplify the neoliberal turn in Finnish education in the 1990s. Education remains a fundamental feature of the Nordic welfare state; however, through liberalising the welfare state, school diversity and parental choice became a feature of Finnish education. Decentralisation in the 1980s and 1990s aimed to dismantle the central governance of education (West & Ylönen, 2010). While Finnish municipalities enjoyed autonomy during this time, from 1993, municipalities received a "lump sum" of money, and decided autonomously how to spend it on welfare services. During the recession it allowed tough austerity decisions to be made at a local, rather than a national level. This devolution facilitated the neoliberal turn in Finnish education. As no central regulation exists as to how schools and local authorities spend welfare services funding, this has led to school markets, or the marketisation of comprehensive schooling (West & Ylönen, 2010).

School choice, one such feature of this decentralisation in Finland, has arguably led to a middle class flight (Lundahl, 2016) from schools in underprivileged areas, thus creating more homogenous schools with fellow students of higher socio-economic backgrounds. Furthermore, in Helsinki, the local education authority decreed that funding would follow the pupil, thus further creating a market for schools. This, in turn incentivises schools to compete for students. In fact, half of the students in Helsinki apply to schools outside of their catchment area in lower secondary school, and in other large cities, this is one-third of the pupils (Antikainen, 2010). Unsurprisingly, these children are from upper- and middle-class families. However, due to the decentralised nature of school governance in Finland, some municipalities actually discourage this practice (West & Ylönen, 2010), making this "middle class flight" type of school choice difficult to generalise around the entirety of Finland.

Decentralisation also has allowed schools to specialise in a certain subject. The national curriculum reforms of 1994 allowed for more flexibility and local control over the teaching in schools. This coincided with the encouraging of schools to concentrate on subject areas. The implementation of the 1998 Basic Education Act granted parents the power to choose a school outside of their local catchment area (West & Ylönen, 2010). Although priority is given to the pupils living closest to the schools, this allows parents to apply for schools outside of their immediate area. This, in turn, has led to some schools implementing aptitude tests, creating a selection process for pupils. This has allowed for selective schools to emerge. As with school choice, this is best utilised by the middle class (West & Ylönen, 2010) and further adds a neoliberal element to Finnish education.

Chapter 2 discussed the recession of 1991 to 1993, and concurrent neoliberal policies and austerity measures. While Finland's education system previously reflected the socio-democratic values of universalism and comprehensiveness (Lundahl, 2016; West & Ylönen, 2010) representative of the golden age of the welfare state, the 1990s brought about a new era. The "radical decentralisation" of Finnish education and other public services and the "introduction of management by results" (Simola et al., 2009, p. 163) coincided with the economic recession of the early 1990s. Interestingly, the neoliberal policies for education overlapped with a wider, changing political landscape and the recession. For example, as discussed in Chapter 2, a conservative turn came to Finnish politics in the late 1980s and early 1990s. This included the Ministers of Education, who, at that time, fell on the political right (Simola et al., 2009).

Thus, the decentralisation of education coincided with a more conservative view of Finland, general decentralisation in Finland, and a more consumer-based view of society. As stated previously, the recession of the early 1990s also led to savings and austerity measures (Simola et al., 2009). To blame the educational restructuring entirely on neoliberalism is a flawed view, according to Lundahl (2016), as it was partly a reaction to the government's insistence on comprehensive schooling in a top-down manner. Decentralisation also stemmed from a more democratic approach to compulsory education. This paved the way for a neoliberal interpretation of education, allowing for school choice and managerialism. Therefore, a neoliberalist approach to education was not a sudden reaction to the economic downturn of the 1990s, but rather a reaction to the times; this occurred in all public services, and not just education.

Neoliberalism in Finnish education must be viewed in context, as suggested by Sadler's speech (in Higginson, 1979) earlier in this book. Furthermore, the decentralisation of Finnish education should not be viewed entirely in a negative light. One could argue that decentralisation of the Finnish education system increased the autonomy of schools, and therefore self-governance for schools and teachers. The schools have the responsibility of producing learning outcomes, while the government has the responsibility of providing for the schools in order to meet their goals, therefore creating a cycle of trust in the governance of Finnish education (Sahlberg, 2007). Additionally, the decentralisation of Finnish education governance and school choice remains relative to the Nordic context, and within the Nordic socio-cultural values (Lundahl, 2016). Citizens still support high taxation levels for social assurances, and Finland is among just a handful of OECD countries that provide higher education for free. On the other hand, one could argue that this decentralisation and marketisation of education is undermining the Nordic welfare state and education model, albeit slowly.

3   Educational Legislation in Finland

Finland's education system enjoys political consensus on the major issues by its political parties. Seven key policies encapsulate the main issues under agreement:

1. Depth: The importance of knowledge and learning
2. Length: Long-term educational goals, rather than short-term gains
3. Breadth: The responsibility of education falls at all levels of government
4. Justice: Equity of quality and access of education
5. Diversity: Strong principles of inclusive education and heterogeneous classrooms
6. Resourcefulness: Trusting that creativity and competency override "routine experience"
7. Conservation: Balancing proven, efficient education methods with new innovations (Sahlberg, 2007, pp. 166–167).

In the Finnish constitution, educational rights come under section 16. Children have rights to education free of charge. Under this decree, public authorities must guarantee equal opportunities for education, despite special needs, for all students no matter their economic background. The Basic Education Act, effective from 1 January 1999, states: "Education shall be provided according to the student's age and capabilities and so as to promote all students' healthy growth and development" (Finnish National Board of Education, 2008, p. 7). This Act, purposely simple, functions as a starting point for education and takes differences into account. The Basic Education Act also maps out the minimum and maximum time spent in school for students. For example, Finnish students in compulsory school have 190 days of school, from four to seven hours of school per day. The Basic Education Act also encourages integrative, interdisciplinary themes in education and encourages good basic competencies. The organisation of teaching and learning in Finland comes from four areas: first, the Basic Education Act and Decree, as already discussed; the government's decree, which gives more detailed goals of education; the National Core Curriculum, and the municipal and school curricula; the implementation of the national curriculum according to local needs. Expenditure in education comes at about 10 billion Euros per year. Within this expenditure, Finland spent the following percentage of the budget in each educational sector in 2005:

– Pre-primary (six year olds) – 2.9%
– Basic education – 36.5%
– Upper secondary general education – 6.4%
– Vocational education and training – 14.7%
– Higher Education: Polytechnics – 7.8%
– Higher education: Universities – 17.9%
– Other education – 3.9%
– Administration – 2%
– Financial aid – 7.8% (Chung, 2009).

The current educational legislation in Finland reflects the consistency in the country's educational values over centuries. For example, early twentieth century researchers found a level of educational autonomy incongruous with neighbouring countries (Thornton, 1907, in Whittaker, 1983). Also around that time, the high literacy levels of the Finns were noted, along with the egalitarian nature of the system, and the near-universal access to tertiary education (Bacon, 1970; Fox, 1926). The respect for education was also recorded at that time, along with "international recognition of Finnish scholarship" (Fox, 1926, p. 132). The strong welfare provisions for children were also recorded, as health and dental care, along with transport, were provided in the 1930s (Binham, 1968). Furthermore, the practical application of Finnish education and its applicability later in life also made their mark on researchers (Gilmour, 1931). In the mid-twentieth century, writers observed the lack of time spent in schools, especially compared to England (Bacon, 1970). Even the OECD's PISA data took note, decades later, that the Finns also spend very little time in the classroom compared to their counterparts in other countries, showing consistency in the continuity of the education in the country.

4   The Current Education System of Finland

The present Finnish education system, the object of so much current interest, actually has a straightforward structure. Finns hold education in "high esteem" and acknowledge "its significance for the development of society and the economy" (Herranen, 1995, p. 323). Traditionally, Finnish education aimed to "raise the general standard of education and to promote educational equality" (ibid.). The system consists of basic school, upper secondary school, and the university level. Finland also enjoys extensive preschool provision and day care. All of these sectors are discussed in this section.

4.1   *Early Childhood and Compulsory Education*

In terms of early childhood education, the concept of kindergarten was brought to Finland in the 1860s by Uno Cygnaeus, as stated in the previous section. In the 1970s, the government passed the Child Day-Care Act, which decreed that all day-care centres provide supervision by registered child-care providers (Nurmi, 1990). Furthermore, a study in the 1970s initiated by the Ministry of Education and that for Social Affairs and Health allowed for a preclass consisting of six-year-olds to begin the first year of comprehensive school, if seen relevant by the local council (Nurmi, 1990). In the 1990s, it became a goal for all six-year-olds to have the right to attend preschool education (Herranen, 1995).

The Finnish Ministry of Education sees preschool as part of the early childhood education process and as assisting in the goal of equal educational opportunities for all. In 2014, 96% of children partook in the preschool system. The curriculum is prescribed at the national level but carried out at the municipal level (Ministry of Education, n.d.-a). The transitional year for six-year-olds provides the strong foundation for high-quality education for the Finnish people (Sahlberg, 2007). Today, six-year-olds have the right to free schooling, under the organisation of the municipalities. School for six-year-olds takes place in either schools or day-care centres. This way, students have preparation before basic education. All day-care teachers have university training. Since 2001, the Basic Education Act has administered the "provision of preschool education [which] is an obligation on the local authorities and a right for families" (Ministry of Education, n.d.-a).

Today, the basic or compulsory school covers nine years and begins at the age of seven. The government finances the education, but the municipalities control the spending of the money for their local schools (Ministry of Education, n.d.-b). Local authorities assign a place in a school for each student, close to their homes. However, the students have school choice and can apply for a place at another school. Basic education remains the responsibility of the municipalities (Chung, 2009). The system has full, public financing (Sahlberg, 2007). The current system of education comes from the reforms in the 1970s. The reforms combined the Finnish equivalent of primary school, secondary modern school, and middle school into this nine-year compulsory school (Nurmi, 1990). Compulsory school breaks down into two sections, the lower stage and the upper stage. The lower stage lasts six years and the upper three. In the first six years of compulsory school, the students have classroom teachers, and in the last three years, they have subject teachers. In the upper stage, children have both mandatory and optional subjects. The curriculum in the current system came from a combination and an adaptation of the former primary and middle schools.

The National Core Curriculum, created by the Finnish National Board of Education, provides teachers with a plan of educational objectives as well as assessment criteria. Although the Board of Education lays down the guidelines, the municipalities and schools place the curriculum into the local context, and the teachers hold the responsibility of carrying out the national curriculum as they see fit (Finnish National Board of Education, n.d.-a). In 1970, Finland introduced the first national curriculum, with strong centralisation (Chung, 2009). The curriculum has undergone four reforms since its inception thus far, in 1985, 1994, 2004, and 2012. In 1985, the National Curriculum became the National Core Curriculum, with increasing emphasis on a municipally-based syllabus. The reforms also abolished ability grouping and increased eligibility to studies after compulsory education. In 1994, the reforms delegated power further to the municipalities and schools. Furthermore, the changes abolished school inspections, encouraged cooperative learning, and created a "thinner" core curriculum. The 2004 reforms reversed the curricular reforms and strengthened the core curriculum. It also re-distributed the lesson hours, emphasising goals instead of content. The reforms in general have heightened the roles of local authorities and schools, and stress the relevance of local and school-specific curricula. They have also increased the role of student welfare and special education, in addition to individualised student learning. They have stressed the importance of cooperation between home and school. Although the reforms of 2004 to the National Core Curriculum have increased the control of the local authority over the curriculum, the latest reform has applied more regulations to the National Curriculum, for the Board of Education felt it needed to provide more guidance (Chung, 2009). In 2012, the National Board of Education announced a new distribution of lesson hours, and schools will implement these along with the National Core Curriculum in 2016 (Finnish National Board of Education, n.d.-a).

Although schools in Finland vary in size, most primary schools have fewer than 300 students. In order to illustrate the range in size, over one-third of comprehensive schools have fewer than fifty students, while 4% of schools have 500 students or more (Sahlberg, 2007). Schools today still follow the values of equity and provide free hot lunches, free health care, free transportation for students living far from school, and free counselling.

Finnish schools also provide extensive special needs education. The schools provide special support for students with difficulties, disorders, and disadvantages (Chung, 2009). All students have the right to the same educational objectives and possibilities; therefore, students with various difficulties have the right to individual support. The extent of this support depends on the extent of the difficulties. The Basic Education Act defines students with special educational needs as those affected by illness, disability, or reduced functional ability, those who need more mental or social support, or the students who have risk factors in their development that affect their learning. The special education philosophy in Finnish schools aims first to include the students within the mainstream classroom, in order to best provide them with the same educational opportunities as their peers. The second option will provide special education in a separate class, group, or school. In 2006, 7.7% of Finnish students received special education, while in 1998, 3.8% of students obtained more attention in schools. The Board of Education attributes this to better diagnosis, as with disabilities such as dyslexia. Boys most often attend special education classes due to behavioural problems, while girls receive more instruction in mathematics. Students receive part-time special education when they exhibit slight difficulties in learning or when they need support in some areas to overcome learning difficulties. 21.9% of students receive some sort of part-time special needs education. Some 99.7% of students complete basic school in Finland, which gives it one of the lowest dropout rates in the world (Chung, 2009). In the 2006–2007 school year, the entire country had 350 school dropouts. Even this was considered to be too many by the Board of Education and the Education Ministry. The importance that is placed on special education and education in Finland reflects the importance of education in the country, and that education helps prevent disaffection and further isolation in society.

4.2 Upper-Secondary School

After compulsory school, the students can choose between upper-secondary school and vocational school. Students may choose an optional tenth year of compulsory school, if they feel they need more time in compulsory school to improve grades or better select post-compulsory school options (Chung, 2009). Approximately half of the continuing students choose upper-secondary school and half choose vocational education. Students applying to upper-secondary school fill out an *yhteiskaku*, an application based on their marks from school, which also lists their preferences for upper-secondary school. Assessment is discussed in the next section, but, as there are no national tests within compulsory education in Finland, teachers themselves determine these grades, which are based on the national core curriculum. These teacher-assessed grades, along with student preferences, help determine their applications for upper-secondary school. Numbers in both sectors of upper-secondary education have increased in the past few decades. As previously stated, 97% of students completing compulsory education continue on to upper-secondary school. Students completing the vocational track of upper-secondary education sometimes enter the academic track after the completion of their course (Nurmi, 1990). In both sectors, students have both mandatory and elective subjects. In general upper-secondary school, students have compulsory courses and choose at least ten advanced courses in the three-year duration of school (Finnish National Board of Education, n.d.-b). Much like compulsory school, local authorities have responsibility for general upper-secondary schools. A matriculation examination takes place after the completion of upper-secondary general education. This is the only national, standard assessment that students face in Finnish primary or secondary education. The National Curriculum provides the basis for the examination, which has a minimum of four tests: the compulsory mother tongue examination, plus three assessments chosen from the second national language, mathematics, foreign language, and general studies. The matriculation certificate at the end of upper-secondary school gives eligibility to enter tertiary education (Ministry of Education, n.d.-b).

Those who continue on to upper-secondary education also may enter the vocational sector of upper-secondary education. Students who choose the vocational track learn in a school environment, but do have some work-based learning as well (Chung, 2009). The apprenticeship schemes in vocational schools have expanded recently, and approximately 10% of the vocational course takes place in an apprenticeship environment. Institutions carrying out vocational education receive a licence from the Ministry of Education, but municipalities and companies carry out the education itself. In initial

vocational education, students can receive 53 qualifications out of 116 study programmes. The qualifications come under seven sectors of vocational study:
1. Natural sciences
2. Technology and transport
3. Social sciences, business and administration
4. Tourism, catering, and home economics
5. Health and social services
6. Culture
7. Leisure and physical education
8. Humanities and teaching (Chung, 2009).

Vocational education and training in Finland believes in giving students knowledge and skills necessary for vocational competence and employment, in addition to knowledge and skills needed for further studies and lifelong learning (Chung, 2009). Therefore, students in the vocational sector have one third of their curriculum filled by general studies. Currently, a movement has been gaining momentum whereby students gain qualifications in both the academic upper-secondary school and the vocational sector of upper-secondary education. For example, 10% of students in the vocational education stream take classes in the general upper-secondary school, and 8% take the matriculation exam. Furthermore, 5% of university students come from vocational upper-secondary school.

4.3 *Assessment and Evaluation in Compulsory and Upper Secondary School*

Assessment in Finnish schools comes strictly from the teachers. The decentralised nature of Finnish schools allows for this. Primary schools do not use testing in order to concentrate on teaching, which allows for flexibility in curriculum design for teachers (Sahlberg, 2007). This lack of testing may relate to Finnish success in PISA, as the PISA data show a low level of anxiety among Finnish students. The Finnish National PISA Report cited that 7% of Finnish students felt anxiety when working on mathematics at home, compared to 52% of Japanese students and 53% of French students. Students are assessed continuously throughout the school year, with coursework and a final assessment in the subject areas. As previously stated, Finland does not nationally assess their students in compulsory education; rather, the teachers generate their own assessment according to national core curriculum guidelines. Students are also encouraged to self-assess, in order to reflect upon their learning, and instigate self-awareness (Finnish National Board of Education, n.d.-b).

Each student receives a report once a year, and teachers may administer an additional report halfway through the year. At the end of compulsory school, students receive a certificate of completion, also designed by the teachers. As stated previously, students completing the academic upper-secondary track take the only nationally administered testing in Finland. Students in the vocational track have the option of taking the matriculation exam as well, to provide opportunities to access universities.

Finnish schools self-evaluate; in other words, they have no school inspectorate (Finnish National Board of Education, n.d.-c). The government entrusts the schools, the providers of education, to carry out the National Curriculum and to evaluate and monitor their own quality. This school self-evaluation occurs every three years (Chung, 2009). It consists of surveys with parents, personnel, and students, in addition to teacher meetings over different issues within the school. This ethos of self-evaluation comes from a similar philosophy within the teacher education programmes. School evaluation in Helsinki, for example, takes into account these factors: school achievement compared to national samples, parental opinions, health reviews, curriculum evaluations, and evaluating the annual plan. Schools start the academic year with an annual plan, and use these self-evaluations to ascertain if they have achieved their goals. The ethos of self-evaluation implies a culture of trust within schools, and therefore eliminates the need for inspectorates and league tables. The Evaluation Council for Education and Training works with the Ministry of Education to aid the self-evaluation of schools (Finnish National Board of Education, n.d.-c).

4.4 *Tertiary Education*

At the tertiary level, students can attend a university or a polytechnic. Polytechnics focus on a more practical training of professionals for their careers. Finland has twenty-nine polytechnics, most having good connections to business and industry. Finland developed polytechnics in order to have a more practical focus in its tertiary education sector (Ministry of Education, n.d.-c). Finland's first university was founded in 1640 in the city of Turku. When the capital moved to Helsinki in the early 19th century, the university moved as well. However, not until Finland gained independence did more universities emerge (Nurmi, 1990). Today, the university network includes nearly every subject and enjoys geographical distribution all around Finland (Ministry of Education, n.d.-c). The state administers the universities, but they have widespread autonomy. Polytechnics at the higher education level come under municipal or private administration. Students enter university through entrance exams. The polytechnics differ from universities as they have a more practical focus. For example, doctors receive their education through universities, while nurses do so through polytechnics. Engineers can take either path, and are referred to as either *insenööri* or *diplomi-insenööri* in Finnish indicating whether they have studied at polytechnic or university, respectively (Chung, 2009).

Participation in the Finnish education system has increased dramatically in recent years. In 1960 only 8% of adults had an upper-secondary qualification, and only 4% had a tertiary education degree. In 2005, nearly 50% of adults had finished upper-secondary education, and 25% of adults received a tertiary education (Sahlberg, 2007). Nearly 70% of today's younger generation aims at tertiary education, while approximately 70% of their grandparents held an elementary school certificate (Simola, 2005).

4.5 *Influence of Reforms*

The 1990s were a time of reform for the Finnish education system. The upgrading of polytechnics to the higher education level was one of the biggest changes in Finnish education of the 1990s. Polytechnics also gained the ability to grant Master's degrees, undertaken after three years of work experience by the candidate (Ministry of Education, n.d.-c). The Finnish National Board of Education considers the year 1994 as marking a paradigm change in Finnish education. In this year, the National Core Curriculum underwent the aforementioned reforms, which strengthened the role of the municipality (Chung, 2009). This "revolution" in Finnish education also marked the end of school inspections and inspections of school material (ibid.). Along with delegating the responsibility locally, the "thinned" national curriculum entrusted the municipalities, schools, and teachers with implementing the curriculum within their schools. In fact, the "thin" curriculum of 1994 only had approximately two pages of goals and content per grade level and study area. The reforms also stressed cooperative learning. The 1990s also gave birth to LUMA. The LU in LUMA stands for *luonnontieteet*, or natural science, and the MA stands for *matematiikkaa*, or mathematics (University of Helsinki National LUMA Centre, n.d.). LUMA began in 1996 as an attempt to improve skills in science and mathematics (Finnish National Board of Education, 2007). Jointly supported by the general school and vocational school tracks, LUMA attempted to raise interest in science and mathematics as well as achievement in those areas, especially among girls. The Ministry of Education, National Board of Education, universities with teacher training courses, municipalities and schools all had stakes in the project. The reforms of the 1990s illustrate the ongoing efforts of Finland to continuously improve the education system.

5 Education Provision for Minority Groups

5.1 *The Saame*

The *Saame* (Sami), the indigenous people of Lapland, have constitutional rights to cultural autonomy (Finnish National Board of Education, n.d.). They have their own parliament that does command educational influence (Chung, 2009). For the municipalities located in the Sami areas, pupils learning the Sami language must have the provision of primary education in the language, if wanted by their parents (Finnish National Board of Education, 2001). Education in the Sami language, therefore, does exist in the Sami-speaking areas of Lapland.

5.2 *Education for Swedish-Speaking Finns*

Swedish-speaking Finns, called *finlandssvenskar* in Swedish, or *suomenruotsalaiset* in Finnish, hold a unique place in Finnish society. The Swede-Finns, constitute a "declining cultural, economic, and social elite [which] has sought to maintain ethnic identity boundaries through control of a separate Swedish-speaking school system and widespread non-formal educational efforts" (Paulston, 1977, p. 181). Separate schooling allowed the Swede-Finns to maintain the survival of their minority group. Although a minority, Swedish-speaking Finns had an atypical role compared to other ethnic minorities. They constituted "a high percentage of Finland's economic and social elite [...] with [...] superior resources, historical dominance, and psychological advantage" (ibid., p. 182).

In response to the Finnish nationalist movement in the mid-nineteenth century, the Swedish-speakers started their own counter movement, but only in the interests of the upper classes. The common Swedish-speakers did not have a part in this movement (Paulson, 1977). Many viewed the Finnish language as the language of peasants and felt superior to Finnish speakers. In 1906, Swede-Finns founded the Swedish People's Party in order to unite the entire Swedish-speaking population in Finland, irrespective of social class. This uniting of Swede-Finns supports their view that Finland, much like Switzerland or Belgium, has a culturally and linguistically pluralistic society, and "that both nationalities in Finland have existed side by side since the beginning of Finland's history. Both have contributed to its development" (ibid., p. 183).

With Finnish independence came official bilingualism, and with this legal status the Swedish-speaking Finns "aggressively pursued a policy of separatism and cultural autonomy" (Paulson, 1977, p. 183). Legal bilingualism and separatism led to separate Swedish-speaking schools. The Constitution of Finland clearly declares the rights of education in the Swedish language. In Section 17, the Constitution confirms the two national languages of Finland, Finnish and Swedish. The Section also asserts the right to use the mother tongue in official capacities, such as in courts of law and government documents. It also affirms the provision for cultural and societal necessities, on an equal basis, in the mother tongue. In 1920, with the founding of the Swedish Department in the Central Bureau of Schools, both Swedish schools and Finnish schools held, legally, an equal position (Paulson, 1977). This advantageous minority position does not find a parallel with the Finnish-speaking minority in Sweden. The Swedes have the vision of assimilating and integrating the Finnish minority into Swedish society.

During the 1920s and 1930s, Finnish-speaking university students battled for the "Finnification" of the University of Helsinki (Paulson, 1977, p. 184). The prevalence of Swedish-speaking professors and Swedish as the language of instruction placed a great onus on the Finnish-speaking students. Furthermore, the large number of Swedish schools and the "disproportionately large size of the Swedish-speaking educated class" encouraged "an overproduction of Swedish-speaking university students in comparison to the total Swede-Finn population" (ibid.). Nevertheless, today's University of Helsinki still does have a quota for Swedish-speaking students and professors, and Åbo Akademi in Turku caters only to Swedish-speakers.

The original dominance of the Swedish-speaking population's needs is clear. Economically and intellectually, the Swede-Finns held great power in Finland. "The penetration of ethnic or nationality sentiments into the field of economic and financial activities [...] that have successfully provided the funds necessary to support [...] educational work in popular education, folk high schools, cultural activities, and in the media" illustrates this power held by the Swedish-speakers in Finland, and in so many realms (Paulston, 1977, p. 186). Efforts for separate education secured a mutual acknowledgement that the Swede-Finns were different from Finns. Nordenskiöld (1919) cites that between 1880 and 1881, Swedish-speaking students in schools numbered 1,764 while the total of Finnish-speaking students came to only 786. In 1908–1909, however, the Swede-Finn numbers remained nearly constant at 1,771 while Finnish students grew to 4,756.

More recently, the "resettlement of Finnish refugees and post-War reconstruction, along with increased economic power and [the] legitimacy of Finnish nationalism, has meant increased intermarriage and the rejection of Swedish culture for a national identity by a relatively small but growing number of young Swede-Finns" (Paulston, 1977, p. 186). In other words, the events unfolding after World War II lessened the stronghold of Swede-Finn identity and allowed for mixing of the two language groups. Although the number of Swedish-speakers has remained consistent over the years, their percentage of the overall Finnish population has decreased. Language shifting has become more common, as the Finnish language gained recognition in Finnish society, and became the language of the labour market. Intermarriage also influences this trend. Swedish-speakers also emigrate to Sweden, further decreasing their percentage in the Finnish population. As recently as 1919, people still believed that "Finland is permeated with Swedish culture. The majority of the leading men still have Swedish as their native tongue." However, "the Finnish element is coming more and more to the front..." (Nordenskiöld, 1919, p. 376). Less than 60 years later, in 1977, Paulston could say "the Swede-Finns continue to surpass national educational norms, and especially those SF [Swedish-speaking] youth who live in towns and regional urban centres [...] The continuing high priority of urban Swede-Finns on formal schooling is apparent" (p. 184). Upon investigation of current PISA results, where Finnish-speakers outscore their Swedish-speaking counterparts, we must question if this superiority still exists.

6 Teacher Education in Finland

6.1 *The Historical Context of Finnish Teacher Education*

Earlier, this chapter explored in depth the context of the Finnish education system, as, "to understand the Finnish people you must study their educational system" (Gilmour, 1931, p. 63). Therefore, this chapter explores Finnish teacher education in a similar manner. The teacher education programmes of Finland reflect the high status of teachers and the professional reputation of the teaching profession. Kivinen and Rinne cite how various occupations professionalised themselves, so to speak, by "squeezing themselves inside the definition of the professions and evolving their own professional ideology" (1994, p. 516). In the Scandinavian countries, teaching has an element of professional competition, as those unqualified for teaching become excluded from the job market. The trend towards professionalism and the movement towards university preparation also affected teacher education in Finland. The "academic drift" of teaching and other professions to the university level provides examples of this new trend of "neo-academic higher education curricula" (Kivinen & Rinne, 1994, p. 518). In both Sweden and Finland, the movement of teacher education to the university level coincided with the reforms of the comprehensive school, showing some consistency between the two countries.

We can see the history of Finnish teacher education in three phases. First came the "quasi-monastic" training, "being groomed to civilise the ignorant masses of an agrarian society" (Kivinen & Rinne, 1994, p. 518). The second phase saw teacher training moved to seminaries, and the third, and current phase, is that of university teacher education.

Under Russian rule, there existed a movement to nationalise education and teacher training. A Finnish-speaking teaching seminary opened in 1863, while a Swedish-speaking institution opened in the 1870s. The development of a basic national school increased the need for more structured teacher training. Although Finland made basic education compulsory in 1922, it was the last of the Nordic countries to do so, and the country did not implement compulsory education fully until World War II, when children even in the most remote districts enrolled in school (Kivinen & Rinne, 1994).

Despite the enviable position that Finnish teachers enjoy today, the ascent to this place in society took a great deal of effort. This feat of endurance included a resistance from the land-owning peasant class to having schools within their municipalities until the early twentieth century, when, at that comparatively late time, nearly every municipality had a school (Simola, 2005). Unfortunately the bitter Civil War in 1918 divided the country and, eventually, its view of teachers and education. The loyalty of some teachers to one side or the other left a feeling of bitterness and lack of trust. The Civil War led some to believe that only missionary-style teaching could save the immoral masses, some to stop believing in a universal society, and the elite to no longer believe in education for all. Not until after World War II did the country begin to re-unify in its view of teaching and education, as teachers and "ordinary people" once again became worthy of trust. Finnish teachers have been on the conservative side of the political spectrum, unlike their colleagues in other countries.

Finnish independence in 1917 further emphasised the need for a united teacher training system. In 1934, the Jyväskylä College of Education trained teachers after completion of secondary education. Even at this early time, teaching and teacher training held great respect in Finland. "It has been a very characteristic feature of Finnish teacher education that it has leaned on the legitimacy of the educational sciences [...] Teacher training thus in fact eventually legitimated its gradually growing status by leaning on the established academic status of educational research" (Kivinen & Rinne, 1994, p. 519).

The reforms of teacher education in Finland illustrate the educational change so closely interwoven with politics, the economy, and society, and the reassessment and reconstruction the Finnish government underwent in the twentieth century (Begrem et al., 1997). Post-World War II forced Finland, along with many other countries, to reconsider the role of education in social and economic development. Putting education under a microscope revealed the inadequacies of the education system, triggering the reforms that followed.

Despite the founding of post-secondary school teacher training institutions, many of the teaching seminaries continued to exist. In 1968, however, a committee determined that all teacher training courses require an upper-secondary school qualification and that they would consist of a four-year course of study, culminating in a Master's degree in education. Therefore, all teacher education would take place within the universities (Kivinen & Rinne, 1994).

In 1971, the Teacher Training Act moved all teacher preparation to the university level. These teacher education reforms mirror the school reforms of the 1970s. Seven universities at that time had teacher education departments, one of them Swedish-speaking. These programmes all led to a Master's degree in education, the formal education for all teachers in Finland, including the primary school level. Primary school teacher training, originally a three-year programme at teacher training colleges, expanded to four-year, and finally five-year programmes in universities in the late 1970s (Sahlberg, 2007). The impetus to prepare teachers as professionals and researchers created the foundation of the teacher education reforms. "The interaction between teaching and research, it was hoped, would lead to an improved level of scholarship among the teachers" (Kivinen & Rinne, 1994, p. 522). The attention to teacher education within the general educational reforms illustrated the objective of professionalising and "academising" teacher training (Begrem et al., 1997, p. 434). It also closed the gap between educational science and teacher education. Finnish teachers, even those not currently engaged in any educational research, thus maintain a strong knowledge of educational theory. In 1982, only 10% of applicants found themselves selected for a teacher training programme, implying good quality of teacher education and popularity of the profession (Whittaker, 1983).

This process further cemented respect for teachers in Finland. "The long march of teachers from despised and underprivileged civil servants to the core of the academic elite has been more glorious and successful in Finnish society than in most other countries in the world" (Kivinen & Rinne, 1994, p. 521). The "march" of primary school teachers illustrates this fact. Even as far back as 1890, primary school teachers wanted their education within universities, and not in seminaries (Simola, 2005). Before World War II, more primary school teachers had an upper-secondary education than their colleagues in any other country. After the founding of the Jyväskylä College of Education in 1934, more universities developed faculties of education, eventually including the education of primary school teachers, and raised the level of their preparation within the educational hierarchy. In the 1950s, the teachers' union insisted that primary school teachers have education at the same level as grammar school teachers, within a university. The educational reforms of the 1970s finally fully supported the education of primary school teachers at the university level. The aforementioned comprehensive school reforms (1972–1977) and the teacher education reforms (1973–1979) had a sister reform, the General Syllabus and Degree Reform in Higher Education (1977–1980), which abolished the Bachelor's degree and subsequently raised the level of primary school teacher education to the Master's level in 1979 (ibid., p. 461). The educational reforms of the 1970s, which included teacher education reforms, finally ended the rift begun in the early twentieth century. The "teachers' middle class war" culminated in a "triumph for popular schooling" (ibid.).

The teacher education reforms seem to have achieved the overarching aim of improving the quality of teachers and their status within society (Begrem et al., 1997). This enviable position in Finnish society reaps great benefits for the education system. The respect and high status of teachers come from people of all types of socio-economic backgrounds as well (Simola, 2005). "Today the success of the professionalisation strategy can also be seen in the comparatively high status of teachers, and in the huge numbers of undergraduates wanting to launch their career as teachers" (Begrem et al., 1997, p. 434). Along with high status of teachers come respect and satisfaction from the consumers, the parents. A 1995 survey showed that 86% of parents had high satisfaction with teaching (Simola, 2005). For the most part, Finnish parents supported principles of equity.

Teaching, with its respect, appreciation, and high status, also enjoys popularity. A 2004 poll of upper-secondary school graduates cited 26% of students naming teaching as the most sought-after profession (Sahlberg, 2007). Even though, as in most countries, teacher shortages prevail, especially in mathematics and science, teaching still remains the most popular profession and overtakes such careers as medicine, law, engineering, and journalism (Simola, 2005). The popularity of teaching, according to Sahlberg (2007), comes from the requirement of a Master's degree. The degree benefits both schools and the broader society. A qualified teacher can gain employment not only in schools but also in occupations within both the public and private sector. A teaching degree also allows entrance to other postgraduate degrees, which explains an increase in PhDs among both teachers and head teachers. Master's degrees also indicate the depth, breadth, and general high quality of teacher education, in addition to reinforcing trust on the part of society and parents.

The professionalising of teacher education and teaching in general stems from both the shift of teacher training to an academic subject within universities, and the educational reforms that decentralised decision-making for schools (Begrem et al., 1997). Professional teachers:

1. Perceive personal enrichment as a professional asset

2. Appreciate cooperation and interaction with students and colleagues
3. Realise their responsibility and value their autonomy
4. Dedicate themselves to their work (ibid.).

The decentralisation and devolution of school control also add to the increased responsibility of teachers. The current Finnish school curricula "reflect a clear transition to decentralised educational decision-making, being much less prescriptive than the previous curricula" (ibid., p. 437). They allow teachers freedom and autonomy, and a culture of trust within Finnish society for the teaching profession. This trust among the Finns includes politicians and economists, something rare in other countries (Simola, 2005). Recent periodical publications in Finland have indicated this unanimous support for education and its equitable distribution among all students within the country.

Teachers today, perhaps because of their long road to high status and becoming the academic elite, perceive themselves as members of the upper-middle class (Simola, 2005). Their aforementioned conservatism still seems to exist today. The teachers in comprehensive schools "appear to be pedagogically conservative and somewhat reserved or remote in their relations with pupils and their families" (ibid., p. 461). A 1996 report from a visiting group from England found the Finnish schools surprisingly conservative and traditional, with the teacher in the front of the classroom teaching to the entire group of students. The visitors from England rarely observed individualised or student-centred learning. They did, however, notice a great amount of consistency between the schools (ibid.). A Finnish head teacher remarked how Finnish teachers did not want to give up their traditional forms of teaching if they did not have to. Finnish teachers, however, showed a strong commitment to their work and good work satisfaction.

Currently, twelve universities have teacher education courses in Finland. Moving all teacher education to the university level shows the unification within the teacher education programmes, no matter what the level or discipline (Begrem et al., 1997). The country has more professors of education than the rest of the Scandinavian countries combined (Kivinen & Rinne, 1994). Does the system produce better teachers? The former Director General of the Ministry of Education, Jaakko Numminen, believed that the promotion of teacher training to the university level, on the whole, failed, as "a university training offers no better guarantee of good teaching than that provided by the old seminaries or even the crash training programmes" (ibid., p. 523). Even so, Finnish teachers enjoy high status in society. Currently, as we have seen, teacher training courses still accept approximately only 10% of around 5,000 applicants each year (ibid.; Sahlberg, 2007).

6.2   *Current Teacher Education in Finland*

Today, all teachers within the Finnish education system, despite the level, have a tertiary degree education. Teachers for pre-primary school have either a Bachelor's degree from a university or a polytechnic. Teachers in vocational education need to have a higher or postgraduate degree within their specific subject, either from a university or a polytechnic. If a higher degree does not exist within the field, they must have the highest possible qualification within that discipline. In addition to the academic qualifications, vocational teachers must have at least three years' experience within their field of study, as well as the pedagogical coursework.

Research attributes Finnish PISA success to the high quality of Finnish teachers and the rigour of Finnish teacher education (Chung, 2009; OECD, 2010). The aforementioned popularity of the teaching profession relates to the low admissions rate to teacher education programmes. As stated previously, typical admissions rates to teacher education programmes hover around 10% of the applicant pool (Chung, 2009; Raiker, 2011). Primary teaching courses are the most selective. Those wanting to become subject teachers for lower or upper-secondary school have the option of "direct selection," meaning the university accepts them for both their subject and for teacher education. This also indicates that the applicant must pass two sets of entrance examinations. Teaching has proved an extremely popular profession in the country, and those aspiring towards a teaching career must undergo a tough admissions process (Chung, 2009).

Although the admissions process differs from university to university, applicants wanting to enter teacher education programmes often must first pass an aptitude test. This usually means a test based on a book that candidates read before the test, predominantly based on educational theory. Those who perform well on the book test then have interviews with the university staff. Primary teaching candidates also undergo a psychological test, which is used in addition to the interview. Some students studying secondary school subjects may apply for educational science and teaching practice during their university studies. Students for both subject and primary teaching programmes always have major and minor subjects. A university course lasts for five years, including a Bachelor's degree, a Master's degree, and teaching practice, which is included in the programme credit distribution. A degree includes research conducted by students at both the undergraduate and Master's level in the form of a dissertation.

A teaching degree in Finland covers subject education, educational sciences, and teaching practice. Primary teaching students have more teaching practice, spread out throughout the five year programme. Subject teaching candidates typically study their subject and pedagogy, and undertake their teaching practice during their fourth year. The students mainly carry out their teaching practice at the *normaalikoulu*, or university-based teacher training school. Students also undertake some of their teaching practice outside of the *normaalikoulu* setting. It is up to the students to find such placements; however, the university used for this case study does have a standing partnership with a "field school" in the area. These placements have proved very popular with the students.

This *normaalikoulu* differs from a municipality school as it receives its funding through the university. The head teachers and teachers are employed as part of the university, and a head teacher's job involves cooperation with the university. An example of this partnership is that head teachers and deputy head teachers serve on university committees, as their colleagues in the teacher education faculty would do. Teachers within the *normaalikoulu* elect the head teachers from within the school, and they serve as head for six years.

Teachers at the *normaalikoulu* must have a Master's degree, teaching qualification, and a minimum of two years of experience. Teachers' salaries are higher than average, in order to accommodate their extra responsibility. Many teachers within *normaalikoulu* have a degree higher than the minimum Master's degree, whether a PhD or a Licentiate degree. Teaching at the *normaalikoulu* has proven very popular, and competition for these positions is high. Teachers' highest priority at these schools must be the training of future teachers.

The Finnish teacher training philosophy perceives the teachers as researchers, and therefore takes a research-based approach to teacher education. As stated previously, qualified teachers in basic school and upper-secondary school have Master's degrees. Teachers of the first six years of comprehensive school have a Master's degree in pedagogy, while subject teachers have a Master's degree within the subject, although they can choose to write a Master's degree in pedagogy. Successful completion of a teacher education course allows the candidate admission to doctoral programmes.

Despite the careful attention paid to teacher training, Kivinen and Rinne worry about the future of Finnish teacher education. They believe that the too-rapid expansion and reform of teacher education requires a reassessment, and wonder whether the professionalisation of teaching "blocks from view the needs for greater flexibility on the educational labour market and the real demands generated by a teacher's work" (Kivinen & Rinne, 1994, p. 525). While these debates continue, Finland's high PISA outcomes and its connection to teachers, teaching, and teacher education have quelled the criticisms of the current state of teacher education in the country.

7 Summary

This chapter provided an overview of the Finnish education system. It delved into the historical developments of both the education system and examined the entire education system, from early childhood education, through compulsory, secondary, and tertiary education. It discussed tertiary education as well. In addition to the structure of Finnish education, this chapter included the analysis of major educational reforms. The impact of these reforms can be seen in Finland's PISA outcomes. This chapter also examined education for the two main minority groups, the Swedish-speaking Finns and the *Saame*. The rights of the Swedish-speaking minority are exceptional and uncover the group's privileged standing within Finnish society. The rights of the *Saame* acknowledge the country's indigenous settlers.

Finland's oft-admired teacher education also merited exploration, from its historical roots to its current provision. The Finnish education system, teacher education, and education for the Swedish-speaking minority all stem from historical contexts and Nordic philosophies. In order to understand Finland's present situation and its education system, one must investigate Finland's past. Later in this book, it will become evident that the reasons behind Finnish PISA outcomes refer back to the discussions in this chapter.

Note

[1] Uno Cygnaeus. (n.d.). Retrieved August 15, 2007, from http://www.britannica.com/eb/article-9028391/Uno-Cygnaeus. Uno Cygnaeus. (n.d.) Retrieved August 15, 2007, from http://www.jyu.fi/tdk/museo/unoe.html

CHAPTER 4

The Programme for International Student Assessment: The Birth of an Achievement Study that Captured Worldwide Attention

1   Introduction

The Organisation for Economic Cooperation and Development's Programme for International Student Assessment, or PISA surveys have created a sensation in both the educational and political worlds. The tests, administered every three years beginning in 2000, have revealed Finland as one of the top performers. Triggering global curiosity, the PISA tests have placed Finland on the travel itinerary of those wishing to discover the influences behind educational success. Finland has shared the top spots with educational powerhouses such as South Korea and Japan. Finland outscored even its Nordic neighbours. The country's performance in PISA has created a great attraction to the country's education system. In order to investigate the strength of Finland in PISA, we must also explore the assessments themselves, their aims and goals, as well as the criticism and praise of the project. Furthermore, we must delve into the OECD, the phenomenon of Finland in PISA, and the interest this has triggered in its educational system.

The first administration of PISA in 2000 has undoubtedly changed the face of education, placing it in a more political, global context. However, other international educational surveys existed before PISA. Before PISA, the International Association for the Evaluation of Educational Achievement (IEA), headquartered in The Netherlands, conducted surveys in mathematics, science, and reading achievement. IEA, established in 1967, believes education must not only take into account inputs into education, but also observe outputs as well (IEA, n.d.). The IEA views "the world as a natural educational laboratory, where different school systems experiment in different ways to obtain optimal results in the education of their youth" (ibid.). The organisation began studies with the First International Mathematics Study (FIMS) in 1964. Over the years, IEA has generated many studies involving different subject matter and grade levels. Most notably, in the 1980s, it surveyed both mathematics and science in the Second International Mathematics Study (SIMS) and the Second International Science Study (SISS).

In 1995, the IEA conducted one of its most visible surveys, the Trends in International Mathematics and Science Survey, or TIMSS, which involved forty-five countries and approximately 500,000 students. In that study, the IEA aimed to measure mathematics and science achievement and "identify the major in-school and out-of-school determinants of the educational outcomes" (IEA, n.d.). TIMSS was the largest educational survey to date. The IEA repeated administration of TIMSS in 2003, expanding the number of countries to fifty, many coming from Africa and the Middle East, and participating in international educational assessments for the first time. In 2007, the IEA produced yet another round of TIMSS, this time with sixty participating countries. The TIMSS 2011 survey included sixty-five countries.

TIMSS measures mathematical and scientific knowledge at the fourth and eighth year of compulsory schooling. After its first administration in 1995, the IEA has conducted the study every four years. The sampled students answer questions covered within the mathematics and science curricula at their grade levels. Experts from various countries collaborate to collate curricular matter from all around the world in order to create the assessment material. TIMSS seeks to measure curricula in schools around the world on three levels: the intended curriculum, the implemented curriculum, and the achieved curriculum. TIMSS has expanded from small, separate studies of mathematics and science achievement to a large, multi-country survey with a large range of participants.

IEA also assesses reading skills. Its assessments of reading literacy started in 1970, and in 1991 it conducted the Reading Literacy Study. The Reading Literacy Study evolved into the Progress in Reading Literacy Survey (PIRLS), initiated in 2001, which measures the reading levels of pupils in thirty-five countries, and forty in 2006. The 2011 survey included fifty countries. PIRLS, generated at a five-year cycle, measures achievement in reading literacy in order to provide benchmarks for measurement, and uses three main foci: comprehension, purposes for reading, and attitudes towards reading. These new participants in the IEA studies mark a new wave of countries participating in international assessments. While the original participants came from traditionally wealthier countries, the new countries have more modest economic situations and different social and political contexts. The participation of such countries and growing uptake indicates the widening of the international education context, both in terms of international comparison and in the increased participation of countries in these surveys.

While the IEA quietly produced various educational studies over the years, the OECD instigated a more high-profile survey. In 2000, the OECD surveyed students from around the world with PISA. The OECD, principally an economic organisation, initiated the survey at the request of its member countries. Despite the existence of IEA surveys such as TIMSS, PISA made a huge impact in the educational world, the political world, and in the media. PISA took a different approach from its counterparts in the IEA, by reinventing the notion of literacy.

This self-described "innovative" approach "is concerned with the capacity of students to extrapolate from what they have learned and to analyse and reason as they pose, solve and interpret problems in a variety of situations" (OECD, 2007, p. 3). This "forward looking" approach measures the ability of "young people to use their knowledge and skills in a variety of real-life situations, rather than merely on [sic] the extent to which they have mastered the school curriculum" (OECD, n.d.-a, p. 6). PISA, therefore, does not use curricula from various countries as testing material; rather, it assesses the students' ability to use the knowledge gained in schools. PISA uses the testing age of fifteen in order to measure "how far students approaching the end of compulsory education have acquired some of the knowledge and skills essential for full participation in the knowledge society" (ibid., p. 4). PISA has helped redefine educational goals by assessing "what students can do with what they learn at school and not merely whether they can reproduce what they have learned" (ibid.).

PISA's new concept of literacy breaks down into a rubric, allocating students into six categories, measured on a scale. For example, the 2006 survey, which focused on scientific literacy, used this rubric to distribute the participating students into the six scales for science (OECD, 2007, p. 14) (see Table 4.1).

TABLE 4.1   PISA proficiency scale (1–6) for scientific literacy

Level	Percentage of students able to perform at level	Description of what students can do at specific level
6	1.3% of students from OECD countries can perform at Level 6	Students can consistently identify, explain and apply scientific knowledge and knowledge about science in a variety of complex life situations. They can link different information sources and explanations and use evidence from those sources to justify decisions. They clearly and consistently demonstrate advanced scientific thinking and reasoning, and they demonstrate willingness to use their scientific understanding in support of solutions to unfamiliar scientific and technological situations. Students at this level can use scientific knowledge and develop arguments in support of recommendations and decisions that centre on personal, socio-economic, or global situations.

(cont.)

TABLE 4.1   PISA proficiency scale (1–6) for scientific literacy (cont.)

Level	Percentage of students able to perform at level	Description of what students can do at specific level
5	9% of students from OECD countries can perform at Level 5	Students can identify the scientific components of many complex life situations, apply both scientific concepts and knowledge about science to these situations, and can compare, select and evaluate appropriate scientific evidence for responding to life situations. Students at this level can use well-developed inquiry abilities, link knowledge appropriately and bring critical insights to situations. They can construct explanations based on evidence and arguments based on their critical analysis.
4	29.3% of students from OECD countries can perform at Level 4	Students can work effectively with situations and issues that may involve explicit phenomena requiring them to make inferences about the role of science or technology. They can select and integrate explanations from different disciplines of science or technology and link those explanations directly to aspects of life situations. Students at this level can reflect on their actions and they can communicate decisions using scientific knowledge and evidence.
3	56.7% of students from OECD countries can perform at Level 3	Students can identify clearly described scientific issues in a range of contexts. They can select facts and knowledge to explain phenomena and apply simple models or inquiry strategies. Students at this level can interpret and use scientific concepts from different disciplines and can apply them directly. They can develop short statements using facts and make decisions based on scientific knowledge.
2	80.8% of students from OECD countries can perform at Level 2	Students have adequate scientific knowledge to provide possible explanations in familiar contexts or draw conclusions based on simple investigations. They are capable of direct reasoning and making literal interpretations of the results of scientific inquiry or technological problem solving.

(cont.)

TABLE 4.1   PISA proficiency scale (1–6) for scientific literacy (*cont.*)

Level	Percentage of students able to perform at level	Description of what students can do at specific level
1	94.8% of students from OECD countries can perform at Level 1	Students have such a limited scientific knowledge that it can only be applied to a few, familiar situations. They can present scientific explanations that are obvious and follow explicitly from given evidence.

PISA and the IEA assessments have in essence created an educational Olympics. Previous to these assessments, most could only speculate about the best features of education systems, and which countries had the most successfully educated citizens. In terms of the visibility of education, the possibility to see strengths and weaknesses within a system, and the observability of successful systems, the quantitative, international assessments have made a significant contribution to the field of education. PISA, TIMSS, and PIRLS, large, sweeping educational surveys, also serve as a catalyst for further educational research. Seeking the reasons behind the outcomes in such studies or comparing in-depth a few educational systems can stem from these international surveys, providing a different, more qualitative viewpoint on educational matters. The advent of these studies has expanded the possibilities for educational policy borrowing, stemming from the attraction some countries exhibit towards "enviable" education systems. A relatively recent phenomenon, such international surveys will surely change, and have already changed, the future of education.

2   The OECD

The creator of PISA, The Organisation for Economic Cooperation and Development (OECD), with thirty member countries, commits itself to "democratic government and the market economy" (OECD, n.d.-b). It also "plays a prominent role in fostering good governance in the public service and in corporate activity" (ibid.) Furthermore, the "OECD produces internationally agreed instruments, decisions and recommendations to promote rules of the game in areas where multilateral agreement is necessary for individual countries to make progress in a globalised economy" (ibid.).

The OECD emerged from the OEEC, the Organisation for European Economic Cooperation, founded in 1947 to help reconstruct Europe after the Second World War. As NATO's economic counterpart, the OECD came to existence in 1961, taking over the OEEC (Chung, 2009). The current trend toward globalisation has "seen the scope of the OECD's work move from examining each policy area within each member country to analysing how various policy areas interact with each other, between countries and beyond the OECD area" (ibid., p. 43). The OECD has also striven to "achieve sustainable economic growth and employment and to raise the standard of living in member countries while maintaining financial stability – all this in order to contribute to the development of the world economy" (ibid.). The Organisation also assists in the world's economy beyond its members, and uses its experience to aid transitional countries and economies.

The OECD's directorate for education views education within a lifelong learning context. The OECD conducts tests to generate statistics and indicators, but its work also aims to cover the qualitative dimensions of educational research. The Organisation describes its educational research as "policy recommendations designed to increase both the quality and equity of education systems" (OECD, n.d.-a, p. 19) and hopes to have wide policy relevance.

3   PISA

Beginning in 1992, the OECD began publishing *Education at a Glance*, which provided the OECD member countries with comparative information about the differing organisation and function of their education systems. The study, published yearly since that date, sparked considerable interest among the OECD member countries. In response to the member countries' interest in comparative student performance and reliable educational data, the OECD initiated the Programme for International Student Assessment in 2000 (Riley & Torrance, 2003). The OECD feels it created PISA in accordance with the wishes of its member countries and that it has considerable use at the public policy level. Through PISA, the OECD wishes to make good educational practice visible to the rest of the world. However, the OECD "acts non-coercively," meaning that countries, whether involved in PISA or not, can set their own levels of reaction and response to the survey (Gruber, 2006, p. 198).

In order for the OECD to execute a survey of this magnitude successfully, it relies on many experts to fulfill the needs of the test. The OECD works in cooperation with the education ministries and education ministers from the participating countries. The team at the OECD has central control over the management of PISA and provides a consistent direction for all the PISA groups. The education ministry of every participating country designates a representative to the PISA Governing Board, which determines the PISA policies (OECD, n.d.-c).

The PISA Consortium refers to an international contractor responsible for the design and implementation of PISA. This Consortium consists of different testing and assessment agencies. National Project Managers, appointed by their country's government, work with the OECD, the Governing Board, and the Consortium to supervise the application of PISA in their home country (OECD, n.d.-c).

Two groups manage the questions set. PISA has two groups of experts, one for subject matter and one for the questionnaire as a whole. An international group of experts make up the Subject Matter Groups for the target subjects for PISA: mathematical, scientific, and reading literacy, and, for the 2003 survey, problem solving. The Questionnaire Expert Group provides guidance in the creation of the surveys themselves. The Governing Board chooses the members of the Expert Group. The OECD encourages all participating countries in PISA to submit possible test questions to the PISA Consortium. The Consortium itself also writes questions for the survey. It reviews all questions and the participating countries review them for any cultural bias. The participating countries also take part in pilot studies to determine the fairness of the questions (OECD, n.d.-c).

The assessment survey, intended for administration every three years, tests students nearing the end of many countries' compulsory education, at age fifteen, on their acquired skills necessary for life in the knowledge economy (OECD, 2004a). Furthermore, it created the tests with the view that school education comes as a part of the lifelong learning process, and it did so not to measure school curricula particularly, but the application of knowledge in everyday life skills (OECD, n.d.-c). PISA also takes into account that "the acquisition of knowledge and skills can be influenced by students' individual characteristics, by features of their schools, and by the structure of their education systems" (OECD, 2004a, p. 5). Therefore, the survey solicits data on students' home background, engagement in learning, approaches to learning, gender differences, social backgrounds, school climate and resources, and school system characteristics and their influence on the results. Head teachers also answer a questionnaire about their schools. Participating countries have the option of administering one of several PISA questionnaires, asking, for example, about parent background or computer literacy. The OECD points out that this survey "does not produce prescriptions for education systems, but makes observations designed to help policy makers think about the effect of certain system features" (ibid., p. 18). PISA also measures student capabilities across academic disciplines, as in their motivation, their attitudes towards learning, strategies for study, and computer skills. The OECD uses this information to clarify the connections between student performance and external factors, such as socio-economic status, immigration, and gender (Lie & Linnakylä, 2004; OECD, n.d.-c).

At the first time of administration, PISA surveyed 265,000 students in 43 countries and measured mathematics, science, and reading literacy. Furthermore, each survey has a focus on one of the assessed areas, and these foci rotate with each administration of PISA. Table 4.2 shows the years of the PISA rotation, focus, countries assessed, and number of students.

TABLE 4.2   PISA overview by year

Year	Focus	Number of countries/ economies	Number of students assessed
2000	Reading	43	265,000
2003	Mathematics (and Problem Solving)	41	275,000
2006	Science	57	400,000
2009	Reading	70	470,000
2012	Mathematics	65	510,000
2015	Science	72	540,000

Note: PISA 2018: Reading, 80 countries, 500,000+ students

According to the OECD, three general themes emerged from the PISA 2000 data. First, they noticed that autonomous education systems performed better than centralised ones. Secondly, they found that education systems that monitored and assessed their performance had better results than those that did not undertake periodic assessments. Lastly, the OECD states that countries that provide support to low-performing students had overall higher academic achievements than those that did not (OECD, 2004a).

The test, re-administered in 2003, added a new section of problem solving to the previous three subject areas. This provided "for the first time a direct assessment of adult competencies that apply across different areas of the school's curriculum" (OECD, 2004b, p. 3). The ideal 15-year-old problem solver "can think about the underlying relationships in a problem, solve it systematically, check their work and communicate their results" (ibid.). Forty-one countries participated with analysable results in this administration of the test. The 2003 test, while covering all four subject areas, focused on mathematics (OECD, 2004b).

The 2006 survey expanded to fifty-seven countries, including both OECD countries and partner countries. It covered 90% of the world's economy. PISA 2006, which focused on scientific literacy, also increased its research on factors contributing towards educational outcomes, such as motivation to learn, learning strategies, and socio-economic background (OECD, n.d.-a). The OECD concluded that PISA had illuminated "those countries that succeed in achieving high performance standards while at the same time providing an equitable distribution of learning opportunities" (ibid., p. 4).

PISA 2009 included seventy countries and economies, and focused on reading literacy (OECD, 2010). This survey marked the beginning of a new cycle of PISA foci, as the first survey in 2000 also focused on reading literacy. The results as discussed in the OECD reports of the 2009 survey illustrated the importance of the value of education in society; celebrating diversity of educational interests, abilities, and socio-economic backgrounds; and individualising student learning. The quality of head teachers and teachers is of utmost importance as well. High-performing education systems also exhibit consistency and transparency in their goals and high standards. These high standards must reach across the entire system, ensuring all students adhere to the expectations.

PISA 2012, the second survey within the second cycle of PISA focused on mathematical literacy. This survey included sixty-five participating countries and economies, representing 80% of the world's economy (OECD, 2013b). The data revealed that mathematics skills impacted a person's life chances, especially with access to well-paying jobs in the labour market. As the 2012 release of PISA scores collected data over a twelve-year period, the findings revealed that some countries improved in the assessed areas, signifying that educational improvement is possible and attainable. Furthermore, the equality in some systems indicated that education systems can have both many high performers and few low performers, illustrating how educational improvement policies do not need to choose between the two. Similarly, the results showed that education systems can be both high-performing and equitable. PISA 2015 focused on scientific literacy and assessed 540,000 students in 72 countries and economies. The PISA survey of 2018 collected data from 80 countries and economies, and involved over 500,000 students. PISA 2018, which focused on reading literacy, releases its scores in December of 2019.

PISA effectively changes the role of the OECD and also alters its relationship with member countries (Gruber, 2006). PISA provides the OECD countries and participating countries with significant educational benchmarks. The OECD's strong reputation for measuring economic indicators presumably has allowed for the high visibility of PISA and its general acceptance as a measure of educational standards. Drawing upon the educational research potential of its member countries, the OECD has created a policy-driven survey, with "hard" empirical data, arranged in a league table format that can embarrass low-performing countries or praise high-performing ones.

3.1 The Administration of PISA

The international contractor, called the PISA Consortium, chooses schools at random within each participating country. According to PISA protocol, the students must be between 15 years and three months and 16 years and two months of age at the time of testing. The PISA Consortium samples schools and students in order to include a wide range of backgrounds and academic abilities. These sampled students take a test on the areas covered: mathematical, scientific, and reading literacy, and in 2003, problem solving. PISA stresses that literacy means measurement of their everyday life knowledge, and not school curricula. Each PISA survey includes approximately seven hours of testing material. While each student takes a two-hour test, the combination of all the surveys allows for all seven hours of testing material to be covered. The OECD has conducted some computer testing, in anticipation of future PISA surveys (OECD, n.d.-c).

The National Project Managers from each country oversee the test markers. Every participating country has its own test markers for PISA. They grade the surveys according to the protocol determined by the PISA Consortium and Subject Experts. The groups exchange and check the corrected PISA surveys, send them to the PISA Consortium, and ultimately to the OECD. The tests are scored according to a scale, Level 1 for the most basic level and Level 5 for the most difficult. The PISA questions also reflect these five levels of difficulty. In the end, the OECD ranks them according to the mean score on the surveys (OECD, n.d.-c).

3.2 Criticisms of PISA

The complex nature of large-scale, cross-national surveys lends itself to criticism. Many criticisms of the OECD's PISA surveys exist, and these cover a wide range of concerns, from the methodology of the survey itself to the wider political implications of PISA. Many of these issues have escalated since the release of the first PISA scores, and have contributed to some of the major discussions and analyses in this book.

The methodology of any study, especially of one so large, almost inevitably comes under criticism. PISA is no exception. Its sampling, for example, often comes under scrutiny (e.g. Prais, 2004). PISA, as stated previously, samples according to age, and not grade level, across the different countries. However, some critics of this argue that this often spans two grade levels, creating confusion when analysing the results. Countries with rigorous testing regimes may also be more reluctant to enter international testing, due to the stress on the students as well as the price of undertaking such tests, which affects a country's sample size (Prais, 2003). Despite these concerns, PISA continues, and the interest of the press, governments, and education officials seems to grow from survey to survey. Even with these criticisms of PISA methodology, the interest in PISA and subsequent comparative value indicate the staying power of PISA in the future.

Some criticisms target the purpose of PISA along with its methodology. It has been argued that PISA does not actually achieve its goal of measuring skills for real life:

> PISA gives a relatively valid assessment of 'knowledge and skills of students in assessment situations,' but its results cannot validly be generalized to claims about 'knowledge and skills for life.' In other words, the PISA studies do not assess what they claim to do. (Bondup Dohn, 2007, p. 2)

PISA really addresses two questions, how fifteen-year-olds use their competence in reading, mathematical, and scientific literacy in life, and how well compulsory schooling prepares students for life after formal education. This suggests that PISA's methodology is too insufficient and the survey items are too simplistic for the onerous task of measuring one's ability to navigate "real life" situations. All tests, to some extent, can apply to real life.

The criticisms of PISA's methodology also come in comparison to the IEA studies, such as TIMSS and PIRLS. Some countries, such as Finland and the UK, have disparate outcomes in both PISA and TIMSS, which can give conflicting impressions of different education systems (e.g. Schagen & Hutchinson, 2007). Two surveys, even with different goals, can raise confusion among those interpreting the results. Schagen and Hutchinson equate having two surveys to a man having two watches:

> A man with one watch always knows what time it is; a man with two watches is never quite sure. (Anonymous, in Schagen & Hutchinson, 2007, p. 34)

The different foci of the two studies may account for this disparity in outcomes, as it has been argued that PISA aligns closely to the ethos of Finnish education (Chung, 2009). This explains high Finnish scores in PISA, and more mediocre ones when the country participates, albeit rarely, in TIMSS. Therefore, this raises the question of the best way to survey students cross-nationally. IEA assessments differ from PISA through the methodological differences between the two tests, namely the questions asked, differences in target age groups, and the representation and response rate of participating schools (Prais, 2003).

Related to this is the confusion created by these approaches to measuring education cross-nationally. For example, PISA's view of academic "literacy" is also criticised, as it does not directly correlate to the curricula like TIMSS and PIRLS. Those who respond to these criticisms (e.g. Adams, 2003), however, argue that PISA has merit in uncovering how students can apply their education in real life. Furthermore, critics argue that the target age for PISA leads to better data, since seeking out a specific grade level, as with TIMSS, brings up comparability issues across countries, such as starting age of compulsory education. This confusion thus leads to the conclusion that a hybrid study would help overcome the contradictions between the two surveys (e.g. Prais, 2004). Furthermore, the three-year interval of PISA does not allow for a clear view of the changes within and among education systems, and longer cycles, even up to ten years (e.g. Schagen & Hutchinson, 2007), are recommended.

The sheer size and scale of PISA brings up more methodological criticisms, with the difficulty of ensuring comparability in a large-scale, international survey. Many share the view that PISA takes too narrow a view of education (e.g. Riley & Torrance, 2003) with a limited subject matter, meaning just three subject areas. "No measures are produced of performance in other academic areas, far less of attitudes and values across the curriculum as a whole, and whether or not schools are producing decent, tolerant, and curious citizens of the future" (Riley & Torrance, 2003, p. 423). This suggests that the methodology of PISA is too simplistic (e.g. Goldstein, 2004b). Goldstein (2004b) recommends that a multilevel data analysis would allow for more complexity of models and account for more cultural specificity, also a criticism when it comes to PISA.

Criticisms of PISA also stress that cross-national studies do not provide an accurate picture of education systems. For example, "unmeasured 'third factors' can actually be the root cause of both measures" (Schagen & Hutchinson, 2007, p. 35). Critics (e.g. Goldstein, 2004b; Bonderup Dohn, 2007) note a lack of attention to cultural specificities, ambiguities, and errors, leading to cultural bias in the test questions. Cultural context can also affect understanding and test taking in a survey such as PISA. "Situations of everyday life require not only the solving of pre-set problems but the ability to pose such problems, as well as an understanding of their embedding in context" (Bonderup Dohn, 2007, p. 3). Culture, in addition, influences the final outcomes in PISA. Test scores and league table rankings include, but do not necessarily separate, educational differences influenced by social, political, and structural differences between the countries. For example, the high scores of nations such as Japan and Korea in PISA may reflect the strong culture of private tutoring outside of school, and not the education system alone. A country like Finland, however, which does not participate in high-stakes testing and does not have a culture of private tutoring, also performs well in PISA (Sahlberg, 2007). Cultural bias and the influences of society, therefore, do not show up in PISA results, offering an often skewed view of an individual country's education system.

The issue of equity in translation especially has pertinence with PISA. In fact, PISA is used as an example when illustrating the difficulty of maintaining equivalence in an international test (Grisay & Monseur, 2007). While "there is now a recognition of the tentative and approximate nature of translated materials" (Goldstein, 2004b, p. 319), some argue that PISA does not have a robust enough methodology of translation to achieve maximum equity between the surveys for different countries. The OECD utilises an extensive methodology, incorporating both of its languages, English and French, in the processes of translation into other languages. Critics note the impossibility of creating such a large survey and completely eliminating bias (e.g. Bonderup Dohn, 2007). Even though they acknowledge the immense effort by the OECD to reduce bias, especially working in two languages, PISA has more bias than it should. Translation of testing materials is often the point where errors and cultural contexts arise, despite the efforts taken by the OECD to eliminate these (Grisay & Monseur, 2007). The OECD even takes advantage of its position as a bilingual organisation, and uses two language versions, in English and in French, to minimise any translation biases. The OECD encourages the two translators for each country to use both the English and French versions, and reconcile the differences with a third translator. The national versions then go back to the OECD, to the PISA International Centre, to further verify the equivalence of the translated version (Grisay & Monseur, 2007). Despite these careful efforts, however, cultural and curricular differences can skew the equivalence of different countries, even with the same mother tongue. Furthermore, Bonderup Dohn (2007, p. 10) asserts that the OECD created PISA in a vague way on purpose, in order to appease all interested parties. The concrete and absolute results of the surveys contrast with the comparatively ambiguous measurements made by PISA.

The further or more "distant" the language from the Indo-European family, the less equivalence occurred in the PISA surveys (Grisay & Monseur, 2007). For example, East Asian countries had more diversion from the original tests than European countries. Bias also exists among the test questions. Asian countries scored lower on multiple-choice questions than their western counterparts. This comes down to speculation that the Asian languages do not lend themselves to multiple-choice questions, whether in terms of syntax or word order, for example. The Asian countries scored much higher on the constructed response section of PISA. Countries with both low GDP and low reading scores, however, scored better on multiple-choice questions. These linguistic differences and disparate test taking cultures also potentially skew the PISA scores of different countries.

Criticisms of PISA often state that the survey results make education too political. Much literature, including chapters in this book, discusses the politicisation of education as a result of international surveys such as TIMSS and PISA (e.g. Riley & Torrance, 2003). This draws attention to the fact that the OECD actually has no direct responsibility for education, but has had a great impact on education and subsequent policy. While this influence can be positive, it is often negative. The superficial scores generated by such surveys, such as PISA, are "blunt instruments" and often carry too much weight and have become a part of a "new education currency" (Riley & Torrance, 2003, pp. 420–421). For example, Finnish "PISA tourism" could have a negative impact if "politicians seek simplistic solutions to the education challenges which their own countries face and seek off-the-shelf solutions which are highly context specific" (ibid., p. 421). This politicisation of PISA creates the temptation for "quick fix" policy solutions, a criticism of the survey soon after its inception, which will exist until education policy makers begin viewing PISA results in a critical, informed manner.

Since the first PISA scores were released, there has been a worry that education policy makers do not pay any attention beyond the scores produced by surveys such as PISA. International surveys such as TIMSS or PISA can increase understanding of an education system's strengths and weaknesses, and provide useful data for policy makers. However, the allure of the survey results often overshadows these helpful elements, especially when presented as an international league table.

The political impact of PISA, less directly related to the formulation of the tests, remains a source of criticism nonetheless. The PISA rankings, in league table format and the cause of political and media sensation, "are clearly designed to attract attention while the caveats which are included in the reports are routinely ignored" (Riley & Torrance, 2003, p. 423). The many observers of these surveys do not take into account the statistical significance of the results. For example, England, ranked 7th in PISA 2000, could have been 3rd or 9th, as the countries in that range did not produce different scores of statistical significance. In 2003, Riley and Torrance worried that countries would construct new education policies as a direct result of the outcomes in PISA or TIMSS, and the German, Japanese, Norwegian, and English policy reactions to PISA, discussed in the final chapter of this book, show that these worries came to fruition.

Riley and Torrance also feared for a change in the focus of education, the paradigm shift that this book also addresses. Surveys such as PISA and TIMSS "create and reinforce a climate that views education as narrow skill preparation for future employment, rather than as a challenging engagement with the knowledge and understanding that constitutes our culture and the democratic processes which future citizens must control" (Riley & Torrance, 2003, p. 424). These surveys have altered the field of comparative education into "a political tool for creating educational policy or a mode of governance, rather than remaining in the research realm of intellectual inquiry. The publicity and effects of the OECD-led PISA assessment of political debate were a perfect example of this. It is symptomatic of the problem that scholarly discussion has been most vivid in so-called 'hero and villain' countries" (Simola, 2005, p. 456). The critics presciently realised that international surveys may change the future of education. "What physicists realised some time ago, but educational testing people seem averse to acknowledging, is that when you measure something you change it" (Riley & Torrance, 2003, p. 424).

PISA, for all its shortcomings as a survey, was created to be viewed as this:

> Finally, any such survey should be viewed primarily not as a vehicle for ranking countries, even along many dimensions, but rather as a way of exploring country differences in terms of cultures, curricula and school organization [...] Such studies should be treated as opportunities for gaining fundamental knowledge about differences, not as competitions to see who comes top. (Goldstein, 2004b, p. 329)

However, critics of PISA realised soon after its inception that the use of the data moved beyond its original intentions as a cross-national survey. Despite the shortcomings of PISA as a survey itself, and of its use, these international comparisons will most likely remain a fixture in the future of educational policy and research. The surveys "serve as a basis for creating a rich empirical database that has continuing significance for cross-national research in its attempt to understand the potential reasons behind observed differences between and within countries" (Lie & Linnakylä, 2004, p. 228).

4 Summary

The OECD's PISA has garnered much attention, politically, educationally, and in the media. The PISA results thus far have shown that Finland has, according to the survey, a highly performing education system. This chapter intended to explore the background and context of the PISA survey in general, as well as of the OECD.

PISA was not the first international achievement study. Before PISA, the IEA conducted cross-national surveys since the 1960s. PISA and the IEA surveys differ, however. While the IEA focuses on school curricula at certain grade levels, PISA looks at fifteen-year-olds and at "literacy," or the application of mathematics, science, and reading literacy in life.

The OECD, previously a principally economic organisation, has changed the face of education in a global context. The creation of PISA has been a new phenomenon in an internationally and globally comparative context. Conducted every three years, it will continue to provide a longitudinal study of educational achievement and context for various countries in the world, in addition to creating a benchmark for international educational comparison.

A survey such as PISA, however, falls prey to criticism and disapproval. Prais, argued that "immense resources had been invested in carrying out and analyzing the results of this survey – but not, in my view, in fully thinking through its purpose and design" (2003, p. 139). Assessment on this scale inevitably garners negative press. The basic methodology, its validity, cultural and linguistic transferability, among other factors, have all come under attack by PISA critics. Research of this kind cannot ignore its critics. However, others have praised the new approach of cross-cultural comparison in the PISA tests. "It eschews the often-derided model of curriculum testing. Instead, it accesses whether students nearing the end of compulsory education have the knowledge and skills needed for full participation in society" (Lyne, 10 December 2001).

PISA and the success of Finland in the surveys act as a catalyst to investigate many factors, those influencing PISA and the issues that PISA influences. The survey has exhibited wide influence and has affected other fields of educational study. For example, it has provided new benchmarks for school effectiveness. On a grander scale, PISA has triggered considerable interest in the Finnish education system, and an immense degree of cross-national attraction has occurred.

CHAPTER 5

Issues of Policy Transfer

1   Introduction

This chapter delves into the background of comparative education and policy borrowing theory. Finland's top performance in all administrations of PISA thus far has inevitably led to immense interest in the country and its education system. The temptation to borrow Finland's policy and emulate its educational successes may, according to policy borrowing theory, become problematic. This chapter thus explores policy borrowing theory and the problematic nature of policy transfer.

2   Background and Theory

The long and developing tradition in the comparative education field of investigating other countries' systems of education, in the hope of eventual policy transfer, results in the borrowing and lending of educational policy between countries. Noah and Eckstein (1969) describe the field as developing in five different stages, although not discretely:
1. Travellers' tales
2. Travellers with a specific educational focus
3. Understanding of other nations, detailed accumulation of information
4. Study of "national character" and role in shaping national systems of education
5. Quantitative research, explanation of educational phenomena (summarised, in Phillips & Schweisfurth, 2006, p. 28).

Comparative education, although quite nebulous in its exact definition, aims, as Sadler stated, to investigate educational systems not in the "home" context in order to improve the "home" system. The "*copying* or *emulating* successful practice as it is manifest in other countries [...] has become generally known as 'borrowing'" (ibid., p. 17). Identifying good examples in other education systems implies "that such good practice might be seen as potentially adoptable in (and adaptable to) the 'home' context" (ibid.).

Since the time of travellers' tales, a longstanding debate has existed surrounding the transferability and borrowability of educational features. On one hand, some argued that education policy was indeed borrowable, and desirable to borrow. On the other hand, others claimed that it was not possible to borrow or transfer education, for the context of education played too strong a role. Phillips and Schweisfurth (2006) acknowledge the difficult and complex nature of policy transfer. The process of policy transfer, which seemingly takes three simple steps, firstly, with the identification of good practice, secondly, the introduction of the policy into the home country, and thirdly, assimilation into the home context, deceivingly produces problems through its complexity. Sadler's aforementioned speech of 1900 warned of the contextual factors that make policy borrowing a difficult process. Self-improvement, whether on the micro or macro levels, instinctively involves looking elsewhere for strong examples. While countries have long "borrowed" from each other in terms of science, technology, and agriculture, these warnings imply a much more complex process of borrowing.

The word "context," in this situation of policy borrowing, needs definition. As a key point for models of policy borrowing, context may include "philosophical, historical, cultural, religious, social, 'national character,' political, economic, demographic, geographical, linguistic, administrative, and technological" features (Ochs & Phillips, 2002a, p. 16). These factors also have a complex relationship with each other:

> The contextual factors might also interact with one another and compound influence – as economics impacts politics and *vice versa*. The complexity of these features of context, and their essential interaction, will clearly have an influence on the receptability of ideas from elsewhere. (Ibid.)

Therefore, "context must be addressed in any discussion of 'cross-national attraction,' in both the 'target' country and in the 'home' country" (ibid., p. 33). Hence, the lending and borrowing of educational policy depend on the context of both the "target" and "home" countries. The notion of context, especially in terms of policy borrowing models, becomes an underlying thread when considering policy transfer.

The debate over the possibility of policy borrowing has, as stated previously, existed since the first travellers' tales. In nineteenth century France, for example, both Jullien and Cousin viewed policy transfer as a desirable process, and that these foreign examples could improve the French system (Beech, 2006). Much as Noah and Eckstein (1969) documented, the travellers' tales evolved into travelling with a specific focus, as even in the nineteenth century, governments appointed people to investigate foreign education systems to improve the systems at home. This even exists today, for, as stated earlier, "In reforming school, Finland makes exactly the same mistakes as Sweden. Only it happens ten years later" (Välijärvi et al., 2002, p. 3). Finland's traditional observations of Swedish education illustrate this examination of foreign examples. Again, as Phillips and Schweisfurth (2006) summarised from Noah and Eckstein, this interest in foreign education systems eventually took a quantitative perspective. In late nineteenth century France, Levasseur compiled comparative statistical tables of countries' education systems, allowing him to rank them according to measured educational criteria. Interestingly, he considered the Scandinavian countries as the best-achieving systems (Beech, 2006). However, others, including the writer Tolstoy, felt the aforementioned significance of context played too important a role to ignore.

As stated previously, the oft-cited Sadler, among many others, believed strongly in the importance of context in education, and the difficulty of education policy transfer. However, comparativist Holmes, while a follower of Sadler, did note a need for a scientific method for successful transfer. Thus, until the 1960s, comparative education had two views of policy transfer, that of possibility and that of difficulty (Beech, 2006). However, after that time, a search began for a methodology to better secure more successful policy transfer.

The theories behind the models of education policy borrowing or transfer show some consistency. Firstly, a local problem is identified. Then, foreign solutions are sought. Finally, the borrowed policy is adapted and implemented into a new context (Beech, 2006). One hundred years after Sadler, in the year 2000, Alexander (p. 172) stated that education systems are not "hermitically sealed," but that history and culture nearly always play a role in a country's education. Nevertheless, while there is some debate whether comparative education is strictly theoretical or needs to take a practical turn (e.g. Auld & Morris, 2014; Cowen, 2006), transnational organisations such as the OECD help promote this perhaps inevitable practical and scientific focus of comparative education (Beech, 2006). This quantitative element to comparative education and policy borrowing and transfer has now become an obligatory element of the field. Despite this, comparativists still warn that policy transfer remains a problematic process.

Dolowitz and Marsh (2000) noted the increasing interest in education policy transfer, especially with the growing role of transnational organisations such as the OECD, and their role in influencing education policy makers. Their framework for policy transfer involves seven questions:

1. Why involve it?
2. Who is involved in the process?
3. What is transferred?
4. Where are the lessons drawn from?
5. What are the degrees of transfer?
6. What are the restrictions/facilitations of the transfer process?
7. How is the transfer process related to the success or failure of the policy?

Dolowitz and Marsh also argue, much like Phillips and Ochs (2004), discussed at length in this chapter, that policy transfer often stems from quick fix solutions to critical policy issues. Furthermore, these quick fix solutions often come under time constraints, leading to flawed transfer. If a number of interested parties are involved with the borrowing process, this heightens the chances of successful policy transfer. Conversely, if politicians do not consult those interested and affected by the potential policy, more implementation issues may occur as a result.

Dolowitz and Marsh (2000, pp. 8, 13) uncover the differences between "voluntary" and "coercive" transfer, which lie on a continuum. The increased role of transnational organisations such as the OECD has made them agents of coercive transfer by spreading ideas that influence policy makers on a national level. The timing of policy transfer also plays a role. For example, in times of political, social, and economic stability, transfer becomes voluntary, but in times of a downturn or crisis, transfer can have coercive elements. While policy transfer can occur voluntarily, by drawing lessons from other policies, or can occur through direct coercion, most often policies transfer voluntarily, but with some alleged obligation, "such as the desire for international acceptance" (ibid., p. 13). This echoes the "negative external evaluation" impetus discussed later in this chapter.

However, comparativists, as stated previously, have warned repeatedly of the difficulty in policy transfer. Not all policy borrowing ventures result in successful policy transfer. In this case, Dolowitz and Marsh (2000) call this policy failure. They give three reasons for this: uninformed, incomplete, or inappropriate transfer. Uninformed transfer occurs when there is insufficient information about the borrowed policy. Incomplete transfer happens when critical factors of the policy are not included. Finally, inappropriate transfer transpires when inadequate attention was paid to the context and ideology of both the borrowing and lending contexts. This assertion echoes that of Ochs and Phillips, and Sadler, among others.

Much like Dolowitz and Marsh's continuum of policy transfer, Ochs and Phillips describe this as a spectrum, referring more specifically to the conditions under which countries borrow education policy:
1. Imposed, as under totalitarian or authoritarian rule
2. Required under constraint, as with countries occupied by others
3. Negotiated under constraint, for example, required by bilateral and multilateral agreements
4. Borrowed purposefully, intentionally copied policies observed in other countries
5. Introduced through influence, where countries make policy changes under the general influence of educational ideas (2004, p. 9).

The degree to which countries borrow education policy from other countries varies both in the original intentions as well as the degree to which the policy is borrowed.

Policy borrowing necessitates change from the original, borrowed policy when implementing it into the new context. This metamorphosis must occur when the transferring the policy from one place to another. Phillips and Ochs (2004) use the analogy of filters to describe this policy borrowing process, which distort and alter the original educational policy. The borrowed policy goes through various stages before the policy becomes properly lent. These filters or lenses distort the original policy in four phases:

1. Interpretation
2. Transmission
3. Reception
4. Implementation

These stages of policy borrowing distort the original "image" in order to achieve full implementation. In the end, the borrowing country can have a very different educational practice from that originally borrowed.

Another model of policy borrowing, or more specifically, a cycle, consists of four stages:

1. Cross-national attraction
2. Decision
3. Implementation
4. Internalisation/Indigenisation (Phillips & Ochs, 2004).

The cross-national attraction stage begins with impulses that spawn this attraction, such as internal dissatisfaction, political imperatives, or "negative external evaluation." "Negative external evaluation" often comes from international education surveys such as PISA and TIMSS (ibid., p. 778). Externalising potential also sparks cross-national attraction, as countries may have an interest in certain aspects of another country's education system. For example, Country A may admire the teaching techniques of Country B, or Country X has an interest in the guiding philosophies of Country Y (Phillips & Ochs, 2003), providing the impetus for interest, or cross-national attraction, in another country's policy.

The second phase of policy borrowing, decision, has four types of decision-making:

a   Theoretical
b   Realistic or Practical
c   "Quick Fix"
d   "Phony" (Phillips & Ochs, 2004, p. 780).

Theoretical decision-making occurs when governments make decisions on policies so abstract that they cannot easily find effective implementation within the education system. Realistic or practical decision-making isolates measures already successful in another country or education system, which does not have the constraints of contextual factors. "Quick fix" borrowing occurs in times of "immediate political necessity," for example, after the fall of Communism in Eastern Europe in 1989. This parallels Dolowitz and Marsh's (2000) discussion of "quick fix" solutions to urgent problems, resulting in flawed education policy transfer. The "phony" type of decision-making refers to interest in external education systems by politicians for immediate political impact. The "quick fix" and "phony" catalysts for policy borrowing decision-making play a particularly relevant role in this book, and are frequently discussed in other chapters. Although the implementation stage does not require much explanation, the internalisation/indigenisation phase can also be seen as the "domestication" of education policy (Phillips & Ochs, 2004, p. 780).

This process, not a linear but rather a cyclical one, implies that policy borrowing does not occur as a one-off process, rather as a continuum of cross-national attraction. Once properly indigenised, the cross-national attraction may begin again, sparking a new cycle of policy borrowing. This educational interest seemingly never ends: it continues as countries, politics, society, and education systems grow and evolve.

Building upon this, Ochs (2005) reveals four motivations for looking abroad when looking for educational motivation. These are to caution against educational reform, to glorify the home reform, to legitimate the adoption of a reform, and to scandalise the policy at home. Rappleye (2006), with his review of previous policy transfer models, reorganises the causes for cross-national attraction, dividing them into structural reasons, for example, the launch of *Sputnik*, or based on human grounds, such as those using the examples of foreign education systems. The obstacles to transfer are also expanded and recategorised, by dividing them again, into structural and human categories. These include structural issues, such as a country's legal hindrances or tradition, and human issues in the form of resistance actors, who contest the educational reform. Rappleye (2006, p. 238) argues that policy borrowing has become an extremely political process, and argues that cross-national attraction is used in a "big 'edu-political' chess match." In addition to this, he notes that globalisation had added new dimensions to the policy transfer process, by further complicating the influence of context. While the origins of policy borrowing began with travellers' tales, the newer, quantitative research phase has added another element to policy transfer, that of globalisation. Globalisation has included the influence of transnational organisations, such as the OECD, and their international achievement studies, for example, PISA, on cross-national attraction. Thus, looking across borders for educational inspiration has become more intricate, as even more complexity and subtlety has been woven into the highly problematic, and now political, process of cross-national attraction and policy transfer (Beech, 2006; Rappleye, 2006).

3   Examples of Cross-National Attraction

Attraction to Finnish education, although quite compelling, does not mark the first time where a country became the focus of educational cross-national attraction. Many other cases of cross-national attraction exist, despite the fact that "educationists in 'target' countries often react with scepticism to the outside interest expressed in their home systems" (Phillips, 1989, p. 271). For example, Japan originally borrowed Western models before its education system became the educational envy of many countries in the 1980s. Cummings (1989) attributes this to the publication of *A Nation at Risk* in 1983, the Japanese economic boom, and US economic decline around the same time (in 1989). An American report attributed this to the "superior quality of [the Japanese] labour force, and especially the work ethic and intellectual capabilities of the average participant" (ibid., p. 294). The "negative external evaluation" of this situation created an impetus to visit Japan. Thus, this established an "educational pilgrimage" of Americans to Japan (ibid.). These pilgrimages by American educational scholars resulted in ascertaining the salient cultural characteristics of the Japanese system, such as the "education mother" and high competition (together with the apparent downside of elevated suicide rates among high school students) (ibid., p. 297). They also determined the strengths of the system, for example, integrated science and mathematics, and a sequential curriculum.

Ichikawa (1989) responds to Cummings and demystifies the characteristics of Japanese education as perceived by the American researchers. The juxtaposition of the articles illustrates the different perceptions of an education system from the "home" country and the observing country. A Japanese periodical at the time found the interest baffling, since the Japanese looked to other countries for models of creativity in schools (Phillips, 1989). These examples illustrate the difficulty of a Japan-to-US "borrowing" situation. Cummings states, "Despite the rising American interest in Japanese education we have yet to see a significant impact on the way Americans solve their educational problems" (1989, p. 301). Ichikawa comments on his statement: "I agree that the United States will encounter difficulties in borrowing ideas and practices from Japan without modification" (1989, p. 304). Although the interest on the part of the US in Japan would allow for educational improvement, Cummings, at the time, did not see any. Ichikawa acknowledges the difficulty in borrowing Japanese practice, especially without modification and indigenisation into the home context.

England and Germany also form another classic example of cross-national attraction, especially in terms of secondary education (e.g. Phillips, 2000a, 2000b). Gruber and Pollard, however, take a different perspective on this matter and account for the attraction, or lack thereof, towards British primary schools from their continental admirers, namely Germany and Austria. Gruber (1989) praises the philosophy of the child-centred primary school and the autonomy behind the school administration. He wonders why continental European countries do not look towards British primary schools as good models of early childhood education and cites three reasons why they have overlooked the example of Britain:

1. Governments overlooked primary school reform in German-speaking countries due to energies devoted elsewhere
2. The admirable autonomy of the British schools does not translate well into the tradition of "standardisation and uniformity" of school culture in Germany and Austria. The school-to-school variations in British primary schools "are appreciated with difficulty"
3. German-speaking countries tend to concentrate their educational energies on theoretical research, while British educationists analyse real-school processes.

Gruber asserts that the "silent revolution" of British primary education has remained the object of admiration of experts (ibid., p. 364).

Pollard, in response, argues that the German and Austrian perspective on primary schools represents a degree of "idealistic romanticism" (1989, p. 365). He feels that the autonomy of schools that should, according to Gruber, allure continental admirers also has downsides: large variations in school quality and then limitation of central governments to intervene with failing schools. As a result, Pollard supported the Education Act of 1988, which implemented a National Curriculum in Britain. Gruber's (1989) three assertions about the overlooked British example come under scrutiny from Pollard. He agrees with the first point, but feels that the second point does not ring true in his opinion. He believes that continental European teachers also have encouragement to assert their individuality. On the third point, Pollard (1989, p. 366) agrees with Gruber, as he "note[s] with great sadness" that the "abstract and detached work which Gruber portrays was left behind some time ago by most educationalists in Britain." The analysis of these two articles raises two interesting points. First it illustrates how cross-national attraction can go both ways. Phillips accounts for English attraction to Germany (2000a, 2000b), while Gruber describes attraction from Germany and Austria to England. Secondly, this raises the issue of the cycles of cross-national attraction. The articles, published in 1989, praise a British system characterised by autonomy and decentralisation. However, the reforms of 1988 created a more centralised system. Pollard presciently writes,

"Perhaps in 2007 [...] Karl Heinz Gruber will be led to wonder why we too failed to appreciate some of the finest qualities and achievements of British primary education" (ibid., p. 367). In other words, so many years after publication, does the same admiration of British primary schooling still ring true, or does Britain regret the educational reforms of the late 1980s? Interestingly, this book has discussed the Global Education Reform Movement in an earlier chapter, and noted how the 1988 Education Act acted as the catalyst for GERM. The policy reaction of Germany to PISA, discussed throughout this book, would indicate that this cause for admiration may have taken the opposite route, that of resentment.

4   Finland and Cross-National Attraction

Previous examples of cross-national attraction provide a good base for the exploration of Finland as the "new" target for policy borrowing. Pollard, in 1989, astutely wondered if, in the future, the same attraction from Germany and Austria to British primary schools would exist. Clearly, however, Finland has taken over the position of educational admiration because of the interest generated through its participation in PISA.

PISA has generated great amounts of interest in the Finnish education system. "Finland has recently been basking in educational glory [...] The recent PISA 2000 project in particular turned Finnish comprehensive schooling into a success story" (Simola, 2005, p. 456). Before PISA, little interest surrounded the Finnish education system. In fact, in the Second International Mathematics Study (SIMS), Finland ranked only average among the eighteen participating countries (Sahlberg, 2007). In the 1999 repeat of the Third International Mathematics and Science Study (TIMSS-R), 38 countries participated, and Finland ranked only slightly above average. However, owing to its performance in PISA, Finland's education system has become a popular travel destination for educational policy makers, teachers, researchers, and the like, observing how Finland created a high-performing education system while maintaining its commitment to the welfare state. The educational achievements of Finland, especially taken into account with its financial struggles of the 1990s, are worthy of praise. "The overall social and economic progress has often been judged as indicating that a relatively small, peripheral nation can transform its economy and education system into a showcase knowledge society only if policies are right and if sufficient hard work supports the intended visions" (ibid.). International surveys such as PISA have become one of the biggest reasons for educational change in recent years, triggering an "educational pilgrimage," as seen in the case of Finland (ibid., p. 163). In fact, "several countries changed the direction of their education reforms by borrowing education policies and practice from well-performing nations" (ibid.).

Finland's success in PISA has sparked interest among educationists and the mass media. For example, around the time of Finland's European Union Presidency in 2006, *The Economist* published a piece entitled "In Praise of Finland":

> In Finland now, everything is all right. Fifteen years after one of the worst recessions any European country has seen, triggered by the collapse of the Soviet Union, Finns are not exactly merry (that would hardly suit the national temperament), but they are content. Their small country (5m people) is at or near the top of most league tables: first in the World Economic Forum's list of most competitive countries, and second in its business-competitiveness index; first in the OECD's world ranking of educational performance; second-highest share of R&D spending in the European Union. The country is reversing its demographic decline: its fertility rate is one of the highest in Europe. A Finnish group even won this year's Eurovision song contest. (The Economist, 6 July 2006)

This article not only commends Finland's education system, but also other aspects such as its economic achievement. In response to the release of PISA data, *The Economist* published an article called "Educational Standards Compared: Britain Scores." Although in praise of the UK's performance on the 2000 PISA survey, it mentions that Finland "won the whole tournament" and also suggests that Britain can aspire to Finland's small gap between their high achievers and low achievers (The Economist, 6 December 2001).

Following the same vein of "negative external evaluation," *The Economist* printed another piece, "Back to School: Some Remedial Lessons are Needed for European Leaders." This article states "Europe is failing its students" (The Economist, 23 March 2006) and mentions that European educational institutions find themselves falling behind their American and Asian counterparts. Citing PISA to illustrate the decline, *The Economist* describes the decline of European education, with Finland as an exception to the trend. The article mentions that most European countries have a larger gap between their weak and strong students than the United States, traditionally a country with a large distribution between the two. Even though the article admits Finland's faults in education in the 1960s, today's Finland "has the best schools in the world. Finnish 15-year-olds have the highest level of mathematical skills, scientific knowledge and reading literacy of any rich industrialised country" (ibid.). In order to achieve this, Finland had to make reforms, including allowing more responsibility and independence for its teachers. The Finnish education system also has no streaming, no selection, and few national assessments.

The article has these words of advice: "European governments should go back to school. In Finland" (ibid.). These examples show just a small fraction of the power of the media when portraying the PISA results, and ultimately, influencing education reform. The final chapter of this book discusses this further.

5   Negative External Evaluation

Germany's reaction to its PISA outcomes has become a classic example of "negative external evaluation." This PISA-Shock, which occurred after Germany scored below the OECD average in the 2000 survey, has had much the same impact as *Sputnik* or *A Nation at Risk* (Ertl, 2006). In fact, Gruber believes the PISA-Shock, resulting after the 2000 results, eclipses the impact of *A Nation at Risk* (Gruber, 2006). He cites how the *Bundestag,* or German Parliament, held special "PISA sessions" in order to discuss PISA-triggered, educational worries, and how PISA marks different educational eras with BP (Before PISA) and AP (After PISA), much as BC and AD also denote a significant change in temporal measurement and history (ibid.).

The media reaction to PISA, especially after the release of the 2000 scores, illustrated "how calmly Finland dealt with its champion status" and "how deep the German PISA-*Schock* went" (Gruber, 2006, p. 196). The German performance in PISA 2000 contradicted "the German and international expectations of a nation with a high standard of living and a school system which had enjoyed a high international reputation since the nineteenth century" (ibid.). The PISA performance illustrated the disparities in performance among PISA literacy levels and the varied educational achievement across Germany's *Länder*. In addition, Germans found that socio-economic background, immigration, and the tripartite system held positions as strong factors affecting educational success (Ertl, 2006). In fact, Germany had the highest rate of social inequality in education, even more than the United States (Gruber, 2006). On a more positive note, this PISA-Shock triggered the unilateral decision by the federal government, in addition to the *Länder*, to agree to educational reforms and national standards. Previously, they were at a standoff (Ertl, 2006). The great "taboo" subject of German education, the *Gesamtschule,* or comprehensive school, however, is still a source of contention (Gruber, 2006). Despite great disparities in educational attainment, socio-economic disparity, and the low educational attainment of immigrants, the tripartite system still remains intact. The PISA-Shock, however, did prompt the German curricula towards a more practical focus. The formerly respected German system admitted to its ossification and began looking outwards, generating comparative research, in order to improve. The Germans especially look to Finland and Sweden as successful models of good education (Ertl, 2006). PISA triggered a "mass pilgrimage" to Finland from German politicians and educational authorities viewing Finland as the "promised land" (Gruber, 2006, p. 203). Despite these positive reforms, they do not address the socio-economic problems and subsequent educational inequalities in the country, instead focusing on the future increase of PISA outcomes (Ertl, 2006).

6   Examples of Policy Borrowing

After all the discussion of policy borrowing, one must ask, what is the importance of educational policy borrowing? How does the cross-national attraction and eventual policy transfer have importance for educational policy makers? This brings us back to the points made earlier in this chapter, stating that we study other systems of education to improve our own, and how a country has the ability to improve its own shortcomings by adopting the virtues of another. Despite the cyclical phases and the distorting lenses, an education system can adopt policy from another.

Problems do exist in this process of policy borrowing. These external factors and "battles long ago" make the adaptation of an education system difficult. However, examples of policy borrowing do exist. For example, Ochs (2006) investigates a case of successful policy borrowing, where a London borough internalised and indigenised the educational practices of Switzerland and Germany into its own system. The Japanese education system contains a more historical example. This rare, "unambiguous" example of policy borrowing comes from not one but two cases of educational policy borrowing. Under the Meiji era, between 1868 and 1912, Japan borrowed the then-admired Prussian education system, then again borrowed the educational structure of the United States after the Second World War (Phillips & Ochs, 2004). Even today, Japanese children wear Prussian-style uniforms to school, and the current students also use terminology such as "junior high school," much like their counterparts in America.

International tests of attainment provide even more concrete evidence of transferable educational policies and practices. PISA has undoubtedly changed the face of education, placing it in a more political, global context. International achievement studies have placed the spotlight on countries with high educational performance. PISA, especially, has had a huge impact in the educational world. Finland has attracted much attention due to its performance in PISA. In other words, Finland's performance in PISA has created an educational frenzy manifest in considerable attraction to the Finnish education system. Finland's performance in PISA has already taken a conspicuous position in examples of cross-national attraction, since it provides a good educational example from which other countries can learn (Phillips & Ochs, 2004). The research of Chung (2009) revealed that small-scale borrowing from Finland has already occurred. In Beijing, for example, a new school has recently been started following exactly the Finnish model. Japanese teachers have also copied the Finnish language teaching model. Takayama (2009, p. 51) also cites this "Finnish Method Promotion Association," which translates Finnish textbooks into Japanese. This is discussed more fully in the final chapter of this book. On a larger scale, England's Master's in Teaching and Learning, launched in 2010, aimed to raise the level of teachers' education to the Master's degree level, emulating a salient feature behind Finnish PISA success (Chung et al., 2012).

7   Dangers of Policy Borrowing

The case of Finland in PISA and the subsequent interest in the education system require re-examination of Sadler's speech, where he warns that the exploration of foreign systems of education needs to take into account that external factors influence the characteristics of the education system. In other words, in addition to the structure and governance of the Finnish education system one must delve into the "things outside the school."

In the early nineteenth century, Jullien generated a series of questions in order to identify "good educational practice" and aid in its "transfer to other systems" (Phillips, 1989, p. 267). Jullien sparked an educational interest in other countries that continues to this day. Continuing along this vein, Sadler stated that studying other systems of education creates a better understanding of the home system, but warned that, when investigating another education system, it becomes necessary to take into account the societal and cultural factors of the country. Halls takes it a step further by stating, "The grafting of features of another educational system into a different cultural context, like transplants of the heart, is a difficult and sometimes unsuccessful operation" (1970, p. 163).

In fact, when attributing success in education many have the tendency to credit individuals, "their psychologies and pedagogies, rather than [...] phenomena characterised as social, cultural, institutional or historical" (Simola, 2005, p. 455). "Schooling is not confined to pedagogy, didactics or subject matter [...] it also, even mainly, incorporates social, cultural, institutional and historical issues" (ibid., pp. 456–467). Simola also believes "a comparative study in education purporting to be something more than a mode of educational governance should be a historical journey" (ibid., p. 457). Often interest in another country baffles the subjects of observation. Phillips (1989) cites the example of the Japanese system, which gathers interest for its high achievement, yet looks to other countries in order to seek out examples of creativity.

The subject of policy borrowing generates much debate. Since the time of Jullien, the "attitudes to the feasibility of educational policy borrowing have ranged from scornful dismissal to enthusiastic advocacy" (Phillips, 2006, p. 551). Many have used the foreign model to exemplify a successful education system and to warn against change. The same country can also come as a positive or a negative illustration of an education system, as in the case of Germany. Phillips raises a central question: "Can country x solve its educational problems by adopting policy or practice deemed to be successful in country y? And if so, how is such policy or practice transferred and implemented?" (ibid., p. 553). Furthermore, the use of foreign models to solve educational problems adds to the politicisation of education, education policy, and international achievement studies. Thus, the issues surrounding policy borrowing and transfer, outlined in this chapter, add to the politicisation of education, as discussed at length in the first and last chapters of this book. The additional dimension of globalisation and international achievement studies in policy transfer further emphasises the complicated nature of informed, critical policy transfer, and the temptation for quick fix policy solutions.

8 Summary

The field of comparative education, while having roots even back to Ancient Greece, has recently exploded with the onslaught of international assessments. The field has evolved from travellers' tales to international, quantitative, educational research. Until the 1960s, comparativists debated the possibility of successful policy borrowing. However, after this time, they have searched for a methodology of successful policy transfer. This has led to a more practical, scientific slant to the field of Comparative Education. While seemingly simple in its definition, transfer has a deceivingly complex process, due to the importance of an education system's context. Transfer can occur under voluntary or coercive conditions. The impetus, according to this model, falls under a continuum, where most policy transfer transpires for voluntary reasons, but often flavoured with a "desire for international acceptance." Policy failure happens when the policy makers are uninformed, the transfer process is incomplete, and the transfer is attempted in inappropriate conditions. Quick fix solutions can lead to this policy failure. Policy transfer can also occur in four stages: cross-national attraction, decision, implementation, and internalisation/indigenisation. Cross-national attraction has occurred in educational situations since these travellers' tales of the past. A major catalyst for cross-national attraction is "negative external evaluation," which often occurs with poor performances in international assessments such as PISA. The decision phase can occur for "quick fix" and "phony" reasons, stemming from political necessity and impact. Globalisation has added another dimension to policy transfer, as do politics. This had led policy transfer to become part of a highly "'edu-political' chess match."

Cross-national attraction has occurred throughout time. Classic examples include the attraction between Japan and the US, and England and Germany. The advent of PISA has introduced new classic examples of cross-national attraction and negative external evaluation. Germany, and its PISA-Shock after the release of the first PISA rankings of 2000, has become a new classic example of negative external evaluation. Finland now holds the position as the object of educational cross-national attraction. This has resulted in PISA tourism and a media frenzy. However, the Finns perceive this attention with some bemusement.

The implementation phase does not need further clarification, but when a policy is properly borrowed, then it becomes "internalised" or "indigenised" into the borrowing country's context. A borrowed policy should appear different from the original policy. A borrowed policy can also pass through lenses, or filters, which have a similar distorting effect. Less critically-borrowed examples include the Japanese borrowing of Finnish textbooks and possibly the Master's of Teaching and Learning in England. Overall, comparative education theorists warn of the difficulty of policy borrowing. External factors and context play too important a role in a country's education system.

CHAPTER 6

Strengths of Finnish Education

1   Introduction

Previous chapters of this book have focused on the global context of education policy formation, the background of Finland and Finnish education, the PISA survey itself. In addition the previous chapter investigated the policy borrowing and transfer, in light of the recent and renewed interest in the topic, especially in response to the results of international achievement studies such as PISA. This chapter delves deep into the strengths of Finnish education from the perspectives of Finnish Ministers of Education, professors of education, head teachers, teachers, and OECD officials. The evidence provided for this chapter, and for the following two chapters, stems from empirical research investigating the reasons for Finland's high PISA scores. These strong points, it is believed, have allowed for high quality education, as indicated by consistently high outcomes in PISA. The salient factors divide into four categories: teachers; equality; value of education; and structure, organisation, and characteristics of Finnish schools. Each section discusses the salient factors at length and provides firsthand, qualitative evidence from the participants.

The participants contributing to the findings, whose names have been changed, included two former Ministers of Education from Finland; six head teachers of lower secondary schools; seventeen teachers of the PISA subjects: mathematics, science, and reading literacy of PISA-aged students; eight professors of education responsible for the execution of PISA in Finland; and four OECD officials.

2   Teachers

All of the participants agreed that the teachers hold much responsibility for Finland's PISA success. Outstanding teachers, along with their Master's degrees, aid in the overall learning of Finnish students. Even the teachers show appreciation for their situation, along with appreciation for their profession, by citing the high quality of their profession and their colleagues as a strong point of Finnish education. For example, Maarit, a mathematics, physics, and chemistry teacher praises the Finnish system in trying new ways to teach over the years:

> We have had quite many [sic] ways to teach. In the '70s we had different teaching methods to what we have today. And in the '60s and '50s we had a very different way. Maybe we try nowadays cooperative learning, sometimes group work, and we try these methods.

This willingness to try new techniques allows for educational improvement and the avoidance of educational stagnation. The teachers also specialise in their subjects, and are not spread too thin in terms of their subject expertise. Krister says, "I just have math, physics, and chemistry. In some countries one teacher teaches many subjects, and that, I think, is not so good. They can't get so deep into something. I don't think my class would want me to teach in other subjects." The narrow, focused specialision of the teachers allows for more expertise within the subjects taught. This allows for both deep and meaningful learning. The positive perspective of teachers concerning their own profession reinforces the attention Finnish teachers have received due to PISA outcomes.

Finnish teachers' abilities stretch beyond the classroom. Professor Laukkanen, for instance, speaks of the many talents of teachers today. They exhibit strong skills at academic subjects; she cites how many have talents in the arts and in sports as well. She says: "Wonderful that the Finnish teachers see that their work is really producing good results. I know they work very hard. They are very responsible. I feel proud for the teachers."

2.1 *Teacher Education*

Finland's teachers anchor their country's exemplary education system, and related to this, is the much-lauded Finnish teacher education. Former Finnish Minister of Education, Minister Halonen, mentions that Finland has especially strong teacher-preparation programmes and highly qualified teachers. He states, "I strongly believe that they are very motivated, well educated, and committed to their work. That is definitely a benefit." Minister Jussila concurs. He believes that excellent teacher training remains one of the great strengths of the Finnish education system. He describes the process of acceptance into teacher training programmes, which involves two rounds of tests:

> The first test has been done on the basis of papers from secondary papers, or level of qualification from [the] secondary level. Then [from] that group, there are people who will take the applicant test. They are interviewed. They are put to play a teacher's role in practice and they have writing tests and then practical tests. On the basis of these two tests there are really top applicants that can be adapted for academic study. In the beginning, the level of applicants is very high. Then the education

is quite good from our point of view. If you have good students and good teaching, the results must be good.

Chapter 3 also discussed this rigorous method of selection to teacher training programmes. In addition to this extremely selective rate of acceptance, teachers strengthen their skills with in-service training. Minister Jussila describes these opportunities as reinforcing the strength of teacher education programmes, and heightening the level of more experienced teachers.

Aino, a biology and geography teacher, also attributes Finland's top outcomes in PISA and the high level of teacher education as the overall strength of the Finnish education system:

> I think it is because the teachers are so good, and the teacher training [...] The basic education of teachers is high, and it is so good, because we do the higher, upper exam at university and then we go one year [...] we do the teachers' education after that. It's because [of] that the education is so high.

The teachers greatly affect the high quality of Finnish education, since all have undertaken many years of study to receive their teaching qualifications. The policy changes which resulted in university education and the Master's degree for teachers, and the professionalisation of teaching show their positive outcomes in the minds of the teachers. Juho, a Finnish language and literature teacher, thinks teachers contribute to the high quality of Finnish education, but modestly says the entire system works together as a unit, so teachers cannot take all of the credit. Nevertheless, he credits Finnish teacher training for its contribution to the education system:

> It is the qualifications of [teacher] education. We have high standards for teacher education [...] Teacher motivation for their work is not dependent on the price they are paid but their inside motivation. We don't have to watch each other, 'Are they doing their work?' Everybody is motivated by himself or herself [...] Every teacher is responsible, I think.

Juho's observations outline the cycle of trust within the Finnish system, and the positive effects of a lack of accountability in an education system. Here, we see how teachers can thrive in an education system resistant to GERM.

The professors similarly viewed teacher education as an important factor in terms of the strengths of the Finnish educational system. Professor Virtanen states how the high quality of teacher training leads to a strong education system:

> The quality of teaching and teachers is extremely important [...] and it explains also why differences between schools is [sic] quite small in Finland [...] They are trained, our teachers, at university level, and they get Master's degrees. I think that is a very important part of the explanation, the quality of teaching. It's homogenous compared to some other countries. That has kept also the status of teachers quite high in Finnish society.

Finnish teacher education aims to create independent thinkers, problem solvers, and researchers. These skills allow teachers to apply various pedagogical theories to help inform their own practice, within their own style. The Master's degree, especially, helps qualify new teachers in these various good methods of teaching different students. The low acceptance rate, again, illustrates the high quality of teacher education candidates. Furthermore, the acceptance rate to teacher training programmes in Finland is surprisingly low. Professor Virtanen states, "If you look at what kind of students we get to teacher education programmes, especially primary teacher programmes, it is quite high, very popular, only ten to fifteen percent of the applicants are approved." Professor Rantanen says, "We have very straight-A students in teacher education." Professor Laukkanen also speaks of the low acceptance rate into teacher education programmes and the high quality of students:

> We have the best students in high school to apply to the classroom teacher programme. For example this year, at this university we have the teacher training college, and there were so many applicants, thousands, that we could only accept eight percent. So when you take eight percent of the already good students, you can have very good teachers in our programme.

A 2004 *Helsingin Sanomat* newspaper survey illustrates this popularity of teaching. Professor Rantanen refers to this when saying, "I guess that you have heard about [...] high school graduates, they were asked what they would like to work with, and what job. [The majority] said [...] they would like to become a teacher." The survey, which asked one thousand upper-secondary school students which career path they would most like to choose, ended with teaching topping the list of thirty-seven professions. Teaching, with 26% of the responses, came first on the list, followed by engineering with 19% and psychologist with 18% (Liiten, 11 February 2004). Minister Jussila, much like his colleagues at the university and school institutions, cites that the number of applicants to teacher education programmes far exceeds the quotas at the universities. This low acceptance rate, in addition to the Master's degrees, leads to capable, professional teachers.

In contrast, Professor Sundqvist describes how other countries have trouble finding enough teachers to fill their needs, but in Finland "we have the luxury of selecting the best of the best." Finnish teacher education not only demands more from students, but the educational system also commands much effort from the teachers. A Master's degree adds to further academic expertise for the teachers, adding to their capability in terms of subject knowledge and pedagogy. For example, Christer, a biology and geography teacher, describes the dual nature of teaching, both as an academic and as a teacher. He considers himself as a biologist with a Master's degree in pedagogy. Here we see how the Master's degree, as according to Kivinen and Rinne (1994) helped academise and professionalise teaching in Finland.

Teacher autonomy, also cited as one of the strengths of Finnish education, stems from the popularity and professionalising of the teaching profession, along with the high level of education for teachers. Teacher autonomy relates to the strong teacher education, as parents, teachers, administrators, and policy makers trust teachers to carry out their duties. Related to this, Minister Halonen mentions that, in addition to the strong teaching, high-quality educational materials also contribute to the success of Finnish education. These educational materials do not receive the acknowledgement they deserve. Minister Jussila also believes that this contributes to the teaching quality in Finland:

> The teachers have autonomy in choosing their teaching methods, in choosing their textbooks [...] That is why even if the teaching profession is not very well paid in Finland, it is very popular. It gives you freedom to utilise your high level of education in practice.

He relates teacher autonomy, and the culture of trust in Finnish schools, to the high quality of teachers. The strength, capability, and education of the teachers allows for autonomy, trust, and responsibility.

2.2 *High Status and Respect*

The quality and capability of the Finnish teachers, in addition to their excellent teacher education and Master's degrees, result in high status of the profession and respect for the practitioners themselves. Professor Virtanen speaks about the high status of teachers in Finland:

> The status of teachers in society is quite high. If you compare the status of teachers, we have a survey, I think every third year, made by some

leading newspaper [...] asking people how we value these professions, and teachers are on a very high level compared to lawyers or medical doctors and something like that. That is very exceptional compared to other countries.

OECD official Chadwick agrees that first and foremost teachers are the dominant factor behind PISA success for Finland, as well as the level of respect for the profession in Finnish society: "Teachers are very highly respected in Finland. It is a very highly desirable occupation. They reject ninety percent of applicants from secondary school into teacher training programmes. Most of them have Master's degrees, and so on." The high level of education leads to high respect in the Finnish culture. Professor Laukkanen agrees. "Since they are academics, they are considered academics in society." All classroom teachers and even supply teachers have Master's degrees. This provides a good background and foundation for teaching. This high status of teachers in Finland exists despite their salary, on par with the OECD average. Professor Karpinen says, "Teachers think that their salary is not good, but even though they do very good work. Perhaps we have quite high expectations from teachers." Professor Sundqvist agrees with his colleagues. He describes the high status of teachers in Finland, how "it is still glorious to become a teacher in Finland."

3 Equality

Finland's success in PISA also stems from the egalitarian values of the country, discussed at length earlier in this book. Minister Halonen describes how the lack of social stratification in Finnish society helped create an equal education system. The education system in Finland can create possibilities for everyone. The benefits of the Welfare State manifest themselves through the success of Finnish education, and the egalitarian nature of Finnish society lends itself to a strong educational system. In Finland the system of education tries to provide a good-quality education to all. The integration of high levels of support for weaker students, as well as a lack of streaming, contributes to this. Maintaining this type of cohesive education comes with difficulty. Professor Karpinen admits, "Of course it's a demanding task."

The Nordic countries hold in high esteem the principle of equity; therefore countries such as Finland readily spend money on achieving an equal system. The equal opportunities for education in Finland are illustrated by the lack of private schools, no separation of sexes, and free education for all. Education does not depend on parental income and does not pre-select students into schools. This comprehensive education system follows the egalitarian ideal. The school system also provides children with the advantages of a welfare state, giving them health care, dental care, and free lunches. These factors, all part of the education system, help the well-being and learning readiness of pupils.

Many of the teachers view the equality of the education system as an advantage. Finns have great pride in their education system, because of its equality and access to all, no matter what the family background. Terttu, a chemistry and mathematics teacher, says, "We have opportunities for all children. That is the best thing about [our] education." This equality leads to even results. Furthermore, this leads to the equal chances for education provided for both males and females in Finnish society, and students from differing socioeconomic backgrounds. For example, Pia, a Swedish language and literature teacher, views the equality of the system as a great asset. She says, "You don't have to be rich or you don't have to be talented or you don't have to prove that you are something before you enter the system. Then you can go as far as you want."

Pentti, a head teacher, praises Finnish school culture, since it places high value on education. He feels this comes from the equality of educational provision for all students:

> The Finnish school culture, it has evolved during many years, and one of the benefits of the Finnish school culture is that it gives the same education equally to all of the students. It also takes care of the less capable students. And the Finnish education system is very equal. If you compare it internationally, elsewhere in the world students specialise already when they are very young, for example [they go] to high school education or vocational schools, which means that they have to make choices very early on. In Finland these choices are made only after the comprehensive school, meaning after the ninth year.

In other words, the equality of Finnish society and schools allows for a culture that values comprehensive schools, respects education, and provides support for weaker students, all factors which contributed to the strength of the Finnish education system.

The equality of education and equal access benefit all; for example, the Finnish welfare state, which provides free lunches to every student, fulfills a basic need to every student in order to prepare them for a day's learning. Access to education, as well as uniform standards, helps all students achieve a similar level of education. Related to this, a teacher, Maarit, praises the consistency and continuity of the Finnish system. She thinks having the National Curriculum and similar textbooks helps Finnish students reach a comparable level of education. Similarly, the matriculation examination also provides continuity for all Finnish students and forces them to achieve a uniform standard of education. The equality of the Finnish education system is an advantage for the students as well as the country in its PISA outcomes. Juho, a Finnish language and literature teacher, sums it up well: "When I got older and older I learned we are in a quite extraordinary situation to get this kind of schooling and totally free. We can study in university and it costs quite nothing."

The equality of the Finnish education system stems from carefully considered effort and policy change in the 1970s. For example, Juho thinks these reforms to change the schools to a comprehensive, egalitarian model benefited Finland tremendously:

> We have made mistakes. In the 70s there was a system that we really don't want to talk about. It was not a bad thing that happened, but it was something that was not equal for all of the students. After that, we wanted to give equal education to all and also give those talented students the possibility to learn on their own level. In the 70s there was the intention to make different levels [with] different ability students. It was not equal, so it really didn't make good results. [The inequality] was totally reduced.

Although the Welfare State comes at an expense to the Finnish government, according to Minister Jussila, "it is not so costly as if the pupil would be excluded from active life. Later, she or he will cost a lot. We have, by the way, counted if the young boy, for example, will drop out, he will be excluded from active society; he will cost at least 1,000,000 Euros. School is cheaper, much cheaper." His sentiment echoes the philosophy of the Welfare State discussed in Chapter 2. The Welfare State views early intervention as a way to prevent more severe problems later.

The nature of Finnish society lends itself to educational success. Professors Karpinen and Koivula, for example, attribute much of the success in PISA to societal factors, to the society of Finland as well as to the homogeneity of its people. Professor Koivula, in addition, also stresses that Finland lacks an immigrant population, with only 2% of students with an immigrant background. PISA indicates that students of an immigrant background do not score as high in PISA as their peers, although with differing variation in scores. While countries such as Canada, New Zealand, Australia, and Finland have low variation in these scores, countries such as the United States and Germany have high variation from immigrant students (Entorf & Minoiu, 2004, p. 357). She cites how many countries have trouble educating their immigrant population, which does not really come as an issue in Finland. Similarly, Professors Virtanen, Laukknen, and Rantanen also comment on how the lack of immigrants emphasises this cultural homogeneity and they imply that this aids in administering an equal and high-quality education to all students in Finland. The immigrants that Finland does have, however, score very high in PISA. In the 2006 PISA survey, for example, only 3% of the Finnish students sampled came from an immigrant background, but scored up to fifty points higher than their immigrant counterparts in other countries (Viitanen & Peltonen, 22 February 2008). This book, in Chapter 10, discusses the possible role of increased immigration and changes within Finnish PISA outcomes.

The OECD officials also credit Finland's equality and egalitarian society with its PISA success. For example, OECD official Chadwick believes that Finland succeeded in PISA by eradicating the reasons that cause inequities in other education systems. For example, Finland does not have large inequities due to socio-economic background. He also describes the socio-economic equality as "brilliant." The Finnish government provides equal resources to all schools no matter what the geography or location. Finland's tiny performance variation struck OECD Official Schroeder most significantly, with only a 4% variation occurring between schools:

> I think the most amazing finding for me was not the absolute top-performance of Finland but the fact that only four percent of performance variation lies between schools. Every school succeeds, whether it is in a rural area or an urban area, a rich area or in a poor area, you don't see the performance differentials that you see in other countries. Actually, they are very good at making success a predictable outcome of the system. Parents can rely on the quality of the system rather than worrying about the school to which they send their children. That's a really [...] striking figure.

According to Schroeder, Finland has achieved high levels of equity, quality, and a high level of consistency in its education system, an admirable feat and a difficult achievement. The equality in Finnish society allows all of the schools and all of the students to achieve a high level of academic success.

4   High Value of Education

The high value of education in Finnish society is another salient point behind the strengths of the Finnish education system. While this does relate to the high value of teachers in society, Finland's history plays a strong role in this, as do the characteristics of the country itself, such as politics and the small population size.

4.1 *History*

Both former education ministers feel strongly that Finland has a good educational culture. As stated in Chapter 2, the country's history as a part of the Kingdom of Sweden and also as a Grand Duchy of Russia made the movement for independence a compelling notion among the Finnish people. The aim for independence necessitated the increase of the educational level of the whole population. Minister Halonen states, "It wasn't the idea to educate a few, but it was to make sure that the overall educational level [...] was a possibility for everyone." Finland's history also adds to the value of education in society. He confirms that at the time when the idea of Finnish independence first started to take hold, in the 1860s, the concept of education for all began to appear. The preparation for independence intended to raise the level of education for all Finns, not just for a lucky few.

Juho also describes how Finland values education, not with money, but with respect. He believes this respect for education comes from Finnish history. In the times of Swedish and Russian rule, the educated in Finland were either Swedish or Russian. The educated Finns came from the Swedish-speaking community. He describes how, beginning in the late nineteenth and early twentieth centuries, the Finnish speakers had more opportunities for education, therefore creating this value and respect in the society today.

Similarly, Professor Virtanen speaks of the pride in the Finnish language, the national language, and its expression through literature, newspapers, and the like. The nationalist movement during Russian rule also helped influence this and instilled a need for education in Finnish society, in order to spread literacy in the Finnish language. The nationalist movement and pride in the Finnish language also bled into teacher training. "We have to force [*sic*] that teachers are teaching, creating pupils, which they did. The national language [and] teacher training [are] working together." Finland's strong tradition of literacy helped lead the country to considerable success in PISA, especially in the reading literacy section of the survey. The professors mention Finland's strong tradition of literacy, which led to highly engaged readers within the PISA data. According to Professor Virtanen, Finnish students exhibit high engagement in reading, especially the girls. Many of the youth in Finland list reading as one of their favorite hobbies, and spend a lot of time on that activity. Similarly, Minister Halonen remarks that Finns read a great deal, and acknowledges the importance and influence of reading on eventual educational attainment.

This love of reading, however, is not unique to Finnish culture. A similar love of reading, he admits, exists fairly consistently across Nordic countries. Krister, a teacher of mathematics, physics, and chemistry, thinks that reading really provides a good basis for success. In the early years, he describes, the schools place a great emphasis on reading. This helps them understand texts and perform better in all subjects. Related to the equality of Finnish society leading to consistently high PISA outcomes, universal education and equal access helped promote literacy in the entire Finnish population.

Although counterintuitive, Professor Rantanen describes how television aids reading literacy: "I think one of the [good] things [...] is our TV. We have subtitles. If [children] [...] watch TV they have to have a good reading speed, a fast reading speed." Finnish television imports many programmes from other countries, but does not dub the original language into Finnish. Rather, subtitles in Finnish translate the television programme. In order for Finnish children to watch television, they need to know how to read, and at a rapid pace.

The strength of Finnish education also comes from the value and tradition of education ingrained in Finnish through families. Minister Halonen describes the importance of education in his family:

> My father was a teacher also, and the atmosphere at home was that we valued very highly education and knowledge and all of that. I think many good things have happened to me because of education [...] like the challenges I have had in my life. The reason was because of the possibilities to educate yourself.

Minister Jussila mentions the importance of the family in the Finnish educational culture. The tradition of education, he states, has roots within society and families. The appreciation for education passes down from generation to generation. He says that, typically, parents want their children to attain a higher education level than their own, no matter what the social class. Finland's positive attitude towards education maintains consistency in their society.

Pia, the Swedish teacher, agrees that Finland's culture values education, but attributes it to Finnish history:

> I think it is the history, and for my generation, or for my family, they wanted me to go to university because not a lot of people from my family had the opportunity before. My mother, she couldn't go to *gymnasium* [upper secondary school] and do the *studentexamen* [matriculation examination] because of lack of money. They couldn't afford it, and she was always keen for me, 'You have to do it, you have to do it!' [...] I think

that it is more or less that everybody gets some education. I'm not sure that the kids today appreciate it though. They don't understand how much they get for free.

Hans, a physics and mathematics teacher, tells a similar story. His parents, peasant farmers, encouraged him to pursue his education, since they believed education provided the best preparation for the world. The way of his parents' existence could not continue in a more modern Finland: "There were lots of small agricultural units with no possibility to survive in the world where we are living now, so education is the answer."

This salient factor became a common theme among the participants. Professor Virtanen spoke of the high regard that Finns have for education:

> Basically, I came from a very small, country, poor area. Of course education has been very important to me, to my parents and to myself. That was the way out to get a better position in society. That belief has always been very deep in the heart of Finnish people, and I remember that from my childhood also when I went to school. It was important to go to school.

Professor Laukkanen also describes a similar story: "[When] my father died in the war, my mother was alone with two children, and without anything, just one bag. But she had her education [...] She always emphasised that education was very important."

The role of the Lutheran Church throughout Finland's history also contributes to the high regard for education in Finnish society. For example, Toni, who teaches mathematics, physics, and chemistry also thinks Finnish society makes Finnish education a strong system. He says, "We are hardworking and I think that is the reason. We make work, and we calculate, calculate, calculate. It shows [...] Maybe it is the religion, the Lutheran religion. Work hard and be happy." Professor Sundqvist agrees. He mentions the "multitude of different explanations" behind Finnish success on PISA, such as the history of Finland and the influence of the Lutheran Church. He cites, for example, the tradition of reading from the Bible in order to marry. The role of the Lutheran Church and its role in achieving high rates of literacy still have influence in the people of Finland today.

Professors Tantanen and Koivula also speak of the excellent tradition of literacy in Finland and cite the law where engaged couples needed to prove literacy in order to get married. This law, discussed at length in Chapter 2, helped cement the tradition and importance of literacy in Finland. The Lutheran Church promoted the Finnish language and also literacy. Originally, Lutheran priests were the only group expected to learn the Finnish language, in order to communicate with their congregations, and only religious books such as the Bible and Psalm Books could be printed in Finnish (Gilmour, 1931). This illustrates how Finland's history has had a major impact on its education system today. The high value of education in society shows how closely a country's context relates to its education system. Chapter 2 delved into Finland in depth in order to better uncover the relationship between Finland's context and its high esteem and value for education, which contributed to the consistently high PISA outcomes.

4.2   Small Size of Country

The value of education in Finland also stems from the country's small size. Magnus, a head teacher, states, "That means that we have to do something special with our people, and one special thing could be that we are very [highly] educated here." Finland's philosophy, therefore, tries "to educate not our best people but people best." Finland's tradition of education has concentrated on this philosophy, especially since the aforementioned comprehensive school reforms of the 1970s. He warns, however, that the Finns can always improve their level of education and cannot become complacent.

Seppo, also a head teacher, attributes the value of education to Finland's small population. This small population, in addition to the unique language, requires a high level of education in order to maintain competitiveness in the modern world. Head Aino, a biology and geography teacher, agrees. She says, "We need to make sure we have a good education [...] to preserve the whole reserve of intelligence." The welfare state and the Finnish government also require that the education system take care of all of the students. Similarly, teacher Krister credits Finland's more marginal place in the world's geography: "We are so aside, if we don't get good knowledge, I think we are going to go back [...] I think the whole of Finland wants to learn and the students go to school to learn." Class size also plays a role. In terms of pedagogy, Magnus thinks small class size improves the level of education of the Finns. Small class sizes and small schools aid discussion between classmates, which in turn helps the learning process. He says, "I think that this is the key to education, to discuss and to learn to discuss. In my opinion, teachers shouldn't have a monologue, just talking all the time. In my opinion, the students and the teacher should discuss these problems together, then you can learn a lot."

Jonny, a mathematics teacher, believes that Finnish culture values education because "it is a matter of life and death for the Finnish state and the Finnish culture." Finland, with only five million people, contributes to the success of administering a strong education system, since the small population size better allows the education system to serve the needs of its students. Professor Laukkanen says, "We are a small country. We have to do well. It's a survival game." This references not only Finland's small size, but also its war-ravaged past and tenacity to eventually break through to success and prosperity.

4.3   Political Consensus

Unlike in other countries, Finland's different political parties enjoy political consensus concerning matters of education. Finland's political system, discussed in Chapter 2, lends itself to consensus, which in turn influences the continuity and consistency in Finland's education system (Chislett, 1996). However, the importance of education to Finland most likely enhances the political consensus on this matter. Minister Halonen states, "It was very important in the Finnish educational policy and has been and is a consensus. There are no political disagreements about that." Minister Jussila also places importance on political consensus as a role in Finland's success in PISA:

> We don't have any political party; we don't have any government; we don't have any family who could say that education is not important. If there would be a politician that would say he didn't care so much about education policy, he will be a former one. It is inside the Finnish society, that education is important. There is a political consensus between various political parties on that.

Jukka, a mathematics teacher, also speaks of the consensus of the entire country about the value of education and their ideas about it: "I think the whole nation has more or less a very good consensus about the values and ideas [of education]. We feel that the world around us, at least in our society, our nation, is very democratic." Political consensus prevents problems when creating policies for political clout, or quick fix policy solutions. Furthermore, this helps eliminate the "'edu-political' chess match" discussed in the previous chapter.

Do the participants anticipate any change in Finland's education culture? Mai-Len, a head teacher, believes that Finland's culture values education and has always done so. The culture has emphasised the importance of education and has admired those who have an education. She worries, though, that the younger generation will not have the same regard and respect for education: "The new generation I don't think feel quite the same [...] For my generation it was very important to go on to university. Nowadays young people want to be pop stars or something else. Becoming a professor isn't the first thing they talk about." Similarly, Professor Koivula not only cites a change in attitude among Finland's youth, but also states how education still leads to advancement and social mobility in Finland. Although she feels this importance has declined in recent years, this belief still exists in Finnish society today. In other words, Finland's history, pride in the Finnish language, the influence of the Lutheran Church, and political consensus all positively influenced the high value of education within Finnish culture.

5   Structure, Organisation, and Characteristics of Finnish Schools

When addressing the strengths of the Finnish education system, many of the factors contributing to Finnish PISA success came from the structure and organisation of Finnish education.

5.1   *Decentralisation*

School and teacher autonomy relates to the decentralisation and devolution of the education system in Finland. For example, Minister Jussila thinks that the decentralised system and the local responsibility and accountability for education also provide a strong foundation for the system of education. He states that, at his national level of educational administration, they only look at the results. The responsibility for teaching and learning ultimately lies with the local authorities. Minister Halonen agrees. He believes that national educational organisations should set the standards for education, but should allow freedom for the local authorities to best execute these standards according to their needs. He states, "You should give quite a bit of freedom to the municipalities and the schools. The expertise is there. They know the local circumstances and the experts of teaching and learning are there." Although the Finnish government executes a national curriculum, it remains just a framework for classroom lessons. The local authorities, head teachers, and teachers decide the skills most pertinent for their pupils.

The decentralised system of education in Finland as well as the devolved control makes education relevant for students in each municipality and even school. Professor Virtanen explains how the devolution of control allows municipalities and teachers to create learning environments most significant for and pertinent to the needs of their students and the community:

> In Finland, the tradition is that municipalities have taken control over the educational system. That is a very strong and long tradition […] Even when they have difficulties in their economy, as they have in many cases nowadays, they really value their education system on a really high level. It seems to be, so that municipalities cut their funding of education,

parents get easily quite angry and aggressive. It only says that education is really highly valued by parents and municipalities.

Similarly, Professor Laukkanen says, "We tried to listen to students' needs and their abilities and their dreams and try to teach that way." Even with this devolution, Professor Virtanen notes how no real disparities exist between schools in Finland: "There are no systematic differences in Northern or Southern or Eastern or Western parts of the country, country schools or city schools, their average level is quite similar. It only [indicates] that municipalities are taking their educational responsibilities quite seriously." With the decentralisation, education has the ability to become more meaningful to each student. Despite the decentralisation of control, however, Finnish schools maintain an enviable universal standard around the country.

5.2 Teacher-Student Relationships

The relationship between teachers and students positively affects the education in Finland. Minister Jussila mentions that the teachers manage to maintain a close relationship with their students while upholding a position of authority. He says the visitors to Finland, the "PISA tourists," become surprised at the relaxed relationship between teachers and students. He states, "They are good friends normally." However, they maintain a distance and gain the respect of their students. He believes the students respect good teachers and professionalism. The students "immediately find out if the teacher is not a professional teacher, a less capable [teacher]. It is very important to have that kind of trust between teacher and pupil." From a head teacher's perspective, Magnus believes that Finnish classrooms have a good balance between a relaxed atmosphere and structure. The teachers have a fair amount of authority over the students and can enforce rules without being too strict.

Linda, who teaches Swedish at a Swedish-speaking school, speaks highly of student-teacher relationships:

> We have quite [...] good contact with our students. We know who they are and they know who we are and we talk to each other by name [...] We are not called teacher, we are called by name. That gives a certain feeling of familiarity or being at home in a way. I think that these students feel safe and secure here [...] I think that could be a part of a good learning environment.

According to Professor Rantanen, teachers "are not on the podium" but rather stay on a similar level with their students. Students and teachers respect each other in schools and within the classrooms, maintained with good discipline, with few disturbances from pupils. OECD official Chevalier also credits the teachers and teacher-student relations:

> Another reason for success in Finland is the strong relationship between the teachers and the kids. In some countries, kids don't have the feeling they are believed in by the teacher. In some countries there is much repetition. In Finland there is no repetition [...] You have the teacher that is able to work with an individualisation of the teaching. They can adapt their programme [to] the level of the kids.

Professor Rantanen also cites excellent school-home relationships between the teachers and the parents. Through their relationships with students, and even parents, teachers maintain a high level of trust in Finland, within the society and within school walls.

5.3 Reforms

Within his own academic research, Minister Jussila explored the "talent resources" in Finland. He remarks how in the 1950s and 1960s, he found that these "talent resources" did not always have the opportunity to go to school at that time. The education reforms of the 1970s, however, changed opportunities for Finnish students. The results of these reforms manifested themselves after thirty years. In other words, it took a generation to truly observe these equal opportunities for Finnish students. He carefully mentions the attitude towards reform within the Finnish Ministry of Education:

> When you reform a system, you need a long time for results. We have here in the Finnish Ministry of Education, that if you need a reform, it has to be done quickly. You can't be all the time on the reform. In education you need both continuity and change. How to find the balance between change of reforms and continuity, this is one key issue. Change and continuity, education needs both of them. Continuity is very important but sometimes you need change.

This outlook towards the reforms succinctly describes a very astute attitude towards education reform. According to Minister Jussila, the education reforms of the 1970s allowed for social mobility. Magnus also describes the balance of Finnish education between flexibility and tradition. He says that Finns use an amount of self-criticism and always try to improve their education system. However, "it is very important that you don't change things all the time." His perspective, much like Minister Jussila's, allows a balance between continuity and change in Finnish education.

Professor Kallio also noted the need for sufficient time for reforms to transpire, but used the example of teacher education reforms. He said, "We got very motivated students, but among those were some who thought it takes too long, four years [now five] in the beginning [...] it [a teacher preparation course] was earlier being three years." The addition of the Master's qualification also proved to be difficult. "Then doing Master's thesis was a very difficult job. It still is, for all the students [...] let's say the first five years [of the reform] were quite difficult." The teacher education reforms were not without their critics. Professor Kallio states how the press was often very critical of the high education standards for teachers, but went quiet after the release of the first PISA scores in 2001. Despite the criticism, the reforms continued along their trajectory, and PISA has now reinforced their success. The "continuity and change" attitude to education reform also shows its astute vision with the teacher education reforms of Finland.

Professor Huttunen also spoke of the slow nature of true education reform. During the beginning of his career, in the 1970s, he calculated that major education reform would take approximately 15 years. Decades later, he states, "I still believe that that was a good estimation: that it takes one generation, in one sense, if a generation is 20 years, to make a major reform. Small things can change easily, but mainly in local circumstances." Even on a more local level, he believes a smaller reform would take more than three years: "The first year, you make silly mistakes, then you make something better, and the third year should flow quite nicely." Much like his ministerial colleague, he also believes in the "continuity and change" mantra: "Quick results cannot be achieved. It has taken a long time for our system to evolve." This echoes the arguments from the previous chapter, how quick fix solutions cannot lead to informed policy transfer, and often lead to policy failure. Finnish education success, as outlined by PISA, has uncovered the rational view of policy reform in the country.

The reasons behind PISA success for Finland, according to OECD official Schroeder, come from the reforms and transformations of the education system and teacher training in the twentieth century. He attributes much of the success to the teachers, who collaborate with each other and have achieved high status through their "knowledge-rich profession." The school system, with lots of transparency, allows everyone to see clear goals and standards. Students have access to a great deal of support and individualisation of learning. The national government has entrusted the municipalities and schools with responsibility and autonomy, but can intervene if needed. For these reasons, he expected Finland to perform well in PISA, and was not surprised at the results.

5.4 Positive Assessment Culture

Unlike other countries that implement high stakes testing and league tables based on these assessments, Finland actually has a positive assessment culture. Minister Jussila mentions how assessments, whether international or national, benefit the Finnish education system. The local authorities welcome assessment and eagerly participate in evaluations. He states, "They don't oppose them. Because, you know, in Britain, they are against [them] because they are afraid of being punished later." As Finland does not have the equivalent of Britain's league tables, the negative connotations of an assessment culture do not exist. Rather, Finnish schools welcome assessment in order to see their strengths and weaknesses.

Professor Laukkanen cites the example that prior to cross-national assessments such as PISA and TIMSS, teachers generated and executed their own assessments of students. Although Finland does have national assessments, she describes how they do not measure all students; rather, they take samples, and do not assess every year. The rest of the assessment comes from the individual teachers. This lack of assessments remains a strong point for Finnish education and points to success in PISA. Students, who do not usually take tests, conscientiously undertake tasks such as PISA when they arise. Here, again, we see Finnish immunity to GERM, and more specifically, a lack of testing culture, benefiting the education system as well as the country's outcome in PISA.

5.5 Support of Weaker Students

The support for weaker students is an asset in Finnish education. Jukka, the mathematics teacher, frequently mentions special education, a broad term used by Finns for their support for weaker students in the education system, when describing the best points of the education system. He says how it does not overlook these students. He describes it as a caring system, one that wants the students to do well in society and in their futures. He himself has pupils who receive extra support in mathematics. Jukka describes the school atmosphere as friendly and uncomplicated, a relaxed environment where the students can receive support for work and study.

The professors agree with Jukka's salient point, the lack of weak students in Finnish schools. For example, Professor Virtanen believes that "the obvious trend of the Finnish educational system is how we take care of the poorly performing students, how every teacher, not just some teachers, how every teacher takes all students very seriously and how they take care of the weak ones." Professor Rantanen concurs: "We can see easily from the [PISA] results, how the weakest are the ones who actually keep the Finnish results the best

[...] in the world." Professor Laukkanen takes it a step further, by pointing out that the lack of low achievers in Finland came about because of hard work:

> One of the reasons is that we have so few low achievers, that we have achieved so few low achievers. I would like to emphasise that. It doesn't come by nature. It comes by teachers and good work and all the investments for special education, because we have also very good special education.

Furthermore, Professor Koivula believes that the special education system supports the Finnish "ethos of trying your best." Effort placed on learning leads to better success for Finnish students. She emphasises special education's role in Finnish education and in PISA. She cites how a quarter of students receive some sort of extra support at school. The extensive special education leads to very low class repetition among Finnish students, and therefore to strength among weak students, as illustrated in PISA. Most fifteen-year-olds in Finland study at the proper grade level, unlike their French counterparts, where 46% have repeated at least once before taking PISA at fifteen. In Finland, even the weakest students perform the minimum work required. Professor Koivula implies that this leads to high PISA scores. She also feels that the special education and the support for weaker students encourage them to try, at the very least to complete the minimum requirements for their grade level. This emphasis on effort probably filtered through for those students sampled for the PISA surveys:

> There has been talk in Finland that the special education students are 'counted out' [in PISA] but that is not true. By accident, [...] some of the Finnish samples [...] had SEN [Special Educational Needs] students who should have not even been in the samples. I think that is a [reward] for supporting the low end.

In other words, she describes how the Finnish sample for PISA included special education students, even though they should not have been in the samples, which reinforces the education system's commitment to special education and supporting weaker students. Chapter 3 illustrates in detail this commitment to special education and the practical application of special education in Finnish schools. Professor Sundqvist takes a more statistical view of this issue. He also feels that the support of weak students comes as a strong point of Finnish education. He finds that high results in PISA come from having few low achievers. In Finland, the lack of low achievers has led to PISA success. Countries with high achievers in PISA but many weak students cannot have overall high scores on PISA. Thus, the dedicated support for weaker pupils, coupled with the egalitarian view of education, allows for a strong showing in PISA for the Finns.

5.6 The National Curriculum and Its Alignment with PISA Measurements

The curricula for Finnish schools do not fall far from PISA goals, which would explain also Finnish success in PISA. Professor Virtanen states how science, mathematics, and mother tongue in the National Curriculum do not differ greatly from the definitions of literacy in the PISA frameworks:

> Both curriculum in mother tongue and mathematics and in science, they are quite close to the idea of PISA, how these subjects, these different types of literacy are defined in PISA frameworks. They are not very far away from how they are defined in [the] Finnish National Curriculum. If I compare how mathematics is stressed in [the] Finnish National Curriculum compared to some Asian countries or Eastern European countries, our definition is much closer. That is one explanation why we are doing so well in [PISA] math and science.

In other words, Finnish education strives for a pragmatic education. Professor Koivula also describes how PISA questions more closely reflect the Finnish curriculum than those of TIMSS. She cites how Finland never did particularly well in international assessments, especially in mathematics and science: "I think the socially constructed ideas of education which have been strong in Finland [...] favour the type of tasks that PISA [has] had than TIMSS [has] had. TIMSS has been more dominated by the kind of hardcore math and science curricula." Along the same vein she also says, "I don't really believe that Finnish children are more intelligent than the children anywhere else, but what makes our school system, it seems to be able to educate them in a way, in the framework that PISA has taken." She does take care to point out that Finland did not design the framework for PISA; rather, all the participating countries in PISA collaborated on the project.

Professor Huttunen also cites how PISA tasks closely compare to the exercises in Finnish textbooks. In both PISA and Finnish textbooks, "you read something and the actual act is not very complicated, but you have to take it out of the text whether the figures should be added or divided or multiplied. We have been using those text forms for items for a long time." Professor Karpinen mentions how Finnish students do not spend much time in school, but manage to learn their subject matter properly: "For example, we have a very small number of mathematics lessons if you compare [us] to other countries [...] We can get more out of these lessons [...] There must be something in that. We do it effectively, I suppose." He also believes that curricular reforms in the 1990s added to the strong outcomes in PISA. Curriculum reforms in 1994 emphasised the role of the students as active participants in their own learning, and the applicability of the curriculum to real-life situations (Tani, 2004). He believes this permeated the teaching style of the teachers and influenced the high mathematical literacy score in PISA.

Professor Karpinen also cites LUMA in the mid-1990s, when the Finnish government installed a programme supporting mathematics and science education in Finland, both in the training of teachers and expanding and improving facilities for science and mathematics. LUMA, as stated previously, an acronym for *luonnontieteet ja matematiikka,* or science and mathematics in English, developed in 1996 to increase math and science skills at all educational levels by improving school laboratories and equipment, as well as more teacher education in these subjects (Välijärvi et al., 2002). He admits, however, that he cannot cite exactly its influence on PISA results. Professor Rantanen finds that one cannot find a connection with LUMA and higher achievement in mathematics or science. Nevertheless, initiatives such as LUMA cannot hurt a country's education efforts.

5.7 *Individualised Learning*
Teachers in Finland have the flexibility to individualise learning for the students. This allows for student-centred and student-controlled learning, taking the devolution and decentralisation to another level. Professor Laukkanen describes her days as a teacher, when she struggled with engaging the pupils in the curricula. She states, "I sort of decided that [...] I had to start to listen to [the pupils]. I think that is really the change of our pedagogy [...] We tried to listen to students' needs and their abilities and their dreams and tried to teach that way." Today, these teachers, with their high qualifications and subsequent trust in their abilities, provide their students with student-centred teaching and a school-based curriculum, to better serve their needs. Professor Rantanen describes the individualisation of learning in Finnish schools, tailored to the needs of the pupils. He says how this occurs mainly in the beginning years of comprehensive education. He also states that students can work in groups and that teachers encourage the students to work independently.

OECD official Khan expressed no surprise at the success of Finland in PISA, since he describes the education system as innovative, with individualised learning. He believes the teachers have great interest in educating their students, which helps Finland deliver a high quality of education. The quality of teaching and of teacher interaction with students remains a key factor in the strength of the education system. Finland also uses its vocational training to help ease the transition from school to work. The vocational education stream prevents school dropouts and helps create practical skills for the labour market. Furthermore, the Finnish system recognises that every child has their own rate of learning, and provides funding for the support of those who need extra attention.

6   Summary

Due to the OECD's PISA, Finnish education has become the focus of much interest from around the world. This chapter discussed findings from empirical research conducted in Finland and in Paris in reference to the reasons behind Finland's top performance in all administrations of PISA thus far. This chapter uncovered the strengths of Finnish education, the driving forces behind an exemplary education system.

Finnish teachers must receive credit for the strength of the education system. This most salient finding highlights the connection between high-quality teachers and the attainment of students. Finnish teachers, who face a rigorous and very selective university admission process, receive a high level of education. They are considered academics in Finnish society, and all qualified teachers have a Master's degree. This allows for a culture of trust within Finnish society, where teachers are entrusted to do their job. Finnish teachers enjoy high status and respect.

The Nordic welfare state allows for egalitarian values and equality within Finnish society. This ensures that all students have an opportunity for a comprehensive education. Finnish schools have consistent standards, so factors such as socio-economic level, geography, or an urban-rural divide do not put pupils at an advantage or at a disadvantage. The homogeneous society also aids the execution of a high-quality, consistent education system. With very few immigrants, Finland does not have the same issues as a country with a steady influx of immigrants, and therefore, the associated language and socio-economic issues. Nevertheless, an interesting finding is that immigrant students in Finland outperform their counterparts in other countries.

Finnish society also places a high value on education. The history of the country, with its movement for independence, pride in the Finnish language, the Lutheran Church, and wars ingrained a need and respect for education within the national psyche. It also instilled a love of reading into the culture, and high levels of literacy. The small size of the country lends itself to education for all and to high quality of education. The small population also inspired the Finnish to achieve a high level of education, in order to survive as an independent country. Political consensus on matters of education characterises Finnish politics; this gives educational matters more importance than political agendas.

The structure and organisation of Finnish education also aids the high quality of the system. The decentralisation of the system allows for autonomy and relevance of education to the local area. Healthy and balanced teacher-student relationships allow for good communication between the two parties. A positive assessment culture forgoes high-stakes testing, accountability, and league tables; the assessment culture allows students to try harder in surveys such as PISA. Individualised learning allows both teachers and students to carve out an educational path best suited to the students' needs. Extensive support for weaker students has made the weak students, paradoxically, quite strong, influencing the overall performance in PISA as well as the consistency of the Finnish education system. The pragmatic approach to education in Finland brings the objectives of the National Curriculum very close to the measurements of PISA. Finnish education aims to prepare students for real life, similar to the literacy measurements of PISA.

Generally, the high regard and value of education in Finland contribute to their high results, as well as the egalitarian philosophy of the country. The comprehensive system ensures that everybody attends school and obtains a basic education. The National Curriculum provides continuity among all schools in the country, yet schools have the trust of the system to autonomously complete the curricular requirements in the manner best suited for their students. OECD official Chadwick states, "Putting that all together, they seem to have a system that is dealing [with] and coping well for their particular students." A strong home-school connection and exemplary pre-school education also help, since the students have a late start but manage school easily from an early age. These factors contribute to Finland's PISA results. Chadwick stated, "Fifteen years ago Nokia made boots. Shoes!" This illustrates the rapid ascent of the country from war-induced poverty to a global leader.

The strengths of Finnish education outlined in this chapter point to factors very intertwined with the Finnish context. For example, history has played a very large and important role in the high esteem of education in society. The structure and organisation of the education also contribute to its successes. Egalitarian values of the Nordic welfare state allow for equality and consistency of the system. Upon further investigation, the strengths of Finnish education, much like Sadler warned, have deep roots within the Finnish context.

CHAPTER 7

Weaknesses of Finnish Education

1 Introduction

No system of education is perfect. Even admired, high-achieving systems, as in Finland, have weaknesses and shortcomings. This chapter focuses on the weaknesses of Finnish education from the aforementioned empirical research with Finnish Ministers of Education, professors of education, head teachers, teachers, and OECD officials. As in the previous chapter, the participants contributing to the findings included two former Ministers of Education from Finland; six head teachers of lower secondary schools; seventeen teachers of the PISA subjects: mathematics, science, and reading literacy of PISA-aged students; eight professors of education responsible for the execution of PISA in Finland; and four OECD officials.

Some of the salient weaknesses correspond to the significant strengths of the Finnish system. For example, most respondents listed exceptional teacher education as a main strong point of Finnish education; however, Minister Jussila cites how these exceptional students accepted to teacher education programmes get poached out of teaching. The high education level of those accepted into teacher education programmes at universities leads employers in other sectors to recruit teachers out of the teaching profession. Employers recognise the signal that teachers, with their exceptional educational backgrounds, can work positively in other environments.

The chapter discusses other weaknesses stemming from the Finnish education system. These salient factors divide into five categories: the downsides of mixed ability teaching, decreasing importance of education, the lack of enjoyment in school, budget cuts, and structural weaknesses. Each section discusses the salient factors at length and provides firsthand, qualitative evidence from the participants.

2 The Downsides of Mixed Ability Teaching

Finland's egalitarian society allows for an equitable, consistent system, with few low achievers. This factor, discussed at length in Chapter 6, also has a downside. This section explores the negative factors stemming from a system of education based on egalitarian values.

2.1   Lack of Support for High-Achieving Students

Pentti, a head teacher, believes the great weakness of Finnish education lies in the opposite of one of its strengths. He admits that it cannot adequately provide for its academically gifted students:

> The only problem at the moment, shown by research such as PISA, is that in Finland we cannot yet adequately take care of those students who are gifted in a certain subject. This is the only problem at the moment, but we are thinking about it. Also I have thought about it very much here in this school. How could we organise the teaching in a way which would pay adequate attention to this?

In his school, they have tried to better provide the interested students with more mathematics:

> In mathematics this has been addressed in such a way that students can choose to concentrate more on mathematics. These students study mathematics more than other students, and it seems to be a good solution. Unfortunately this kind of a solution is not at use in all Finnish schools.

The equality of the system does have a downside, both in terms of the lack of support for the strong students, and of the difficulty for teachers to manage different ability levels in a class. Elvi, also a head teacher, believes that the system does not support the academically gifted students. In addition to this, she thinks that the Finnish system should better cultivate the talents of students. She says, "Perhaps the real talents aren't cared for in any special way and that is of course in a way a shame [...] One should find every kid's talent, and one could continue to work on that."

The opposite of the great strength of Finnish education, dedicated support to the struggling pupils, is one of the biggest weaknesses. For example, Jukka, the mathematics teacher, believes that school does not provide enough challenges for intelligent students:

> I think my only concern is that we give lots of support to those pupils who are underachievers, and we don't give that much to the brightest pupils. I find it a problem, since I think, for the future of a whole nation, those pupils who are really the stars should be supported, given some more challenges, given some more difficulty in their exercises and so on. To not just spend their time here but to make some effort and have the idea to

become something, no matter what field you are choosing, you must not only be talented like they are, but work hard. That is needed.

To combat this, Miikka, a Finnish language and literature teacher, describes how he will give extra work to students who want to have more academic challenges, but admits that "they can get quite good grades, excellent grades, by doing nothing actually, or very little." Pia, the teacher of Swedish, also feels that the schools do not motivate very intelligent students to work. She thinks the schools should provide more challenges for the academically talented students. In fact, she thinks the current school system in Finland does not provide well for its students. Mixed-ability classrooms, she feels, are worse than the previous selective system:

> I think this school is for nobody. That is my private opinion. Actually I think so, because when you have all these people at mixed levels in your class, then you have to concentrate on the ones who need the most help, of course. Those who are really good, they get lazy.

Pia believes these students become bored and lazy, and float through school with no study skills. Jonny describes how comprehensive education places the academically gifted at a disadvantage:

> We have lost a great possibility when we don't have the segregated levels of math and natural sciences [...] That should be once again taken back and started with. The good talents are now torturing themselves with not very interesting education and teaching in classes that aren't for their best.

Again, a factor contributing to the strength of Finnish education has its side effects. Aino, the biology and geography teacher, states that the evenness and equality of the education system have a "dark side." Teaching to the "middle student" in a class of heterogeneous ability bores the gifted students, who commonly do not perform well in school. Similarly, Maarit, the mathematics, physics, and chemistry teacher, finds teaching heterogeneous classrooms very difficult. She admits that dividing the students into ability levels would make the teaching easier, but worries that it may affect the self-esteem of the weaker worse than a more egalitarian system.

Miikka describes discussion in educational circles about creating schools and universities for academically talented students, in order to combat this problem:

> Everyone has the same chances [...] One problem is that it can be too easy for talented students. There has been now discussion in Finland if there should be schools and universities for talented students [...] I think it will happen, but I don't know if it is good, but it will happen, I think so. I am also afraid there will be private schools again in Finland in the future [...] [There] will be more rich people and more poor people, and then will come so [many] problems in comprehensive schools that some day quite soon [...] parents will demand that we should have private schools again, and that is quite sad.

He believes this will create socio-economic differences, currently not so influential in Finland.

The professors also mention the lack of support for gifted students as a great weakness. Professor Virtanen says that Finnish education could better reach the academically talented students:

> We could reach better results with the talented students. We are not understanding deeply enough the needs of these students. In many cases they are unmotivated when they leave basic education and they [...] feel school is boring.

Professor Laukkanen attributes this to the Nordic model: "The principle of equity is very seriously taken in Nordic countries, so we invest much more money and effort in low achievers than in talented students. That is [...] [the] problem [...] we don't pay [...] enough attention to the gifted." Professor Koivula also mentions this. In a comprehensive school, all students would share the same academic level. In reality, however, comprehensive schools have heterogeneous class compositions. While the Finnish ethos gives support to the weak students, it also causes oversight of the academically talented students. Professor Rantanen agrees. He says how no support currently exists for the strong students, but wonders "how high would they achieve if they had support?" Professor Karpinen adds that support really should go to the academically gifted students, but it comes down to issues of pedagogy:

> The problem of this kind of heterogeneous teaching is [...] how teachers can divide their time to different students. When [we] put emphasis on weak students, how can teachers give enough support to the best performing students? That is one issue in Finland; we are trying to find some ways to improve.

Professor Koivula addresses pedagogical possibilities that could help the gifted students, but admits the difficultly in implementing them in the classroom. The textbooks illustrate this problem. Many argue that education cannot be equal if different students use different textbooks. Professor Sundqvist describes the logistical difficulty of carrying out gifted education in Finland:

> The simple fact of special education for [the] talented [...] and the question of why not take two percent out of schools and put them into special classes, special schools [...] It would be impossible in Finland, virtually impossible. Two percent of the Finnish school population would be possible to create small classes or a small school in Helsinki but nowhere else. The rest would have to bus or fly all over the place.

The concept of egalitarian education does not cover all students in this sense, and the Finnish context also inhibits the implementation of support for gifted students.

Professor Virtanen worries that the strong students can become bored and leave education. This oversight, he feels, stems from the concentration of support for weaker students: "It seems very difficult to combine these two issues [of weak and strong students], you are taking really good care of weak students when the needs of gifted students become sometimes taboo." The strong students who become bored with education may lose motivation and leave education and not attempt further study or qualifications for the labour market. Professor Sundqvist also describes how academically talented students never learn to study:

> The teaching is geared [...] a little bit towards the average students, or maybe even below. I think that might be growing in the population a number of students who don't learn what it means to study, because they do well without studying too much. This may be a problem one day, that you don't really reach anything if you don't really do some work for it.

Because they do not have sufficient challenges in school, academic matters come too easily to gifted pupils and they never need to study to achieve good marks. Similarly, Terttu, the chemistry teacher, thinks that mixed ability grouping comes at a detriment to the students' learning. She says: "You don't have enough time for everyone [...] All children have to be in the same class. That is not so nice. You have the better pupils. I can't give them as much as I want. You have to go so slowly in the classroom."

Professor Sundqvist believes the structure of the system does not take into account the differing developmental levels of the children. He says how preschool aims to even out these differences in theory, but does not necessarily do so in practice. He describes this as a "politically correct and inefficient model." He acknowledges how the comprehensive education system, especially with the good special education system that Finland possesses, helps an entire population advance in its education level, but it comes at a cost. He believes "some children would, in their personal development […] do better in a system where we go onwards when you have actually understood what you are supposed to understand and learn […] [rather] than just being pushed forward because you are of a certain age."

2.2 Teaching Is too Theoretical

Despite the accolades, the Finnish curriculum does not have benefits for all of the students. Even though the Finnish curriculum takes into account the real world context, much like PISA, many participants acknowledged that the teaching erred on the side of too theoretical. For example, Mai-Len, a head teacher, while describing some stricter curriculum reforms, mentions that Finland's high PISA outcomes came from the more flexible academic environment of the recent past: "It was done at a time when we really could choose within the school how to organise the teaching." While a head teacher in Helsinki, she offered many course options and the students could choose a more individualised course of study. Currently, however, students must all study the same thing, and they also have more theoretical and fewer practical courses than before. She cites how not all students want theoretical courses, and so theoretical courses should be an option for the students who want that direction of study: "It should be optional so that those who want more theory can have it, and those who need more practical things should have that." She believes the government will change the reforms back to the former way: "It will probably change again eventually, once they realise the mistake, because it is a mistake."

Saija, a Finnish language and literature teacher, also thinks that Finland needs to implement more social training in the school curriculum. She thinks the children need instruction on how to express themselves, develop cultural awareness and public speaking skills, and not just emphasise theory and mathematics. She worries that children in Finland suffer from low self-esteem and feel sad in school. She says, "The most important thing is to teach the children to feel good about themselves, so they can be happy people, rather than [just focusing on] these subjects and theoretical knowledge."

Linda, who teaches Swedish, notes deficiency in the amount of time available for subjects. With more time, she would implement more creative activities, such as speech and drama, into her lessons. Saija also thinks that her students need more arts subjects like drama and art. She worries that they consider mathematics as the only important subject. She feels countries such as Sweden, Norway, and England have better arts programmes than in Finnish schools. Arts subjects, according to Saija, help the students get to know themselves. Furthermore, the lack of emphasis on the arts subjects could indicate a narrowing of the curriculum to the PISA literacy areas. One could argue that this shows the narrow focus of the Finnish curriculum led to more concentrated time on the assessed PISA subjects.

Two of the professors believe that the Finnish school system could be too academic. Much like Saija, Professor Virtanen worries about the lack of social development in Finnish schools, and the impact in the future:

> Maybe [the schools] are, in some cases, too much concentrating only on academic achievement and maybe the social side of it; their social needs are not considered. You can see that some students have problems in their sense of belonging and these kinds of social development. Finnish students don't seem to be very active in participating in social life in school. They are in a way, too much concentrated only on the academic part of the education. I think this will be one of the big issues in the future.

He worries about the social development of Finnish students, sometimes overlooked by the Finnish curriculum, although also important in the growth of a person. Professor Rantanen worries that achievement in PISA and the too-academic curriculum in Finnish schools take away from other subjects. Time given to traditional academic subjects reduces hours in subjects such as art and home economics, where students struggling in other subjects may excel. He thinks this creates huge drawbacks in the Finnish curricula.

PISA allows an education system to review both its strengths and weaknesses. Although the academic track in Finnish schools demonstrates high quality, as reinforced by PISA, Minister Halonen thinks the vocational track could improve. He thinks that Finnish vocational education has employed a more theoretical educational ideal, perhaps not suited to vocational education. He feels that the vocational education stream should be combined more with apprenticeships, in order to expand the potential of vocational education in Finland. Similarly, Kalevi, a head teacher, believes that school can be too hard for some of the pupils, who would benefit more from a more applied, practical education. A few students in his school "don't want to read and study so much. I think it is better that they do something more with their hands than read and study so much." He believes the very few students who do not want to study would benefit from more practical training. While Finland has received many accolades for its education system, this chapter thus far has uncovered some shortcomings. For example, perhaps vocational education needs to better serve the needs of the country's youth.

3 Decreasing Importance of Education

The participants mentioned certain factors contributing to Finland's educational weaknesses that relate to a general decline in society. For example, Minister Jussila mentions how drug abuse and other antisocial behavior affect the schools and their communities. This problem, according to him, can become quite serious in some areas. Although this problem has increased since the beginning of the new millennium, he feels that it has stabilised since. Providing education for all and having all schools and classrooms for the learning of all students presents a great challenge for Finnish education. The strong school support helps all students combat these problems and provide educational opportunities for all. Again, a person who dropped out of school costs more than a student needing support to keep him or her in school.

Magnus, the head teacher, thinks students these days have been spoiled by their parents:

> Today's youth, in my opinion [...] are quite spoiled [...] because Finland's economy is quite good, and there are a lot of parents who give them a lot of things. They are very comfortable with the way of living that you can get everything that you want. That is a big thing because now we notice it in school. It's not so nice, because they can't take rules.

Mai-Len, also a head teacher, feels that Finns have become lazier:

> When the children are little, it's so important to teach them to read and write, but we're not always good at that. I think we have gotten a bit lazier [...] The teachers are not so hard working anymore. Some of them are, but many are teaching without caring whether anyone learns anything. I'm not talking about my teachers, of course, but generally, teaching has gone down. When I was young, we had a lot of homework, but that's changed. We had to ask our parents for help because it was so difficult, but now parents don't have time to help their children any more [...]. I don't think we [give] as much time [to] education as we did before.

According to Mai-Len, the young today do not spend time reading or studying; rather, they prefer to see friends or surf the Internet.

Linda, a literature teacher, thinks the love of reading has declined in the younger generation, as they tend to gravitate more to video games and television. Saija agrees. As a teacher of Finnish, she feels that she has difficulty motivating her students to learn: "I think my subject is not the [...] easiest one to teach. They don't read so much, newspapers or novels." Her students, especially the boys, do not like their assignments in Finnish language.

Saija thinks the respect for teachers has declined in this past generation. Miikka agrees that some students lack respect for their teachers:

> They don't respect the teachers. They respect them very little [...] I think it has changed a lot in recent years. In Helsinki, it was actually earlier. When I came here six years ago, I thought this was heaven. I thought it was incredible, how the children were like that after Helsinki, but now I think it is the same.

Pia finds the PISA frenzy about Finland amusing, since she believes the schools have declined in recent years: "I think [the attention] is quite funny because school isn't as good as it used to be [...] I used to be proud of being a teacher and proud of this school, but I can't say I'm proud any more."

Professors Huttunen and Koivula address this issue further. Professor Huttunen worries about bullying in Finnish schools, especially when related to academic motivation and success:

> There is a minor problem which I don't like at all, which is the bullying. The children are not safe [...] Some of the young people do not tolerate others, and they tease them when they are orienting themselves in an intellectual fashion, and I don't know the real extent of that. I believe it is quite common, and that is not nice.

Whether the students actually do not like school or just do not admit it remains in question, and this affects boys more than it does girls. Professor Koivula cites how boys in lower-secondary schools who enjoy learning or have academic ambition find themselves in a socially difficult position. Academically inclined boys find themselves bullied or excluded socially. This leads to boys hiding their interest in school, and a higher number of girls in upper-secondary education. She says, "It enhances the difference between girls and boys attending high school and after that, attending university. It is unfair towards boys because they just seem to be [in] a poorer situation trying to be good students." This shows that Finnish society does succumb to similar worldwide trends such as lack of boys' educational interest, and video game technology taking away from reading for pleasure.

4 Lack of Enjoyment in School

The PISA data cited a lack of enjoyment in school as a worrying trend in Finnish education. Minister Jussila addressed this by saying he feels that the greatest drawbacks in Finnish education lie in the school environment. He considers the lack of enjoyment of Finnish pupils as a shortcoming of the system. The 2000 PISA survey measured the students' sense of belonging in school. In Finland, approximately 22% of the students reported a low sense of belonging in school. Countries such as Sweden, at 18%, and the United Kingdom, at 17%, had the least amount of students reporting this low sense of belonging. However, countries such as Japan, at 38%, South Korea, at 41%, and Poland, at 41%, reported the highest levels of lack of belonging (Willms, 2003). Nevertheless, this statistic worries Finnish officials. Minister Jussila thinks that boys, especially, do not enjoy school. He suspects that boys do not believe that school really suits them, despite good performance in school subjects. This curious phenomenon has the boys going to school and trying to finish as quickly as possible. He also cites how girls perform higher than boys in Finnish education. Minister Jussila feels the real weakness and the real question lie in how to motivate boys to enjoy school and to continue with their studies.

Minister Halonen also mentions how Finnish students do not enjoy school, and cites how many Finns worry about the lack of enjoyment of their pupils. As a father of a teenage son, he adds his own perspective on the situation. He says, "I don't see it as a big problem, I would be more worried if 100% of Finnish pupils say that they enjoy themselves in schools, because I wouldn't think that was true." He has his own interpretation of the lack of enjoyment of Finnish students. He believes that the students perceive school as a place of learning, not of enjoyment:

> They see this role [of school as a place of learning]. I think that's why they say it's not a place for enjoyment for them. I think that [...] I hope what you see in schools is that people, both teachers and pupils are committed, serious about learning. I don't mean that it can't be fun, but you learn things, but they are committed to learning things.

Minister Halonen's personal perspective on the problem sheds light on the situation. Perhaps the lack of enjoyment in school comes as a cultural distinction in Finnish society.

Magnus, the head teacher, worries that the pupils do not like school. The aforementioned PISA data showed that Finnish students had some of the lowest happiness levels in school. He suspects that Finnish students actively admit when they do not enjoy a lesson or school, perhaps unlike their counterparts in other countries. Kalevi also feels uneasy about the lack of enjoyment Finnish pupils have in school. He infers that the students feel this way because teachers have such high expectations of them academically.

According to the teachers, the curious finding in the Finnish PISA results, lack of enjoyment in school, seems to come from a cultural influence. Maarit thinks the students say they do not enjoy school because of peer pressure. She thinks they actually do like school. Aino also addresses this issue: "If you ask a teenager, 'Do you like school?' the mentality in Finland is of course, 'I hate it; I don't like it.' I'm sure [...] they don't like it so much. We have good results, but they don't like it so much." Benny, a mathematics, physics, and chemistry teacher, however, believes his students very much enjoy school. He says, "We have a quite extraordinary school in that way. We don't have many students who dislike coming to school in the morning."

The professors also mention this point consistently, that Finnish pupils do not like school. Professor Karpinen says the visitors to Finnish schools notice this fact, or that the students do not have positive attitudes towards some subjects. He hopes that these "PISA tourists" will have some insight on how to fix this problem. He suggests that this consistent dislike of school comes from a cultural nuance rather than a worrying trend. Nevertheless, he states, "In Finland we think that the students try to do their best even though they can say they don't like to be in school. Even though they say that, they like to go to school and they work quite actively." Professor Rantanen agrees with Professor Karpinen. Students may try their best and actually enjoy school, but do not admit it. Professor Rantanen states, "It is not culturally acceptable to say, 'I love mathematics' in Finland, I guess." He adds, "I think that also may be a cultural feature in Finland, that we are not even supposed to love mathematics, but however, [...] all the kids at the end of the summer vacation, they are waiting to get back to school."

The professors also take a comparative and cross-national perspective on this matter. Professor Sundqvist describes how Danish observers found that Finnish schools did not have a positive climate. He pointed out to the Danes, however, that countries with top results in PISA do not have positive climates. He says, "Perhaps their aim, their goal of teacher education to have a wonderful classroom climate with really efficient work is not a reasonable goal." He also describes enjoyment in school as "the most stupid indicator by a long way." Finnish assessments have shown that the pupils, both boys and girls, have a positive attitude towards school, even though very few admit that they love it. Professor Huttunen points out a negative correlation between school enjoyment and achievement in PISA. For example, countries such as Brazil and Tunisia, which score low in PISA, report high enjoyment in school. Professor Koivula argues that in her observations Finnish students always seem to enjoy school: "I must say, every time I walk into a school, I have never been visiting a school where the students suffer. They look very positive." While the relatively high percentage of Finnish students claiming they do not enjoy school could cause some concern, there seems to be a correlation to the lack of enjoyment of students and high scores in PISA. For example, Japanese and South Korean students have a number of students reporting a low sense of belonging, but these pupils generate high PISA outcomes. Conversely, there is Professor Huttunen's example of Brazilian and Tunisian students, who do not perform well in PISA but seem to be happier.

5   Budget Cuts

Lack of money hinders any education system, no matter how high achieving. Economic downturns and recessions of the first and second decades of the new millennium illustrate this. For instance, Minister Halonen mentions educational budget cuts as a weakness of Finnish education, since the educational system of Finland has seen a decrease in funding. In response to the deep recession of the 1990s and decentralisation of the education system, the Finnish government reduced spending on education. For example, between 1990 and 1994, expenditure decreased in comprehensive schools by 15%, in upper-secondary schools by 25%, and vocational schools by 23% (Rinne et al., 2002). At the same time, enrolment in school increased, for example, by 22% in upper-secondary schools and by 28% in vocational schools. Special support teaching decreased by half at that time as well. Further budget cuts worry Minister Halonen. He notes that many municipalities have decreased their spending on education, and fears that this will affect the quality of teaching in the schools.

Krister, a mathematics, physics, and chemistry teacher, thinks that budget cuts will come as a detriment to the education system:

> In [my city], I think [education] is going in the wrong direction. The cities are independent. They started in many cities to cut down the budget

for education, so next year they are cutting by five percent the school's money, so the city doesn't have enough, and they have to cut it from the school. There are also many schools [where] they are going to cut the money, which will make two or three more students per class. Now we have seven classes [per grade level], and with a five percent cut, we will go to five classes, and that is not so good. I think it is better to have small classes. We have quite small classes, 20–22 students, and in some classes smaller. When I started here we had 32–33 per class, and it is much better now.

Jukka, the mathematics teacher, also says the schools need more resources:

> The resources, economically speaking, they are not the best. They are not at the level I think they should be. The economy of Finland is doing very well. Finland has never been so rich as it has been today. But all in all, I must say that it feels that we don't have enough money for education.

Linda says how Finnish society values education, yet speaks of the difficulty with the tight funding of education. She believes that with more money they could better provide for the students in their schools.

Some teachers feel that the education system could achieve even more with better funding. Aino thinks that Finnish education could benefit from more money:

> I find [the education system] very good, and as I have discussed with teachers from other countries, I think it is quite good, but of course it could be even better – more money, smaller groups, especially when we go outside, working in [...] nature and things, more equipment, and for example, computers. They are very old and only half of them work. Things like that. We could do even better if we had more money.

Sanna, a Swedish teacher, also thinks Finnish education needs more funding. The budget cuts would greatly affect her school, which already has classroom shortages. Miikka, Christer, and Benny all believe their schools could benefit from more computers and resources as well, and they think schools have enough resources to best teach their students. Many schools need more support for their special students but do not have the money for these teachers. Limited resources also mean large class sizes, which are harder to teach.

6 Structural Weaknesses

Some of the shortcomings discussed by the participants reflected the structural weaknesses in the Finnish education system, labour market, and society. Although praised as an advantage in the previous chapter, Magnus admits that sometimes the teacher-student gap can become too large:

> In my opinion, there is too big a gap between the students and the teachers. It could be smaller, but it is very, very important that the students [...] in some way, look up to the teacher... but the level could be smaller. It shouldn't be some garden party or like that but we could be more aware of the students' problems, take care of them more and understand that they have a lot of work to do and so on.

Jonny worries about the possibilities for students after education. The labour market does not provide enough jobs for students: "We have so many young students and university youngsters that are studying and won't get a job in the future. That is a problem that we can't afford in the long term, to continue in this way." He also fears that the small, homogeneous population does not encourage new ideas and becomes stagnant in its thinking. He also feels that Finnish education has no long-term strategies, no plans for the future:

> Our values do not support [the education system] at the moment, not [...] religion and not [...] working values. It doesn't support it, especially not in the South of Finland where far too many are [aiming at] the *gymnasium* and we don't have any long-term planning for how Finland will work after ten or twenty years. We are living hand-to-mouth.

Professor Sundqvist describes the structural weaknesses of the system. In upper-secondary school, the students have a choice as to which subjects to take according to their interests. He thinks this comes as a detriment to a student's learning:

> This is counterproductive in the sense that in the *gymnasium*, those who think they are not good in some subjects will leave them out. They are encouraged even to do this. Then they are selected into further studies on the basis of their selections. This means that structurally, we have built a system that leads to very, very powerful, especially gender and parental background, enhancing or enforcing segregation of further studies.

Even though Finland has a comprehensive system of education, this self-selection leads to disparity in education level, something that worries Finnish education officials. For example, girls often choose not to take much mathematics at the upper-secondary level, causing a discrepancy in mathematical level and in university entrance in these subjects. Professor Sundqvist believes this problem comes from the structure of the system.

Professor Rantanen thinks that PISA has not only been a positive influence on Finnish education, but also a negative influence as well. He feels that the Finnish government tried to hide the PISA results initially. He implies that the high scores in PISA prompted the government to add more instructional hours in subjects pertinent to the PISA surveys:

> I would say that one of the drawbacks in my sense was that the Finnish people were supposed to be the best readers in the world, in PISA 2003, but [at] the same time our weekly instructional hours in mother language were increased by one weekly hour or two. The same happened in mathematics [...] physics and chemistry were started to be taught two years earlier, as independent subjects themselves [...] Those changes might guarantee that Finnish know-how is better and stays at the top of the world.

This increased instruction time in the PISA-related subjects correlates with the lack of time for subjects like art and home economics. The decreased time for more creative subjects and social development may not show up in PISA, but may harm Finland in other ways. This also alludes to a narrowing of the curriculum in order to perform in international surveys. This implies that Finland is not completely resistant to GERM.

Professor Huttunen describes a weakness in the education system but on a more abstract level, the concept of over-education:

> There is also a problem that is called optimal overeducating. We are overeducating our people. The workforce demands but does not require so much *gymnasium* or third degree education. So we are overeducating them, but for a small country this seems to be something which is worthwhile doing, but [we should wonder] whether there should be more vocational elements.

Again, this raises the question of the shortcomings of Finland's vocational education, and whether the system is comprehensive enough for all student needs. Professor Sundqvist states how the debate about over-education has gone on for years, stemming from the education of the peasant and working classes in the past. The debates currently revolve around education and the economics of education. Today, Finnish policy makers worry if they spend too much money on education. However, Professor Sundqvist says, "If anything, the success of the Finnish educational system has been outperformed by the economic performance of Finland. Comparative studies would dare suggest that we are precisely at the right level."

7 Summary

Every education system, no matter how admired or high-performing, has its own weaknesses. The Finnish education system is no exception. The participants mentioned the downsides to mixed ability teaching as a shortcoming. While struggling students receive much support in Finland, high-achieving students do not obtain the same academic care. The system overlooks these academically talented students, causing them to become bored and lack study skills. On a related note, the teachers found mixed ability teaching difficult, as teaching to the middle student neglects the high and low achieving students. Mixed ability grouping also leaves education at a far too theoretical level, according to some participants. Better practical and vocational education would help combat this problem.

An overall decline in society also contributes to the education system's weaknesses. For example, the participants cited bullying, general laziness, declining respect, and loss of interest in reading as factors behind these weaknesses. The PISA data, as well as the participants, stated that Finnish students do not enjoy school. While their enjoyment is higher than some other high achieving countries in PISA, this finding worries many of the participants. Some attribute it to a sense of duty or work ethic from Finnish students in school matters. Others believe that peer pressure of Finnish culture does not allow students to admit that they like school.

School systems need money to operate, and teachers in Finland do not feel that they had enough money to carry out the education system at an optimal level. Budget cuts worried teachers and head teachers in terms of class size, resources, and technology. Structural deficiencies also led to some of the weaknesses as well. For example, despite the excellence of the Finnish education system, students have trouble transitioning into the labour market. Specialising within the upper-secondary school further reinforces gender stereotypes and parental influence on educational attainment. Some participants felt that the government now "tailors" to PISA results, with added hours in PISA subjects and less time in other subjects.

Many of the weaknesses of Finnish education, much like the strengths outlined in the previous chapter, point to factors very intertwined with the Finnish context. For example, the lack of enjoyment in school, while not as marked as in other countries, has explanations related to students' attitude towards school and Finnish teenage culture. The strengths of Finnish education have corresponding weaknesses. While the comprehensive, egalitarian system and extensive support for weak students remain a strong point, as discussed in Chapter 6, lack of attention to the high-achieving students was mentioned consistently as a weakness of the system. Teaching mixed ability groups provided difficulty for the teachers too. Structural weaknesses exist as well. A difficult transition to the labour market after education remains a factor not documented when exploring the Finnish "PISA miracle."

CHAPTER 8

Finnish Responses to PISA

1   Introduction

PISA, a survey with immense size and scope, has garnered much attention and has helped in driving a paradigm shift in education, from a learning-to-learn model to that of education for economic competitiveness. PISA has also aided in accelerating this on a global level, and adding in the educational dimension. As discussed in Chapter 4, PISA falls prey to much criticism. However, the evolution of education due to cross-national assessments has been both positive and negative, and this chapter sheds light upon these positive responses to PISA from a Finnish perspective, in addition to the negative aspects. Thus, this chapter uncovers the positive consequences of PISA in Finland, such as the possibility of measurement, affirmation of the Finnish education system, and good by-products to the survey, and certain policy responses. On the other hand, the chapter also delves into the negative effects, such as the problematic structure of PISA, the negative impact of the survey, and the potentially harmful political implications of PISA. This chapter also weighs up the Finnish perspective of PISA vs the IEA surveys, such as TIMSS, the experience of being a PISA sample school, and the future of PISA.

This chapter stems from empirical research. The participants included two former Ministers of Education from Finland; six head teachers of Finnish lower secondary schools; seventeen teachers of the PISA subjects: mathematics, science, and reading literacy of PISA-aged students; eight professors of education responsible for the execution of PISA in Finland; and four OECD officials.

2   Positive Responses to PISA

Overall, the empirical research did uncover positive aspects of the PISA survey. These can be organised into four sections, including the importance of measurement, good reinforcement for the Finnish education system, positive by-products of PISA, and encouraging policy responses to PISA.

2.1   *Measurement*
The PISA survey allows for measurement of education systems from an international perspective, allowing for benchmarks and comparisons. For example,

Minister Jussila believes that surveys like PISA benefit education and education policy; he even worked with PISA closely from its beginning:

> I was a member of a steering group for the project. For a long time I was the chairman for the group. I was a member and then we there discussed the first ideas to establish the exercise that PISA is [...] It is important to know how your country is compared with others, what is your position compared to the other countries, what [are] the school achievements in our country compared to others. It is very important to know in order to develop education further.

Minister Halonen takes this notion to the next level. He believes PISA provides a good measuring tool from one education system to another, since it helps with decision making, and provides indications of what works and what does not work in an education system. He also states that PISA developed educational tools of assessment that have proved very valuable. Minister Jussila believes that PISA illustrates an education system's strengths and weaknesses, and thinks that PISA clarified some of the needs of the Finnish education system to the ministers. Knowing both strengths and weaknesses allows improvement upon the weaknesses, so that in the future "there won't be any more weaknesses." Both ministers see the benefit of PISA, and acknowledge PISA as an opportunity to observe the weaknesses in Finnish education and as a catalyst for improvement.

PISA has illustrated how Finland needs to have more high-achieving students and reduce the number of low-achieving students. For example, in the 2006 scientific literacy survey, 0.5% of Finnish students scored lower than Level 1, 3.6% of students scored at Level 1, 13.6% at Level 2, 29.1% at Level 3, 32.2% at Level 4, 17% at Level 5, and 3.9% at Level 6 (OECD, 2007). Although quite enviable to other countries, this breakdown illustrates to the education ministers that most students could perform at a higher literacy level. All students, despite their varying levels, need a push forward. Because of this, the Finnish education ministers concluded that they needed to support weak students and those at risk of dropping out, while encouraging the strongest students to keep achieving. In order to do this, Minister Jussila believes teacher education must be kept at a high level.

Overall, Magnus, a head teacher, thinks PISA gives a good overview of education in many countries and provides good comparison between education systems. Similarly, Elvi, also a head teacher, believes PISA allows countries to see where they stand in an international educational context: "It can be nice to know where one stands, that kids can read and write and they have developed as humans, that can be nice of course, and healthy. Also [it is] good to see for national decision makers where one can improve things." Head teacher Seppo thinks PISA gave evidence that the Finnish comprehensive school provided good quality education for all of its students. He also cites that PISA revealed the bad points of Finnish education, as in needing more support for the talented students, as well as illustrating the good educational practices. PISA provides educators such as himself with evidence that they have been working successfully. In this way, they can prove to the government and the educational policy makers that they produce high-quality education and should continue on a similar path.

From the classroom perspective, teachers believe that PISA allows for good comparisons between countries. Christer, a biology and geography teacher, thinks PISA, in addition to centralised standardised testing, allows people to better observe the strong points in education systems. However, he warns that countries must not compete with each other. PISA also allows Finland to see the areas that need improvement. Jukka, a mathematics teacher, speaks of the depiction of Finnish education as the best in the world because of its performance on PISA:

> It is tempting to think [that Finnish education is the best in the world], but I find there is some self-indulgence in the idea that we are the best in the world. In the Finnish minds, when people in Finland are discussing with each other we tend to be very modest [...] We are too modest to say we are the best in the world [...] I think we have a good system, yes, but it would be fantastic to develop it more and more so we have the best system in the world as a goal.

PISA allows Finland to see its strengths and weaknesses, and to improve the system.

In terms of an international perspective, Pia, a Swedish language and literature teacher, thinks PISA comes as an asset for the European Union and provides a good comparison between the EU countries. PISA and standardised tests, according to her, provide good comparisons and help keep educational levels even. Jonny, a mathematics teacher, also believes that PISA has benefits for Finland's EU membership. The European Union necessitates understanding of the other member countries, and PISA aids this. Juho, a Finnish teacher, gives a good summary of the importance of PISA in terms of educational measurement, both nationally and internationally:

> I think [PISA] is important in the international [arena], the OECD, so they can evaluate in different countries, the systems. But particularly in Finland it is not so important for our own school system, because we have seen that we are doing fine. That is one reason it is good. We don't have to really change anything, but if we are okay, everything is fine, we don't have to change anything, that is no progress.

From both the ministerial and school levels, the Finns acknowledge how PISA allowed them to have benchmarks for their own system. Especially for a country without a testing culture, this information has proved invaluable.

2.2   *Positive Affirmation of Finnish Education*

Finland's high outcomes in PISA have provided excellent reinforcement for the education system. Minister Jussila notes that Finns feel that the application of knowledge has great importance in their teaching and learning philosophies, in addition to the theoretical background of study:

> In Finland, we had this discussion about which is more important, to be capable to utilise your knowledge in practice in everyday life or to utilise your knowledge in an academic career. Sometimes the correlation is very strong between the two. We need both of those.

Minister Halonen agrees that the PISA results reflect the Finnish attitude to education and the country's culture of learning.

Pentti, a head teacher, describes how PISA measures practical applications of subject matter, and says how Finland scored well in PISA because Finnish pupils have good skills in the practical applications of knowledge: "This is what we Finns are good at. Top class of the world." However, he warns that PISA did not measure how the students learn the material or their learning processes: "But PISA did not measure how the student had learned all those issues, which are part of the curriculum, things they should have learned in school, for example, for the sake of their future studies. This is where we still should improve." Thus, PISA has shown the strengths and weaknesses within the Finnish education system. Pentti describes how Finland has great pride in its performance on PISA: "We Finns just have to be proud that we are good at what PISA measures [...] Those attributes measured by PISA are valued very much internationally, so in that sense we are very proud." PISA, thus, became a source of pride for Finland, and especially those directly involved with education. The survey also allowed the Finns to learn about themselves and their own education by taking part in surveys like PISA.

Although head teacher Elvi's school participated in PISA as a sample school, she expressed surprise at the results. The PISA questions, not typical school questions, showed that Finnish students can apply their learning to realistic situations:

> I was a little surprised and also impressed [by] the questions that the students did. They were not at all typical school questions in that one, so to speak, sits and crams something and then repeats it. Instead it is more about thinking for yourself [...] and I think it was fairly interesting to see, and it was nice that we did so well. It shows that we probably are on the right track in this country with regards to school.

Although some teachers remain a little sceptical about PISA, they find it strengthens the faith in their education system. For example, Saija, a Finnish language and literature teacher, believes that PISA provided Finland with good reinforcement, but most of all supported the hard work of the teachers. It also rewarded the special education efforts in Finland, whose sample consisted of many students in special education or extra support. Toni, a mathematics, physics, and chemistry teacher, although a little suspicious about standardised tests and international surveys, does admit PISA did good things for Finland.

Professor Laukkanen finds that PISA provided good reinforcements for Finnish education:

> In our newspapers they always complain about education and the students and about the teachers. How young people are terrible and misbehaving and how they don't learn anything, and how the school system is bad and how the old system was good. That is why it has been very eye-opening, to see that our system is functioning very well, that our teachers are doing a good job, and our students are learning more than they used to.

Professor Virtanen agrees with Professor Laukkanen, since he also believes that PISA has increased confidence in the Finnish education system. Traditionally, he says, the public has criticised Finnish education, especially at the lower secondary level. Many thought that the system should re-introduce streaming, rather than following the comprehensive ideal. The PISA results, however, have positively reinforced the comprehensive education reforms of the 1970s. Professor Virtanen describes how PISA compelled Finns to learn more about their system, how the reforms worked quite well for Finnish education and society. He also believes that PISA reinforced the teacher education system, the movement of teacher training programmes to the university level and the requirement to have Master's degrees: "After PISA it is much deeper [sic] accepted by people in the administration and the whole society that investing in teachers [...] will bring good results when we are measuring what students have learned." The previous chapter discussed this as well, stating that the reforms of the 1970s had some difficulty with implementation and acceptance by both those involved and not involved, for example, those undertaking teacher education with Master's degrees. While an opposition to these reforms seemed to exist for decades, the PISA scores quieted this.

Professor Virtanen also, on a more pragmatic level, finds PISA useful because of the amounts of money spent on the project. He mentions how the Finnish government had much more involvement in PISA than in the IEA surveys. The whole idea of PISA, according to him, especially for OECD countries, stems from the notion that education and economic development have a strong relationship, and that they provided the catalyst for the entire PISA undertaking. Professor Sundqvist also argues that PISA provides evidence for debates and discussions about education in Finland, since they had not until that time used evidence-based arguments, but "belief-based" approaches, as Professor Huttunen describes it.

In the same vein, Professor Sundqvist describes how PISA scores came as a shock to Finland. Observing a decline in matriculation examination scores forced many to believe in the weakening of the Finnish education system. They thought they had a lack of success in education, and then the OECD released the PISA outcomes in 2000: "We were talking about how things were going really badly; we are still doing better than anybody else by PISA standards." Those pessimistic about Finnish education did not want to discuss the PISA results of 2000, but the 2003 survey began conversations about education and provided evidence to back up confidence in the education system. Surely the repeat top performances in 2006 and 2009 have added to this positive reinforcement of the Finnish education system. However, the release of the 2012 and 2015 scores may have brought about some negative discourse surrounding the education system.

Professor Huttunen believes that PISA has generated good technical outcomes, such as reinforcing spending on education and educational research, which he feels have more value than "silly economic studies." PISA furthermore shows the value in comparing education systems and paying attention to student in-school variations. Professor Virtanen also praises PISA for making education more visible, by heightening the importance of education, especially in public discussions. Because of PISA, more and more people have an interest in education. He believes people need to realise the importance of education, especially "for coming generations, not only for economic competition but for their personal development and understanding of the world and being able to communicate to each other."

PISA ultimately reinforced education in Finland. Previous to PISA, Professor Huttunen cites dissatisfaction with the education system and discussions about changing the system, especially teacher education. Many argued to remove teacher training courses from the universities and to transfer them to polytechnics. However, "PISA results stopped that discussion [...] That has been a very important effect. No one dares."

2.3 Positive By-Products of PISA

Minister Halonen agrees that PISA provides a good springboard from which further study can emerge, and it needs further study to find true answers to educational problems. He reiterates the point of how PISA not only measures, but also helps people understand more about education, education systems, and the education policies contributing to PISA results. PISA results force the policy makers to really observe the drivers for educational change. He says, "You have to go beyond why is it so in this country and why is it so in that country." Similarly, head teacher Magnus says, "There are [...] a lot of questions that are not so well answered in this project [...] because the only way to really research a school and school activity is [...] go into the school and research it." In essence, PISA calls for qualitative study beyond its results, in order to better understand the factors behind the scores. In this way, PISA aids in the development of education systems.

The professors thought that the creation of PISA was positive. Professor Karpinen, for example, likes the PISA approach, with the focus on "literacy," and not on curriculum content. He finds the application of mathematics, his specialty, in the real world a necessary skill. In addition, Professor Rantanen thinks that the PISA approach, which differs from the IEA approach, has considerable value for education, as it allows people to view education not only in terms of curriculum and the classroom, but how it affects students' future life.

International achievement studies should serve as a catalyst for further study and investigation into education systems. These surveys also help illuminate different educational cultures, as comparisons between Asian countries and Anglo-Saxon countries, for example, become easier. Furthermore, Professor Virtanen finds that the interest in Finland resulting from PISA has forced the Finns to look deeper within their own system and really learn about it. Professor Karpinen feels the international surveys allow people to view education systems as a whole:

In both PISA and TIMSS, the idea is to look at school systems, not students, not separate schools, but school systems. It is good to see what are the strengths of each school system and I think that these kinds of issues have values. After that you can arrange national studies which go deeper [...] We have seen that when people ask from us, what are the explanations of PISA and the good results for PISA in Finland, it is based on this data. It is very difficult to say what are the reasons, what are the explanations.

Professor Rantanen agrees. For him, PISA does not provide a clear message; rather, secondary analysis and further research stemming from PISA should provide better answers. Professor Koivula also praises PISA for triggering more observation of education systems and not just curricula. PISA provides a starting point for further questions about education. Professor Sundqvist admits to PISA's flaws, but says it has good use in the educational world. He believes it has given cause for reflection on the education system of Finland and the politics behind it. Professor Huttunen admits that PISA cannot measure everything and comes at a high price, but acknowledges that PISA boasts a good design constructed by the world's experts on education.

PISA, on the most basic level, has provided the participating countries with a language in which to discuss educational comparison. OECD official Chadwick states how PISA has provided the countries with a forward-looking basis for international comparison. Previous to PISA, "every country [was] convinced that they [had] the best education system [...] When everybody thinks their system is the best, there is no actual basis for communication and discussion." PISA provided not only a language, but also much more information with which to compare students internationally and comparatively.

OECD official Schroeder also believes that PISA has created an active dialogue in education, allowing for debate and discussion among educationists, politicians, and policy makers. PISA has also allowed for educational interaction between countries, and made an insular part of a nation become more international:

> Education has traditionally been an inward-looking business, a very national, cultural business. Now it is becoming more of a domain where people look at alternatives, debate them, not always agree, but [...] [PISA] has served a function, among ministers but also among practitioners that really look outwards.

Although most would have expected Japan to rank near the top and Mexico at the bottom, the importance and interest in PISA comes from the educational policies and practices leading to these differences. Schroeder states:

The ranking of countries, I think that is interesting for the media but it is not that instructive. You see that Japan is on top and that Mexico is on the bottom, but that's what you would have expected. That doesn't give you a lot of new insights, but to see what policies and practices are associated with those differences, that is really quite instructive for countries.

He speaks more about countries learning from each other: "They learn, by looking at other countries, what is possible to achieve, in terms of quality, equity, efficiency, and they get some insights on what they can do to improve." The OECD also works with countries to provide policy recommendations in terms of education. For all of its criticisms, PISA does create positive outcomes, such as the deepening understanding of education systems, both at home and abroad, as well as further educational investigation and research.

2.4   *Positive Policy Responses*
While PISA has come under heavy criticism, some positive consequences have resulted from the survey. For example, OECD official Chadwick admits that some countries see the difficulty in comparing themselves with others:

> A country that has a very high GDP, a very wealthy country, might say, 'What's the point in comparing us to a country that has a very low GDP, and totally different interests and a totally different [education] system?'

Therefore, countries with similar geography and politics, for example, have teamed up to provide collaborative analyses of their collective education systems. Chadwick cites how the Nordic countries have succeeded very well in these cooperative analyses, and the South American countries participating in PISA also attempt these collaborations. Policy discussion and change have become a useful "by-product" of all of this collaboration and discussion. These cooperating countries have used these collaborations for improvement:

> There are particular issues that have come up and have given the countries information to give them a basis for policy improvement, policy change. It might be in the area of socio-economic background [...] It's given information about, for example, migration, and the success or otherwise of migrant students in different countries, information about those other things.

This information relayed by Chadwick may put an interesting spin on policy transfer. While policy transfer may prove difficult to education systems' cultural ties, observing how a similar country handles situations may prove fruitful for the borrowing country. PISA has provided great amounts of information and can hopefully spawn educational discussion, rhetoric, and positive change in the future. PISA starts a conversation but cannot improve education systems on its own. The governments need to initiate the change.

OECD official Chevalier, a specialist in the funding of education systems for *Education at a Glance,* describes the publication:

> *Education at a Glance* [...] cover[s] all the aspects of education starting from pre-primary, the beginning, to [...] compulsory education, primary and secondary, tertiary education, and also lifelong learning opportunities [...] In fact, PISA is part of *Education at a Glance* because PISA is the evaluation of fifteen-year-olds, so it is included in [the] publication.

Previous to PISA's first release, education ministers only had a feeling or a hunch about the strengths and weaknesses of both their own education systems and foreign systems. PISA, however, has changed this and has given countries a concrete view of their education systems, as well as tangible examples of educational success. Chevalier states:

> Before PISA you had a vision, a feeling of what was good or bad in the education system, but it was only a feeling. But with PISA it was the first time some things were compared with students at the same age, fifteen years old, and so many surprises were found with the first PISA results. For example [...] in France for many years, Germany was the best model in the world. After [the] PISA results, PISA showed that Germany was not great compared to Finland or Korea. It changed the perfection [*sic*] for the French people for the German system, and also the perfection [*sic*] of German people for their own system. I think PISA was the beginning of the success of international comparison.

He also cites how the interest in international educational comparison doubled or tripled after the first release of PISA outcomes.

The success of PISA, according to OECD official Chevalier, comes from the need of countries to observe the education systems of other countries: "Now we are in a world with more mobilisation, globalisation [...] It is interesting [...] to know if our system is good compared to another." Chevalier, from France, describes how the French did not express interest in comparison with other countries: "In the past France was not interested to be compared with others, and for the past six or ten years they have been interested to be compared with others, not only in education, but in economy, in all the other sectors." He believes PISA changed this attitude in his country. He acknowledges the difficult methodology involved with such large-scale comparisons, but says the methodology has now improved so that people can better rely on internationally comparative data. These surveys, "show the reality of education systems." Through the perspective of the OECD, the cycles of PISA have allowed them to better understand the survey and its impact. They now know better why an education system has success or failure. He says, "We have many things to improve, but I think we have arrived at the stage where we [are] better able to know the reasons for success and failure in an education system."

OECD official Schroeder, the head of the division at the OECD that runs PISA, started at the institution in 1994. At that time, he was the sole employee undertaking that type of work. Today, however, the division makes up the largest department at the OECD. The larger and more expansive interest in quantitative comparisons, both internationally and nationally, has increased the need for and interest in these quantitative comparisons. He describes the need of OECD countries to know more about educational outputs: "I think governments knew everything about what they invested in education and how large classes are, *et cetera*, all these input characteristics, but they had very little idea on results achievement in a comparative sense." National assessments gave the countries a sense of their achievement nationally, but they needed to know more internationally:

> That was the idea, basically, to get the idea of a comparative functioning of education systems, but also to learn from policies and practices, to see your own policies and practices in the light of what other countries are doing, and you need benchmarks for it. That was the motivation, and that's pretty much what PISA became, so I think it corresponds quite well.

OECD official Chadwick believes that PISA has stimulated countries to conduct policy reviews of their own education systems, in order to identify their strengths and weaknesses. He says, "That is a good thing and a positive thing. It [has] given them this way of comparing that they didn't have so clearly before." PISA comparisons have prompted the countries to explore inwards, but outwards as well. Countries can now look towards other countries to examine their educational strengths, whether from curriculum, teaching methods, funding, or educational structure. At the governmental level, the dialogue will allow for policy decisions based on comparative information. PISA has refined interest in education systems and has allowed for slow change and educational improvement.

Chevalier worries that people perceive PISA only as a ranking of education systems. PISA, however, does not only show rankings and averages. PISA also illustrates dispersions of performance on the survey. He cites the United Kingdom as an example, where they have many high-ranking students but a large level of inequity: "If you look at [the UK's] PISA scores as a whole, you think, 'Oh, it's okay, the education system is fine, the performance is above average,' but if you start to look at the inequities you see another picture." Further study exploring the PISA results is necessary. Overall, the OECD officials cite positive policy responses to the initiation of PISA, such as a common language, a dialogue, and collaboration among policy makers and countries to further discussion about education.

3 Negative Responses to PISA

PISA, a much criticised survey, as discussed in Chapter 4, unquestionably has its negative aspects. These downfalls are thus discussed in three categories: the structure of PISA, the negative impact of PISA, and the negative political implications due to the survey.

3.1 *Problematic Structure of PISA*

The participants, much like with the criticisms outlined in Chapter 4, find the narrow focus of PISA testing problematic. For example, Minister Jussila mentions how PISA only measures one type of thing and does not cover all areas of educational assessment, again warning that one must look beyond PISA scores and investigate successfully performing countries to find their strengths.

Pentti, a head teacher, feels the survey is limited and does not reflect educational strengths not measured by PISA. He describes the case of Hungary, which has an excellent programme for mathematics, but a focus on pure mathematics:

> Hungary [...] is very good at mathematics. In Hungary, mathematics is studied a lot and people study even pure mathematics. However, the Hungarians did not do well in PISA, because it concentrated more on the mathematics of everyday life, practical mathematics. And the result was, really, that the Hungarians were quite average and did not do nearly as well as the Finns, even though we Finns have a lot to learn from the Hungarian mathematics teaching.

Pentti thinks that PISA is just one kind of test and measures one view of education. For example, it does not measure knowledge of curriculum, but Finland has its own assessments to measure this.

Magnus also feels the test is limited. He warns that standardised tests must carefully formulate their questions in order to maintain relevance for the age group and have cultural sensitivity. He believes that very different results could have emerged from another way of designing the tasks for PISA. PISA, according to the participants, does not provide complete educational assessment. Seppo, also a head teacher, speaks of every country having their strong points within their educational culture, and says that PISA only measures a small part of the entire scope of educational provision.

Jukka thinks PISA provides a good measuring stick for education, albeit a bit limited it its scope:

> I don't find [PISA] good since with education, you are never ready. There is a similarity with wines. For example, if you study wines for thirty years, you realise how little you know. A lifetime is not enough. You are never ready. With education it is the same thing. Every morning you have to find the right note [...] If you have a test, it will of course measure something but it will be always a bit limited. If it is measuring, like I said, in Finland we have a great support to the underachievers, to those pupils who are not doing so well in their studies. It's giving us good results in PISA. For my mind, for my idea of the whole educational system, we need to have more support to the brightest pupils, the best ones, to really give them a challenge and give them the idea that you can make something special out of them [...] PISA is not measuring that [...] It is one test. Of course, it is a nice glory to Finland and the whole educational system, but it is only one thing.

Benny, a mathematics, physics, and chemistry teacher, simply feels that PISA suited Finland. A different type of educational survey would not yield the same outcomes. Pia agrees that PISA results and standardised tests do not measure everything in education. She feels that all standardised tests, not just PISA, need further analysis and observation of all factors influencing education in order to provide clearer pictures of the factors affecting education systems. She says, "You can't read this [PISA] as a bible or something [...] I think you should compare schools across Europe and all over the world. But then you have to look at the background, you can't just stare at the numbers and the results." Terttu, a chemistry and mathematics teacher, thinks that PISA needs more research to support the findings from the survey. Jonny agrees. He believes PISA does not show the cultural differences behind the results, such as the values of the students:

> Of course PISA doesn't show values and doesn't show neither the way of thinking nor the reality, what is important, necessarily. It is hard [in]

this kind of quantitative research to see everything. You should also have qualitative research, where you very deeply and in the long term get to know different humans, but how do you compare them? That is almost impossible.

The professors provide a different perspective. For example, Professor Laukkanen had experience prior to PISA of working with the OECD. She represented Finland on the OECD-sponsored collaboration by the Nordic countries on literacy and reading within the Nordic community. She helped develop PISA items for the surveys with the international expert groups. She had the responsibility of assembling the different texts collected from the different Nordic countries and screening the first phase of texts. She notes the difficulty in choosing texts culturally acceptable in all countries. Professor Karpinen also mentions how every country sent in proposals for items for the eventual PISA surveys. The Finnish teachers, he says, were not particularly eager to contribute to PISA. He reveals that the OECD entrusted the experts to do their own work and describes the interesting process of maintaining cultural sensitivity in the PISA items. Professor Rantanen oversaw the problem-solving section and sees problem-solving as a positive addition to PISA:

> I hope that the PISA framework will be changed so that we will not be discussing any more about scientific literacy or mathematical literacy, but it would be problem solving, mathematical and scientific. That would be more dynamic, and it's a dynamic world [...] I think that those skills measured in PISA are really important, but [...] for problem solving itself, all the bigger items are problem solving.

He thinks that creating a test for Finland should not be up to the OECD, but rather to the Finns. He states how surveys such as PISA should be a cooperative effort, and the test items should be "equally unfair to everyone."

Much like some of PISA's critics mentioned in Chapter 4, both Professors Laukkanen and Karpinen think that PISA's administrations occur too often. Professor Laukkanen feels that a five-year interval may improve upon the surveys, cutting down labour and expense. PISA's background questionnaires, she feels, do not ask much because they avoid taking up too much time. She feels they could delve deeper into the students' backgrounds and gather more information.

Professors Huttunen, Koivula, and Sundqvist describe the nuances of the Finnish education system that led to high scores in the PISA surveys. Not necessarily strengths, these features may have contributed to Finland's scores in

PISA. This reflects weaknesses in the PISA survey, as the test does not take into account nor reflect national nuances. Professors Huttunen and Koivula indicate that students in Nordic countries take PISA while still in comprehensive school. They believe this plays an important role in PISA outcomes, since countries that have finished basic school and have already separated their students at the time of PISA testing score differently. PISA, in other words, comes at a good time for the measurement of Finnish students. Professor Koivula cites The Netherlands as an example where students have already separated into their different tracks by age fifteen. The three professors imply that if Finland were in the same situation, scores in PISA would be lower.

To illustrate this example further, Professor Huttunen cites Finland's own assessments of schools, taken at the ages of approximately twelve, fifteen, and eighteen:

> We have from Finland our own results, where we were checking the between-school variations at sixth grade, ninth grade [...] twelve, fifteenth, or seventeen and eighteen years of age. Between-school variations increase enormously at our third measuring point, where the school has been divided into two sectors, vocational school and *gymnasium* track. That creates between-school variation that is quite close to The Netherlands and other countries: forty percent. So, it seems, that because of a good measuring point for us, we are showing results, where the equity is exceptionally high, but within the system there are already extremes.

PISA, therefore, comes at the most ideal time for Finland and the Nordic countries, a time of high equity in the education systems. The Finnish school culture, lacking in high-stakes testing, may factor into high PISA scores. Professor Koivula wonders whether, if a larger testing culture existed, the Finnish students would have done as well in PISA. Her colleagues in The Netherlands said the Dutch results would have been better if they had considered PISA a high-stakes examination. They felt they did the OECD a favour by undertaking the survey, but did not take it seriously. She disapproves of this attitude. She feels the problematic attitude lies in academic motivation solely for money or academic credit. In Finland, however, PISA did motivate the teachers who, in turn, motivated the students. She also thinks that the students in the vocational track would not do as well in these assessments. Since PISA still comes at the comprehensive school level for Finland, the country has an advantage in PISA.

Professor Huttunen further describes details of the Finnish education system not usually mentioned which may have aided Finland's high score in PISA. School choice within the education system and the sparse population of

Finland can influence a student's educational experience. In smaller communities, students may be confined to the local schools, but in bigger cities students can exercise their right to school choice. For example, as of 2000, half of the students in the Helsinki area changing to lower-secondary schools applied to schools outside of their catchment area (Seppänen, 2003). Students who have a particular interest, such as music, for example, can choose a school based on their interests. Professors Koivula and Sundqvist say that some parents may encourage their children to attend a school not necessarily close to home, but based on the strength of the school programme. In a large city such as Helsinki, therefore, the possibilities of school choice result in students coming from different parts of the metropolitan area, creating a more diverse school.

Professor Koivula also mentions the "hidden" streaming structure of Finnish schools. Professor Huttunen reveals that PISA does not pick up on this fact, since the random structure of PISA sampling cannot account for these relative differences. Professor Koivula states how, in principle, each student has the same curriculum because of the National Core Curriculum:

> We have a National Core Curriculum and every school implements that. There is only a leeway of two or three hours a week you can change [...] There are some selective classes especially in the bigger cities, that have an emphasis on math. It does not necessarily mean they have much more math [...] it means they get students that are interested in it. Just because the students are more homogeneously motivated, you reach further.

This "homogeneous motivation" can help certain students excel further in their studies than their peers. She states, "The child gets into a class where the children are of parents who know how to choose the correct things." Even though these opportunities limit themselves to large communities, the professors imply that certain kinds of parents find opportunities for their children from an early age. Professor Sundqvist states, "The players know how to play the game." Professor Huttunen calls this "clever education," implying that those who know the system can take full advantage of it. Professor Koivula mentions, "There are hidden curricula for the children of a given type of parent." Professor Huttunen feels that school consists of "small things" which combine and correlate to make an entire system. When many good "small things" combine properly, a strong education can ensue. He states, "There are no secrets. It is not a hidden mechanism. It may not be known to everybody, but it is not classified information." In other words, students with ambition or parents who seek the best possibilities for their children can use the best offerings of the Finnish education system to their advantage. Even the egalitarian values of the country, and the equal nature of the education system, combined with all of its benefits, do not make Finland immune to parents, especially from higher socio-economic backgrounds, wanting to manoeuvre the education system for their children's benefit.

Even the OECD officials cite weaknesses within the PISA survey. Despite all of these benefits to an international achievement study, OECD official Schroeder does admit that PISA could have a wider focus, as it only concentrates on mathematics, reading, and science, and problem solving in 2003. It does not assess skills such as social competences and the like, which he believes also have equal importance. He says, "Some people think there is a risk that looking only at certain things make[s] you forget about other things that are important." PISA, a very costly programme of assessment, must seem of importance to countries, otherwise, they would not participate in the survey. As a voluntary assessment, perhaps as more countries enter the survey, some would not find it worth the cost and time involved in participation. OECD Official Chadwick describes the difficulty in gathering enough schools to participate in the survey. He does not consider this a shortcoming of PISA itself, but rather a result of too much testing in schools. Because PISA does not come under the category of a high-stakes test, many schools express reluctance in participating.

Schroeder mentions evolution in PISA, doing things differently from cycle to cycle. Even so, he acknowledges the need to improve things further:

> I think sometimes we have been too conservative in the methods we have chosen. I wish we had done many things that we are doing in the sub-cycle of the first one, like using a more interactive approach, taking a more courageous approach to have a larger share of open-ended items which are more difficult to score. We have always taken in PISA a quite cautious approach in order to ensure we don't run too many risks [...] It's a learning process for the countries, for the OECD.

Chadwick also cites how the OECD has continually tried to improve PISA. Although the OECD would like to see more improvements, the governments of the participating countries have expressed a need for continuity. They do not want to change the survey in order to better measure any changes within their system or in the outcomes.

3.2   Negative Impact of PISA

PISA, while with positive impacts, inevitably has negative ones as well. For example, Minister Halonen believes that standardised testing, especially at the international level, presents challenges of comparison and measurement.

Comparing things across countries and cultures involves the difficulty of measurement. He states how one cannot know what goes on in one school compared to another. A standardised test hopes for equality of measurement, but cannot guarantee it. Halonen believes the challenge of standardised tests lies in the interpretation of the results. He cites how someone can look at test results and label one school good and another one bad when, in reality, this comparison between schools remains a difficult task. Despite the danger of jumping to conclusions from PISA, he worries, however, and warns of the problematic nature of believing that Finnish education has done everything right and does not need to improve. He believes many things in Finnish education still need improving. Resting on laurels can become a great downside of Finnish success in PISA.

Minister Jussila also believes that the PISA results made Finland a bit too happy with the educational situation. The society, education policy makers, and parents, for example, may have taken the PISA results too seriously too quickly. He warns that this may be a risk of the PISA results. He states, "We have warned them that we must develop further, otherwise we are dropping down, because all the countries are making a lot of effort at this point."

Mai-Len, a head teacher, has her suspicions about standardised testing in general. She does not believe that tests can effectively assess students because they have received different teaching. Although mathematics may provide a uniform testing base, "all other subjects are based on the values of the teacher and what feels important to the teacher. We can't ask questions about things that might be taught differently in other countries or might not be taught at all." This view also applies to a broader scale. She does not like comparisons with others in general, on any level. Therefore, she finds PISA "pointless" and unnecessary:

> If you compare people on one level but not on another, then it isn't the real truth. If you're good at this one thing but bad at all these other things, then how do you say you're good? I don't think PISA will be able to have such test methods that [allow] you to truly compare different countries.

Mai-Len's sentiments echo those of many critics of PISA, discussed earlier in this book. She feels the differing backgrounds of participating countries do not allow for fair comparisons. She cites the factor of immigration: Finland has very little while other countries have many. She also believes that Finland brags too much about high PISA outcomes. She feels the PISA results just show that Finns have good mathematical skills. A teacher, Linda, expresses a similar sentiment to Mai-Len:

At least some important questions are being asked, but I don't know if the results are to be trusted [...] In different countries, for example, the way you ask the question could be understood in many different ways [...] There are many things that could be understood differently in different countries. I don't know if you can really compare the results between [countries].

These echo the sentiments of many critics of PISA, that PISA has a limited scope and lies vulnerable to cultural bias.

Hans, a mathematics and physics teacher, also expresses scepticism about PISA. He says, "I'm not sure if the results are quite what they seem to be." He feels these surveys provide a reason for the outcomes that really result from something else. For example, many attribute Finland's high reading literacy to the good schools, but he believes that television may play a bigger role than anticipated. In order to watch television, Finns must read subtitles in their own language while listening in another. This cultural aspect may manifest itself in the PISA outcomes.

Much like Mai-Len, the teachers fear that the success in PISA creates a danger of the education system becoming smug and complacent, and worry about a lack of self-criticism. They feel concerned that people will no longer see the weaknesses of the system. This also extends to fears that PISA will lead to a situation where Finland will not change and develop its system to improve, and that the Finns will rest on their laurels as a result of high PISA outcomes. Juho, for example, also worries that PISA will cause the Finns to become complacent with education and stop improving. The economic resources for education, according to Jukka, need to increase in order to maintain as well as increase achievement in education. Jonny also thinks that teachers need continued support from the government to better perform in their jobs.

OECD official Chadwick was surprised at how disappointed countries became when they felt they scored poorly on PISA. The impact of PISA on Germany, for example, gave the country the alleged PISA-Shock. Chevalier continues: "I think it is dangerous to think about ranking and only about ranking. We need also to be able to capture the trends of progress of an education system." He advocates looking at three components of education made visible by PISA: the performance, the inequities in the performance, and the efficiency. A country such as Finland, for example, manages to have few inequities with minimum spending. He also wants observers to notice another factor, the organisation of teaching. This covers the perceptions of school, teaching, and teacher-student relationships. Indicators such as school repeaters, where France has many and Finland very few, come under this category, as well as interest in school. For example, countries such as Japan and Korea have high performance in PISA but low enjoyment in school. Observing and analysing all of these factors behind the average PISA outcomes give a better picture of education systems. The danger, however, lies in overlooking the recommendations of Chevalier and others, and simply looking just at the PISA results.

3.3   *Political Implications*

PISA lends itself to negative political responses. This is discussed at length in the book, especially in the final chapter. Minister Halonen refers to this and says, "Pretty often, what happens also is that you can try to draw very quick consequences of the results. In France, the government fell because the results of PISA were so bad." After the first round of PISA in 2000, the United States and France scored so similarly that France refused to acknowledge the results, even though France scored higher than the US in all three assessment areas. This anecdotal example illustrates the poignancy of the "negative external evaluation" already discussed. Countries often try to implement a "quick fix" solution to education systems, a common reaction to "negative external evaluation." Halonen warns that PISA can cause premature decision-making by people jumping to conclusions simply from the PISA data. He also says by putting things in order or in a ranking, as with PISA, a danger presents itself:

> If you say that it is only something where you put things in order, who is the first, who is the second, who is the third, and then you say that those did it the best and those did it the worst. That is not the way. Sometimes you see the media loves to do it this way. They did it badly. It's their fault. I think that is the bad side of measuring like this.

PISA itself, according to Halonen, does not provide an easy platform from which people can draw conclusions.

PISA prompted policy decisions to maintain or improve PISA attainment in countries, even Finland. Pentti describes a cut in the hours of mathematics teaching in the past, with selected areas of mathematical priority:

> For example when it comes to mathematics, when the number of hours that mathematics is taught was reduced in Finland, a choice had to be made when deciding the curriculum and which issues will be stressed in it. This was when a decision was made, that the emphasis would be on practical uses of mathematics, not so much on algebra and geometry, which – however unfortunately – are important for the sake of further studies of the students […] It is because of this that we are excellent in

PISA, but there are still problems, which we have to deal with. I believe there is a hope we can do it, but it will take a couple of years before this improvement will be visible.

Pentti implies that the policy decisions to focus on practical applications of mathematics, while good for PISA outcomes and possibly tailored to the survey outcomes, remain a detriment to students' mathematical learning. Similarly, although Mai-Len disapproves, the government has added more of an emphasis on mathematics in the national curriculum:

> They added another hour of mathematics to the curriculum, although we're already the best in the world. Why would they do that? They are just putting even more emphasis on mathematics. It's all about these technological skills that Finland is good at, but what might be needed in the future, we don't know.

Aino also disapproves of educational budget cuts due to high PISA outcomes. This further illustrates how the "never ending hunt" (Pongratz, 2006, p. 481) for achievement in PISA affects even a top performer such as Finland.

Professor Rantanen thinks that international surveys lead to political pressure. The political repercussions of PISA may have negative effects in the future: "The assessment results have been evaluated politically. Teachers are horrified that Finland was doing so great and a huge amount of cuts are done in the budgets and the library budgets." Although he admits PISA has placed well-deserved prominence and attention on the teachers, these budget cuts will have consequences in the future: "If cuts are done in a budget for today's kids, the effects are seen in ten and twenty years from now, not immediately." Rantanen also fears that people do not understand much about PISA, simply that Finland did well on it, and that people will jump to conclusions from the results. Although he thinks very highly of the PISA data, he disapproves of the very political use of them. He fears that the political decision makers will not take into account cultural factors influencing an education system. He says, "It is a misuse or a lack of understanding of the data in that sense."

This political impact also affects other countries. Professor Virtanen cites how Germany takes educational standards very seriously, and notes the outcropping of new standardised tests due to PISA. He discusses German PISA-Shock to illustrate the profound impact that PISA had over Germany. Germany's mediocre performance in PISA prompted the country to create standardised tests in order to better assess their education system in reaction to PISA and PISA-Shock. Denmark also has created tests, now compulsory for students, published for the public. Virtanen feels this will increase the competition between schools in a country traditionally quite flexible in its education system. He mentions that, even in Finland, discussions have emerged about more national assessments and stricter standards in different subjects. These possible reforms go against the ideas and philosophies behind Finnish education. He states, "I think that the real trap nowadays is that education is becoming more and more political." He believes this comes from PISA, because of its importance and impact on politics. He fears that, in the future, education will become a more common arena for political quarrels. He believes that teachers should have the freedom to concentrate on pedagogy, but worries about the negative impacts of a highly politicised education system. Professor Virtanen also fears that this will drive away future teachers. Quite astutely, he also asserts that the education standards in the US and the UK, typical of a country with a strong GERM infection, put teachers in a "prison."

4   Additional Responses to PISA

This chapter also examines three additional topics: PISA versus the IEA studies of TIMSS and PIRLS; being a sample school for PISA data collection; and the future of PISA.

4.1   *PISA vs. IEA*

The question of the difference between PISA and the IEA surveys often arises. Minister Halonen discusses how the two surveys measure different things, therefore generating different results. He sees the benefit of diverse educational measurement, as educational systems can vary. Finland scored lower in TIMSS than it did in PISA. Finland's participation in the 1999 TIMSS Repeat, or TIMSS-R, yielded a score of 520 on the mathematics scale. In contrast, Australia had a score of 525, Canada 531, Hungary 532, Japan 579, Korea 587, New Zealand 491, England 496, and the United States 502. The average of the thirty-eight participating countries came to 487. On the scientific part of the survey, Finland scored 535 points. In contrast, Australia had a score of 540, Canada 533, Hungary 552, Japan 550, Korea 549, New Zealand 510, England 538, and the United States 515. The average science performance of the participating countries came to 488. While Finland scored above the average with a respectable amount of points, other countries had much higher scores in TIMSS-R.

Minister Jussila describes how the measurement of TIMSS differs from that of PISA, and how Finns have success on surveys with measurements such as PISA. Finns, according to him, do not necessarily have success in other types of tests. He attributes this success to the importance of application of knowledge in Finnish education. He says how critics of PISA argue that PISA needs more curriculum-based assessment. In Finland, according to Jussila, the debate dealing with the importance of theoretical or applied knowledge has already occurred. He states, "Sometimes the correlation is very strong between the two. We need both of those." PISA, however, does not cover everything, especially the more theoretical background behind the curricula. He mentions that national assessment in Finland focuses more on the curricular objectives. Jussila advocates both kinds of surveys, since the information gathered from them helps further develop the education system of Finland. These surveys provide use to Finnish educational policy makers and enjoy eager participation from Finnish schools. Minister Halonen believes that surveys such as PISA reduce the need for national assessments. PISA undertakes part of the job that countries such as Finland would have to do nationally, and circumvents the need for too many national tests.

The professors revealed their views of PISA and the IEA surveys of TIMSS and PIRLS. Professor Virtanen cites how PISA impacted society much more significantly than IEA surveys. Professor Rantanen does not prefer one survey over the other, since they measured such different aspects of education. Together, he felt, the two provided insights into learning. Looking at the results of PISA and TIMSS together provides a good lens from which to view learning and education. For example, former Eastern Bloc countries, which focus more on content learning, have good results in TIMSS but not in PISA. Professor Karpinen, as previously stated, approves of the "literacy" approach of PISA, and feels that students need to know how to apply their mathematical knowledge. Professor Virtanen believes that Finnish pupils have more motivation in taking the PISA tests as opposed to those of the IEA, because they differ from the tests taken in school.

Professor Koivula cites how many countries, such as Finland, France, and the United States, score differently in PISA, TIMSS, and their own national assessments. Finland's disparity in mathematical scores in TIMSS and in PISA generated much discussion about the mathematical ability of Finnish students:

> In Finland, the kids showed up as good as you can dream of [in PISA], and most mathematicians were pissed off at the results. Their understanding is that the results [in mathematics] are just getting worse and worse all the time, and the kind of math [...] PISA measures does not measure the kind of mathematics that would be of use [in] educating engineers and mathematicians, the higher math in their careers and their work. This gives a false image of the level of mathematical level in this country.

Professor Huttunen also cites how researchers worry that the mathematics in Finland could be more effective and deep. Despite the high scores in PISA, mathematicians in Finland still worry about the mathematical aptitude of students. PISA does not necessarily indicate strength in mathematical skills, and many Finnish mathematicians believe that "math [...] [is] not as effective or deep as it could be and should be."

Observing the different performances of Finland in the two different types of surveys raises the issue of sampling and effect on scores. As previously mentioned, PISA comes at a time when Nordic students still attend comprehensive school, and if given at a later time in Nordic education, the students might not score as highly. Meanwhile, TIMSS samples at grade level, which may cause an age difference of up to two or three years in some countries. Prais (2003, 2004) also questions the issue of sampling and methodology of these two surveys and believes a hybrid between the two would provide the best assessments. Professor Koivula states how no clear answer exists to sampling and methodology of such a large, cross-national educational survey.

Professor Koivula describes how TIMSS measures the "lowest common denominator" of the curricula of participating countries:

> It is subject-based, and it is so that the countries that participate that year make the decision on what can be included based on their curricula. The fact is that they are different countries in different years, so they are a bit difficult to compare year by year because the curricular needs and the curricular denominators are different in different years. I think that just because Finland has never done so well in TIMSS and done so well in PISA [...] I think that one of the fruitful things about PISA is that [it] has shown to begin to look at the education systems but also at the curricula of different countries.

She regrets Finland not taking part in more IEA assessments. The United States, in contrast, took part in both PISA and TIMSS, and in combination with its own assessments, provides good background for analysis and reflection upon the US education system. Although Finland does have some of its own national tests, these strictly assess the curriculum. She praises PISA for triggering further exploration into education systems, since she thinks TIMSS does not provide any reason to look beyond curricula. She feels that with more assessments, Finland can go beyond reflecting on its own education system towards deep reflection and exploration.

Professor Laukkanen, who focuses on reading literacy, thinks that people exaggerate the differences between IEA surveys and those of PISA, and that they actually measure similar things. She cites how the IEA literacy study of 1991 also used life-based questions. The grade-level-based sampling of IEA poses some problems, especially for students in Nordic countries who start school later than their counterparts in other countries. Having served on committees for both surveys, she also found that the two surveys had similar development processes. She believes that many exaggerate the differences between IEA studies and PISA:

> I am the IEA people and the PISA people. The same people are doing both studies, as in many countries. The IEA says it is more research and PISA says it is more economics, [but it is] the same people, the same researchers, in many countries [...] I wouldn't say they are so much different, really.

Professor Karpinen acknowledges the difference of the two surveys on their basic level, measuring curricula or skills for life, but similarly feels the two actually have similarities. They follow similar procedures in formulating the survey questions and adhere to analogous standards. He points out, however, that PISA does not have as extensive a background questionnaire for the students, and illustrates how TIMSS had teacher questionnaires. This lack of student and teacher background in PISA prevents researchers from making close correlations with student achievement. Professor Rantanen looks favourably upon the background questionnaires of these surveys, which set them apart from other national assessments. However, surveys such as TIMSS and PISA, according to Professor Virtanen, instil too much competition between countries. These views support those of Pongratz (2006) who argues that PISA instils an enormous pressure for reform, but pressure in a global sense.

The OECD perspective provides an interesting outlook on the matter. OECD official Schroeder describes the difference between PISA and TIMSS as "another way of looking in the world." TIMSS used a common denominator for countries, the curricula used in schools. Although he thinks of this approach as relevant for educators, he and the OECD did not find it interesting from their perspective. They focused more on the application of knowledge and the transfer of knowledge to real-life settings. This gives attention to the application of knowledge to life after basic education. Schroeder says, "We had not so much in mind how well school[s] had achieved in what [they] intended to do, but to what extent actually schools serve the function on what students are expected to do in the outside world and society." This more external view of education, therefore, did not need to use the "common denominator" philosophy of

TIMSS, but rather the "union effort of what countries do differently." He admits some view this as unfair, since it assesses students on matters not taught within school walls. However, "when students leave school that is what the world will expect from them." He acknowledges that both TIMSS and PISA have relevance and validity, and that PISA simply follows one such view of education. Although the OECD did use the TIMSS data sometimes, the surveys, which concentrated on school curricula, did not fully respond to the needs of the OECD countries.

OECD official Chevalier describes how TIMSS and PISA differ as international surveys. TIMSS measures students at grade four or grade eight, where the students can come from different schools, institutions, or age groups. PISA wanted to measure students at an age level, for one of the "many problems of comparability in TIMSS was that in grade four and eight [...] you are not at the same level in terms of institution and comparison was not really adequate." The success of PISA, according to Chevalier, stems from the age-group sampling. OECD official Khan thinks PISA garnered more attention than TIMSS because it came from a better-known, internationally recognised organisation with greater governmental support. This gave PISA more credibility than surveys generated by the IEA. PISA had more policy makers involved in the process and gained integrity from its more sophisticated methodology, which allowed for better comparison between countries.

OECD official Chadwick cites how TIMSS has different designs and backing philosophy from PISA. TIMSS is based on the learning of curricula and focuses on the students and what they have learned in the past. Assessments such as these give governments an idea of how well students have learned the curricula in school, and provide a good comparison of how students in one country compare to the students in other countries in terms of lessons learned in school. PISA, however, does not look to the past; rather, it looks to the future and assesses how students can apply school knowledge in the real world. He describes the difference: "Ours is a looking ahead philosophy and theirs is a curriculum-based philosophy." He does say how many countries that participate in PISA also participate in TIMSS, in order to obtain two types of information from the assessments. The sampling process also differs between the two kinds of surveys. TIMSS uses grade levels, which, to Chadwick, raises two problems. Firstly, different grade levels denote a different age group in some countries. Secondly, this does not take into account grade repeaters. With PISA, age-based sampling allows them to measure at the end of compulsory school in most countries. He does state that some countries have been extending the time of compulsory education, which will provide a challenge for PISA in the future.

4.2 Sample Schools

Some of the head teachers and teachers experienced their schools as PISA sample schools. This provided additional insight into PISA and the PISA process for these participants. Although some claim that Finland coached students in PISA tests, Head teacher Elvi feels that the nature of the assessment does not allow for preparation:

> It is [...] very interesting that it was a completely random sample of students. One didn't pick out the best or worst or anything, but took those according to a list from these authorities. We got a list like that and we were supposed to pick, was it every third or fourth [...] but it was very random. It was also interesting to see how that would go. It went well.

Krister, a teacher of mathematics, physics, and chemistry, described the process of PISA within his school. The survey called for random sampling, which he recalls as every seventh student from the lists. He feels that having every student in the school take the assessment would provide a better picture of the school: "We have in every class some students with some difficulties, but if you picked a small class the two who go out to small groups, it doesn't show the real standard of the class." Jonny approves of the PISA sampling method, which draws a wide range of students from each school.

Pia's school also participated in PISA as a sample school. She describes the strict process of testing, which called for every other student in alphabetical order. She says, "It was a very strict system. You couldn't cheat. Actually, you could cheat if you just took out some names, if you wanted your school to get the good results." Pia brings up a dark side of PISA, the possibility of cheating for higher scores on the survey. Toni's school also participated in PISA. Although his colleague took charge of the project in the school, he said this colleague, the liaison teacher, followed the rules exactly and picked every tenth student. Maarit, who teaches at the same school as Toni, described the secrecy behind the project. The teachers could not read the tests; rather, they came in envelopes and only the sampled students could access them.

Terttu felt PISA had very easy questions in its mathematical literacy section. Her school, also a sample school for PISA, had many students selected, albeit randomly, who participated in special education or extra support in mathematics:

> There were so many students who were not normal students; they were special students. I was surprised that it went so well [...] But there were such easy questions, but if they were more difficult, then in Finland the pupils would have not succeeded on them so well.

The teachers and head teachers who witnessed the PISA sampling provided good insight into the process itself. They bring up the possibility of cheating on the test, and the sampling process. Interestingly, one teacher who saw the questions found them easy. Even the weaker "special" students found the questions easy, illustrating the depth and breadth of Finnish secondary school students' academics.

4.3   Future of PISA

PISA has already had a massive impact in education, education policy, and politics. This is discussed at length throughout this book. Surely, a survey of this magnitude would continue far into the future. The OECD officials shared their views on the future of the survey. For example, Schroeder hopes to assess a broader range of competencies in the future, which he describes as the biggest challenge for PISA. He believes that those who have the greatest success in the global economy have good skills in collaboration, conflict resolution, and analysing information in an interdisciplinary manner. He also hopes to expand PISA and assess if students can really innovate, create, and produce as well as analyse text. He also wishes to implement more information technology into the survey. He would also like to assess a younger age group in order to measure student growth and consistency in an education system more longitudinally. Measuring at different ages allows one to see "how competencies evolve in education systems [...] [and] to what extent does socio-economic [background] influence [...] performance? Do education systems reinforce those disparities as students grow older or are education systems able to moderate those differences?" Surveys at different ages would better illuminate the answers to these questions. Schroeder also thinks that future PISA surveys should collect more teacher data. He sees the need for closer association between education performance and teachers. He admits, "PISA is weak, still weak today, like TIMSS. These services are far too weak in feeding the results back into improving classrooms and learning. It is a useful instrument for policy, but not yet totally useful for practitioners." In short, Schroeder believes that PISA needs to measure a broader skill set, cover not just one level but the evolution of these skills, and provide a better link between educational results and classroom practices.

Chadwick anticipates more computer testing in the future, and cites how the 2006 survey had a trial run with a computer option for the scientific literacy section. The computer provides more potential for test items, questions that would be difficult to answer on a paper and pencil test. Therefore, a computer-based survey would allow for assessment of more diverse skills than the original test. Logistically, however, this creates implementation issues, depending on the computer access of schools, or whether the OECD itself would provide laptops. This also raises the issue of whether computer-based testing will assess computer skills or the literacy skills measured by PISA. Chadwick also would like to see the expansion of PISA into different age groups. The OECD has contracted an agency to see if an assessment of nine-year-olds could become a possibility in the future. He would also like an assessment at an older age, such as at the university level, but anticipates much difficulty in creating a suitable means of assessment.

Chevalier believes that PISA has already changed the future of education. He cites the example of Finland, the success in PISA, and the influx of PISA tourists. He feels fairly confident that PISA has put Finland on the map, both in general and in terms of education. He says, "When I say that PISA [...] will change the world and the conception of education, it has already started." For example, Germany reformed its secondary education system because of PISA results, which showed that Germany had a high level of inequity in secondary education. Early streaming and the high influence of socio-economic background caused this disparity. Germany, consequently, currently attempts to implement later school selection in order to increase educational efficiency and equality.

The OECD has expanded on their educational testing, by adding the Programme for the International Assessment of Adult Competencies (PIAAC), discussed at length in the first and last chapters of this book, and proposing the Assessment for Higher Education Learning Outcomes (AHELO), also discussed in the final chapter of this book. This illustrates the strong, increasing, and dominant, role of the OECD in cross-national assessment.

5 Summary

This chapter delved into the responses to PISA among the study participants, both within the Finnish educational context as well as from the OECD itself. The participants had positive responses to PISA, despite the many criticisms that are associated with the survey. They cited that it provided good measurement of educational systems and provided concrete benchmarks from which to make comparisons. PISA shows a country's strengths and weaknesses, and allows for comparison, internationally, between countries. In the Finnish context, PISA provided good reinforcement for the education system and the efforts of the politicians, parents, teachers, head teachers, and students to achieve educationally. Finland's top performance in PISA reflected the country's attitude to education and learning. It also reinforced the practical focus of the Finnish national curriculum. Furthermore, it controlled the pessimism simmering in the country before the release of the first PISA scores in 2001. The participants also believed PISA provided positive by-products, for example, the further qualitative study and secondary research that has occurred, and is still occurring, due to a large scale, quantitative survey such as PISA. PISA also provides a language for educational comparison as well as an educational dialogue both within and between countries.

Conversely, the participants also had negative responses to PISA. Many criticised the structure of the survey itself. They felt the survey only tested a narrow array of subjects and had a limited focus. Some thought that PISA did not differ much from other surveys, such as TIMSS or PIRLS. The three-year cycle also came under criticism, as many believed a longer cycle, perhaps a five-year one, would be more beneficial. All of these point to the weakness of PISA's methodology. Interestingly, some of the participants astutely stated that external factors may have responsibility for the actual PISA results. Related to this, the participants cited the difficulty in measuring education systems cross-culturally, and the difficulty of comparison on such a large scale. Finally, some of the participants worried that Finland would become complacent and stop looking for ways to improve its education system. The slight decline in Finland's PISA results, as shown in the 2012 and 2015 surveys, and its implications, are discussed more fully in the final chapter.

The negative responses to PISA also covered the political implications as well. The participants cited negative political responses to PISA, such as "quick fix" and "negative external evaluation" responses to the survey. Some countries have implemented policy decisions to improve PISA outcome, such as increasing class hours for "PISA subjects" such as mathematics, science, and reading literacy. This adds to the political pressure politicians feel to achieve in PISA, leading to more standardised tests and an obsession with rankings.

In addition to these positive and negative responses, the participants addressed additional areas. First of all, they focused on the difference between PISA and the IEA surveys such as PIRLS and TIMSS. Interestingly, Finland performs better in PISA than in TIMSS. Some of the participants felt there was a need for both assessments, although others did not think the two surveys differed very much in content. The OECD officials hoped, in the future, that PISA could broaden in its scope and bring in more critical analysis, strengthen its methodology, and incorporate technology.

CHAPTER 9

Cross-National Attraction and Education Policy Transfer

1   Introduction

The success of Finland in PISA and the subsequent attention to the Finnish education system have triggered questions regarding the transferability of educational features and education policy. Policy borrowing and transfer have long been discussed and debated amongst comparative education scholars. Phillips and Ochs created a cycle of policy borrowing, discussed in Chapter 5, which begins with cross-national attraction and ends with a borrowed policy "indigenised," "internalised," and "domesticised" into the borrowing country's system. Beech also writes of the adaptation and implementation of the transferred policy. The creation of PISA, along with global forces influencing education, politics, and economics, has added to a recent and renewed interest in education policy transfer. Thus, this chapter explores cross-national attraction and policy transfer, but with a special focus on the Finnish perspective and the OECD perspective.

This chapter presents findings from empirical research, where the participants contributing to the results presented in this book were asked about this now well-established cross-national attraction to Finland, and the possibility of education policy transfer. The participants included two former Ministers of Education from Finland; six head teachers of lower secondary schools; seventeen teachers of the PISA subjects: mathematics, science, and reading literacy of PISA-aged students; eight professors of education responsible for the execution of PISA in Finland; and four OECD officials.

The organisation of this chapter differs from the previous ones, by providing the perspectives of each participating group separately. In addition, this chapter also includes a section uncovering the notion of national character and education.

2   Views of Education Ministers

Both former Ministers of Education in Finland mention the difficulty in transferring aspects of an education system from one country to another. Cross-national attraction to Finland, triggered by PISA, brought Finland into the world's educational limelight. These visitors to Finland, or "PISA tourists," travel to the country in order to improve educational conditions at "home." However, the aforementioned importance of context needs highlighting in both theory, as discussed in Chapter 5, and practice, as explored in this chapter. For example, Minister Halonen stresses how education systems have complex relationships with their corresponding national cultures, a structure that "perfects the educational systems." He continues, "The educational system, it is not a machine that you put something in and something comes down. It is so strongly bound to the other things in society that you have to understand those. And a good thing of PISA is that it raises those things." Furthermore, Minister Jussila makes sure he emphasises the differences between Finnish education and the education systems of his guests, the PISA tourists. He warns, "Don't follow technically our system. Don't copy it. What is working in our society is not necessarily working in other cultural and historical circumstances." This illustrates the importance of cultural heritage in a society, since education systems have such cultural, historical, political, and societal ties that these visitors, the "PISA tourists," probably cannot implement features of the Finnish education system into their own.

A survey like PISA encourages education decision makers to really understand the ways in which education systems work, necessitating a deeper investigation into educational systems. Due to its performance in PISA, Finland and its education system have attracted much attention from the rest of the world. According to Minister Jussila, this means that the education ministers, head teachers, and teachers have had to work very hard for the PISA tourists. He feels that the visitors find the relaxed atmosphere of Finnish schools surprising. Minister Halonen finds the attention that Finland's education system has received quite flattering. He feels that the Finns, however, respond to this positive attention with discussions about the shortcomings of Finnish education. He says, "When that kind of attention comes, very quickly it sparks discussion that we aren't that good, that there is something wrong with the results, and actually we should not at all be proud of this kind of attention, that we should try to work harder ourselves." In this vein, he suggests that Finns thrive in the face of adversity: "The culture in Finland is such that we are strongest when there are difficulties. When the times are tough, Finnish people, they are really committed to the future. It is difficult for us to deal with good results." On a ministerial level, the cross-national attraction focused on Finland allows the Finns to concentrate more on their education system. Furthermore, this further illustrates the importance of context, as the aforementioned factors behind the strengths of Finnish education, such as the movement for independence and subsequent importance of education in the Finnish culture, represent external factors that influence the strength of Finland's education system and its success in PISA.

3 Views of Head Teachers

The head teachers took an interesting, and personal view of the immense interest in the Finnish education system, due to the high numbers of "PISA tourists" at their schools. The reaction to the steady influx of visitors ranges from bemusement to irritation. Seppo, for example, looks positively upon the attention that Finland has received, and feels that, in response to the attention to his country, Finland should in turn observe other systems of education to discover factors that could improve the Finnish education system. Elvi speaks of the aforementioned sense of bemusement that some countries experience when becoming the object of educational attraction. She thinks that observing Finland's education system is the new educational trend: "Ten or fifteen years ago everyone went to New Zealand to study the school system. That was where one went; that was the place [...] Planes full of teachers and other school people have flown from Finland to study New Zealand's school system." However, with this new trend in observing Finland, she says "all of a sudden we were a little caught off guard when they started to pour in here and look at the Finnish school system [...] We don't experience it as anything sort of [...] why do they come here? We strive here every day." Much like countries formerly regarded for their education systems, such as Japan and Germany, Finland now holds the position of the country most admired for its education system. Furthermore, this illustrates a new trend in educational interest. Former trends, such as this attention between Japan and the US, and Germany and England, were outlined in Chapter 5.

Head teacher Magnus finds the attention to Finland and its education system somewhat curious, since he thinks Finnish education "is overrated. We are not so good." He hopes that "PISA tourists" can find criticisms about Finnish education in addition to the positive aspects, and can take something home that will benefit their country educationally. He wishes that the visitors will tell teachers, head teachers, or educational policy makers of the strengths and weaknesses they have observed during their trips, so that Finland can further improve on their current system. Similarly, Mai-Len thinks these tourists will not find anything special about the Finnish system, although "it is nice for Finland to have a claim to fame too [...] It is nice for [the PISA tourists] to come here, because it doesn't occur to people to come here."

Pentti cites how the many PISA tourists who have come to his school for observation take a toll on the head teacher. These visits require the head teacher to prepare and spend all day with them, which he admits can be tedious. Similarly, Elvi also feels that all these visitors come as a strain to Finnish educators and thinks that all these visitors disturb school life. The views of the head teachers show how the cross-national attraction, in the form of PISA tourism, can damage the day-to-day life of a Finnish school. Other heads viewed the interest with bemusement, but the head teachers very astutely pinpointed that Finland represented the most recent trend in educational interest. This raises the issue of the slight decline in Finland's 2012 and 2015 PISA outcomes, and the potential decrease in the cross-national attraction paid to Finland.

4 Views of Teachers

Much like with the head teachers, the views of the teachers provide a firsthand view of "PISA tourism" at the school level. The reactions by the teachers showed similarities to those of the head teachers. For example, Hans thinks that the attention from PISA tourists is not worth their time because "We are not that good." Much like the head teacher Elvi, Toni thinks all the attention that Finland has received will soon pass: "There will be another PISA and maybe we will be tenth, or on another study. They come and go. I don't pay so much attention to it. I just teach." He believes the PISA tourists come "looking for something that isn't there. They should know that they have the knowledge to change their own doings." Toni suggests that the PISA tourists are wasting time blindly looking for answers in Finland. Linda views this interest with bemusement, saying the attention "is interesting, and funny in a way because we're just doing what we've always been doing, or that's how it feels. Suddenly there is something remarkable about it." Miikka thinks the attention has benefited Finland, since these visitors from other countries allow Finns to learn from their visitors, and vice versa. All countries could benefit from observing other education systems, not just Finland. He thinks Finnish students should visit other countries to see how things work so that they can learn more about their systems and cultures. Christer, a teacher of mathematics, believes the attention benefits a country like Finland: "It is good for a little country to do something good."

The teachers astutely recognised the complexity involved with a critically informed policy transfer process. For example, Jukka believes the short visits from the PISA tourists cannot yield many conclusions about the system. The Finnish education system has too many complexities that visitors cannot understand in a short time. Pia thinks that the visitors coming to Finland look for the easy answers and easy solutions, but "they can't get it. It's not that easy." The teachers also suggested that the Finns held some sort of secret regarding a successful education system. Christer guesses that the PISA tourists come looking for the "secret weapons that give us these good results, but we don't [have them]." Similarly, Sanna, who teaches Swedish, thinks visitors come looking for "the big secret that everybody wants to know," even though she feels that teachers do not do anything extraordinary. "This is just plain education," she says, "It feels kind of stupid, because these people come to observe and you don't feel like you are doing anything special." She thinks they have received too much attention because of the PISA results. This puzzlement extends to attempts at policy borrowing. Saija describes visitors to her school from Japan: "A group came from Japan and liked our textbooks so much that they are going to translate them into Japanese! It's funny." This repeats the sentiment of bemusement felt by other teachers and the head teachers due to the interest in the Finnish education system.

Jonny thinks the visitors to Finland have different agendas depending on the similarity of the education system in their home country. Visitors with similar education systems "realise that Finland is not the example of education, it is one way, one solution for one country's problems." However, he believes many become tempted to implement aspects of the Finnish system without realising it will not succeed in their home country. This highlights the need for all visitors, or PISA tourists, in this case, to be informed of the intricacies of the policy transfer process.

Pia, who participates in school exchanges with various other countries, has some experience with other education systems:

> I was a member in a group who had a community project, and we went to Slovakia and we went to [the] Czech Republic, and we went to Italy, and it was so different from Finland, so you can't compare. If you look at the results, you can't just look at the numbers, because the school system is so different. The whole society is different and the whole idea about kids going to school, how you look at it, is very different.

Hans similarly believes that Finnish success in education came from a school culture cultivated by teachers and generations of hard work. Educational models from one country cannot transfer to others. Linda thinks different cultures and languages could interpret PISA questions differently, which hinders comparison between countries on their PISA performance, which echoes some of the criticisms of PISA discussed earlier. Miikka does not see much use in comparing systems from other countries, because all countries have their own cultures. He believes that the Finnish education system is the best for Finland, but perhaps not for other countries. He cites how even the Swedish-speaking school in his town has different interpretations of school and the curriculum based on its own needs. According to Miikka, countries cannot really implement the Finnish system into their own.

Jonny believes that PISA necessitates deeper, qualitative research to find the factors behind the results. Even though he thinks that direct comparisons between different cultures and society remain impossible, he hopes the comparisons drawn because of PISA will help the educational authorities in different countries to understand the unique backgrounds of each country, and to "borrow" policies with this in mind. These teachers' perspectives show how they understand the role of context and the complexities of policy transfer, often not realised by the PISA tourists.

5   Views of Professors

The professors' perspectives highlight the issue of cultural transferability. Despite all of the interest in Finnish education, complete with vast numbers of PISA tourists, they warn against borrowing the system and keeping mindful of the context from which the Finnish system has developed. Professor Huttunen states how many perceive Finnish education as the best in the world, but adds, "We are best in that test."

Professor Virtanen acknowledges that PISA allows a country to see what works in their education systems and what could be better. He says no "easy solutions" exist, since "educational systems are so culturally bound that you must be very careful to go deeper in these kinds of issues." He refers to the "quick fix" solutions in cross-national attraction: "You can see people only taking a quick look. It is most important to find the things that are behind the scale points." Furthermore, Virtanen cites the example of hours in school. Finns actually spend comparatively very little time in school, approximately 30 hours a week, but still perform well in PISA. He recommends, "You can't explain [educational differences between countries] only analysing PISA results, you must go deeper into the culture, the educational culture of these countries." In reference to the attention placed on Finland now, Virtanen finds the attraction quite interesting. Originally, Finland modeled its education system after the other Nordic countries, especially Sweden and also Germany. He cites how Germany traditionally held the honour of the exemplary educational model. PISA changed the direction of the attraction. "Suddenly, they are coming from Germany and now other Nordic countries to see how we are organising [education] [...] I think that is one of the positive effects of PISA." He enjoys the increased mobility between countries and the encouragement of learning from each other. The Finns, he describes, have benefited from these visitors since it forces them to learn more about their own system, especially when hearing about the experiences of PISA tourists in their schools. Professor Virtanen remarks how he has learned to value assets such as the social system, health care, free and healthy school lunches, for example, since they all play a role in aiding students and teachers in carrying out their most important responsibilities. He admits it would be difficult to assess what these PISA tourists really learn while in Finland. He says, "You can't move any models directly from one country to another. There is so much connected to the cultural base of the country [...] [education systems are] deeper in the national culture than any other institution."

The professors believe that education systems come intertwined in a country's culture. Professor Koivula explains that a country with a larger population and different social and cultural structure would have no educational guarantees by imitating Finland's education system. Professor Sundqvist agrees. He says, "If you take our education system and transplant it, you won't necessarily get the same results." He speaks of how the investment in factors such as health care of children and expectant mothers has a bigger influence than the investment in education. He describes how even the Finnish assessment authorities have not "looked at what the actual effects of the school system [are], because they are all cultural. They are all intertwined in the situation in the country."

In reference to PISA success, Professor Huttunen says, "It doesn't make sense to say we are the best, but it turned out that we can continue on the way which we have been doing." Professor Koivula agrees that the Finnish education system, a "caring, comprehensive system," seems best for a country such as Finland, homogeneous, with late industrialisation. She states, "There is no basis to speculate that it would be the best solution for something." Despite their doubts, PISA tourists and visitors do come to Finland looking for educational answers. Huttunen, although he admits he does not know the details, describes how China has borrowed aspects of the Finnish approach for a school in Beijing:

> Chinese authorities are trying to replicate a Finnish *gymnasium* somewhere in Beijing or somewhere else. They have translated the material from several of our schools, the core curriculum, and some textbooks used by those example schools. There has been some agreement to train Chinese teachers, several hundred of them [...] If it would be a success, no evidence would be found. Nobody would know why.

This example illustrates the power of cross-national attraction in education policy. However, copying aspects of a successful education system does not necessarily provide the anticipated results.

Professor Laukkanen addresses the steady influx of visitors to Finland due to PISA. As a citizen of a small country, and one not often visited, she enjoys this educational tourism. Even in her city, not as easily accessed as Helsinki, they have up to three tour groups a week since the release of the first PISA results. The Germans came first. "The first year every week a group of Germans came, all different parties and administrators and teachers and different states, because they have so many of these *Länder* [states] inside of Germany." Scandinavians made up the next influx of tourists, coming from Sweden, Denmark, and Norway. Japanese and Koreans came in the next wave of PISA tourists to her city. She says, "It's amazing, even though they are doing so well, they came." Much like the head teachers and teachers, Laukkanen says the visitors to Finland have made her learn more about her system:

> It has been interesting and eye opening to look at your own system and your own culture [...] I learned a lot. I really found out how similar Sweden and Finland are [...] It's not only the visitors that will learn and gain. I am quite sure that the Finns will gain. It is nice to be the focus of attention, but it is also that you learn from other systems of education.

The other professors agree with this sentiment. Professors Sundqvist and Huttunen describe how the visitors coming from all over the world ask excellent questions about the education system, something that they find useful. As with the head teachers and teachers, these visitors and this attention have forced Finland to "look in the mirror" and really learn about themselves. Professor Koivula also describes the trust implicit in the system in Finland, quite different from that of observers. Many educational tourists come to Finland and wonder how they manage without inspectors. She says how the policy makers really do not know too much about the schools, but believe and trust the schools to carry out their jobs successfully. She states, "It is belief-based, not evidence-based."

Professor Karpinen, when citing the evenness, equality, and egalitarian nature of the Finnish system, states how "in Finland, we can produce quite even results and it is not possible to say that if we would move this system to another country, could we have the same results?" Certain systems work in certain conditions, but not others. "They have cultural features, there are historical features, and these always affect the implications and the implementation of the system." He warns visitors to keep in mind that no easy answers exist in terms of educational policy borrowing. Countries can learn from others, "but it is not possible to copy anything as such, to copy this idea and to bring it to some other country, and to use it in the same way." In order for successful policy borrowing to take place, changes must occur to ensure cultural compatibility. "Each culture has to modify their own system so it will suit their own system, their own culture, and their own way of education [...] There are very seldom simple solutions and simple answers."

Professor Rantanen also mentions the necessity of investigating the cultural contexts behind PISA results. In reference to the interest in Finland, he says, "Of course we are very proud to present our system and so on. It is our adaptation of one single instructional activity, and expecting that to work similarly in another country as in Finland is nonsense. It is a stupid thing." He feels that people do not concentrate enough on the backgrounds and cultures influencing PISA scores. The PISA tourists come, according to Rantanen, and focus on small things, like school lunches or that the children take off their shoes in school. "The focus might be on the small things, some instructional things, things that are not easy to be changed in any system. The school type, for example, those cannot be changed easily. A similar educational system cannot be built, for example, in the States, if the bases are not the same as over here." He cites *sisu* as a strong influence behind Finnish education, and describes *sisu* as "Finnish guts." These guts, or "Finnish character," give Finns strength in the face of adversity. "Even if the tasks we have to do and face are not nice, or we do not enjoy those or love those, but we do it anyhow. We are trying to finish the job, any job that is given. *Sisu*, as we call it. Our Finnish guts."

Professor Sundqvist suggests that those observing the success of Finland in PISA need to explore beyond the results. He believes that many trying to decipher the high scores focus too much on subject-related reasons and not more general ones:

> We do a lot of strange things like taking off our shoes [at school], or having a lot of reindeer per capita, and other things that are specific to Finland but have probably nothing to do with any PISA explanation. This would be one way of getting around some of the explanations, and focusing on those [...] that are more general.

In other words, those looking for a quick fix or easy answers to educational success look too superficially into Finnish society, hence resulting in uninformed policy borrowing, and eventual policy failure.

The success of Finland in PISA has triggered its closest neighbour to mimic the system. Ironically, Finland has traditionally looked to Sweden for educational models. The aforementioned Finnish phrase states, "In reforming school, Finland makes exactly the same mistakes as Sweden. Only it happens ten years later" (Välijärvi et al., 2002, p. 3). Following the PISA results, Professor Koivula cites how "the first thing that the Swedish, rightist government decided was to divide their upper secondary school into two like we have in Finland." The original educational trend between these two has reversed itself, with the interest now coming from Sweden towards Finland, showing how cross-national attraction changes throughout time.

6　Views from the OECD

The OECD officials shed light upon the cross-national attraction to Finland. For example, OECD official Schroeder thinks it must be a "nightmare" for Finland, "all of these thousands of visitors coming" to their schools, wanting to see the educational drivers behind the quantitative PISA results. He states how the OECD had to meet with Finland's policy group before the release of PISA results, in order to ensure they knew how to manage their results once released: "I [arranged a] meeting of the policy group, governing [...] Finland to make sure they would have an understanding when they saw the results [...] I knew that three months later they would have the results, and I wanted to make sure that they actually [...] got a sense of it." Schroeder went to Finland to ensure they could handle the results and the consequences it would have.

OECD official Chadwick cites how the variation between the Nordic countries has prompted many visits to the OECD from Norwegian officials:

> The Norwegians are very keen to find out what it is about the Finns that they do differently. We have [...] people who come through visiting because we do presentations to different groups, [and] Norway is by far the country we get most representation from [...] ten times more than any other country [...] It is a very wealthy country as well, and I think they were surprised by the results.

The variation between Finnish PISA outcomes and Norwegian results has Norwegians as the most frequent visitors to the OECD because of PISA. Their performance in PISA could classify as a "negative external evaluation" situation, as discussed in the Introduction. This "negative external evaluation" prompted Norway to seek changes in its education system. Chapter 10 discusses the Norwegian policy reactions to PISA.

The interest in PISA and its outcomes has tempted many countries to make reforms based on PISA results. In fact, Chadwick cites how the OECD has counseled countries not to make changes because of PISA, citing that improvement or deterioration between PISA cycles does not provide impetus for educational change. He feels that countries take PISA too seriously:

> One country, because the [PISA] results had gone down, the prime minister formed a working party to look into this. They came to Paris, and

we had a meeting with them. There were twelve senior parliamentarians, and we had to tell them not to do anything based on a small change from 2000 to 2003. They didn't, eventually. They decided that they would wait.

PISA has provided the danger of a "quick fix" due to "negative external evaluation." He thinks countries observing others, such as Finland, as a consequence of PISA results, only look for a quick fix to transfer into their countries.

The interest in Finland has prompted Finnish officials to focus inward and explore the reasons behind their own PISA success. After the release of the 2000 PISA outcomes, the Finns had to investigate their own system in order to identify the influencing factors that culminated in a high PISA score. According to Chadwick:

> After PISA 2000 results came out in 2001, Finland became flooded with all sorts of working parties and groups and so on. They really sat down, the Finns, and just reviewed what they had been doing that had really brought things to a place where there was a very good education system. They tracked it down to the 1950s and '60s, to changes which had taken place slowly, big changes, and taken place over many, many years. They were able to do that, so they also learned something from themselves ... They actually had been improving their system for a long time [...] They reviewed all that and came up with a plausible answer for why they did so well in all areas [of PISA].

In other words, even Finland needed to figure out the reasons behind its PISA results. Chadwick's statement also echoes the Finnish sentiment of change and continuity in terms of education policy formation, discussed by both Finnish ministers of education and professors of education earlier in the book.

PISA, according to Schroeder, has caused radical change in the educational world. Since PISA, countries have a better idea of the educational pursuits in other countries, and can answer questions based on educational comparison. PISA has instigated borrowing stemming from interest in other countries' education systems:

> I think finally education is doing what other sectors of society have [done] long before. If you are in medicine, nobody would say, you can't operate this kind of disease because it is done in a different way in a different country. I think a lot of the barriers we have in education

today are barriers of traditions, barriers of ideology, all of those things. And I think these things are disappearing. The empirical evidence is starting to replace, get across that. I think that is good. But this is only the beginning. I think education is still a field largely dominated by beliefs, ideologies, traditions, those kinds of things that have to change.

He implies that education has lagged behind other fields in terms of borrowing ideas and policies to better suit their own systems. PISA has allowed for discussion, comparison, and ultimately, policy borrowing. Unlike most interview subjects, he encourages the cross-fertilisation of educational ideas.

Chadwick calls the interest in Finland the "Finland Phenomenon." He describes this as "everybody going to Finland and 'Aha! So this is how you do it. Let's go away and do that.' But it doesn't work." He says that educational changes need to account for the culture intertwined with the education system: "Any change or improvement has to take into account the culture that the education system is operating on [...] I think you have to be cautious with the analyses and the comparisons. You have to take into account the cultural differences." While comparisons between similar countries, such as the Nordic countries, provide useful information from their collaborative work, disparate systems need to observe caution when attempting to make comparisons with differing countries. As the policy transfer theories in Chapter 5 suggested, the cultural differences between countries play a strong role. For example, OECD official Khan states, "We know that with the secondary school level approximately two-thirds of the performance is actually dependent upon outside [factors of] schools [...] So the societal issues come through in the two-thirds part, which is a very large part." He attributes two-thirds of students' performance to external factors, implying that education systems have strong bonds within the societies of the home country.

Chadwick believes some things can transfer into another system, but not others. For example, something like highly qualified teachers, which Finland boasts as part of their education system, can be "policy malleable," but he says that the Finnish language cannot transfer into another country. Aspects of a system such as a comprehensive education system or educational funding can transfer into another when accounting for cultural differences. He states, "I think even within countries, the differences between regions are strong [...] I can't imagine countries will adopt wholesale without taking their own culture into account, their own history, because it is difficult to change things quickly like that."

OECD official Chevalier believes that through PISA countries can learn from each other, such as borrowing the structure and organisation of education systems. He cites the example of his home country, France, which has a high rate of grade repetition. Originally seen as the best solution for weak students France now sees through PISA that a model with low repetition, like Finland, yields better results. These kinds of observations and discussions have become possible because of PISA. However, he thinks that some aspects of Finnish education remain too deeply grounded in the culture to work in other contexts. PISA allows not only analysis of country performance, but also of education systems and teaching philosophies. Chevalier says, "It is up to the countries to decide if they can export or import maybe some of the features [...] in their countries." He thinks that features like individualisation of learning can transfer from the Finnish system to other countries, but the egalitarian quality cannot relocate into another culture.

When asked about the validity in comparing many countries with different backgrounds, Schroeder mentioned the frequency of that kind of enquiry when referring to PISA. He acknowledges the relevance and importance of the question, and addresses the many challenges when comparing so many students from varying countries on one kind of assessment:

> People say, well, you can't compare rich and poor countries. But if you go to whatever country when students leave school, no one asks them if they come from a rich or poor country but they have to be benchmarked on what they can contribute. Some are lucky, some are less lucky, some are born more gifted, more talented than others. There are differences that we can't change. Still, I think the bottom line of what we can do is an important characteristic. I think comparisons are important, and you can adjust them. We do that all the time.

In other words, despite the uncertainty in comparing countries with differing histories and backgrounds, the need for comparison does remain. Furthermore, countries also have varying contexts within their borders that do not receive the same contextual criticism as international surveys. Countries also need to see where they stand and need assessment to see what they can do. Schroeder admits that many do not agree with him, but believes ultimately in the benefits of comparative assessment:

> At the end of the day we need to see where we stand. I am actually convinced that such comparisons are very valuable and that they are pretty robust as well [...] There are different cultures, different ways that students learn in different countries, different forms of tests that they take – all of those things vary. I think at the end of the day, what they can do is what matters. That's what we assess.

He says that others do not believe that comparisons can exist between countries, but that he does. He does not agree that cultural context eclipses the ability of comparison. Quite optimistic about educational transfer, he believes that successful features of education systems can transfer to other countries. Schroeder says, "You can't transfer the context, but you can transfer the ingredients of success." He does not believe in directly copying an entire system, rather, in identifying the drivers of educational success and transporting them to another system. He does not agree with critics who warn about the pitfalls of educational transferability. He says, "You wouldn't have this attitude in industry. You wouldn't say, 'We cannot learn anything from Toyota because Toyota is made [in Japan].' It's an attitude we do not have in other sectors." He does acknowledge, though, that cultural contexts have the most difficulty in transferring to other countries. For example, in Finland, the teaching profession enjoys a very high status. Although a direct transfer cannot occur to another country, in the long-term, others might also instil high value of teachers within their societies. Unlike the head teachers, teachers, professors and education ministers from Finland, the OECD officials seem to have a more sympathetic view of policy transfer, or policy "malleability," as Chadwick described it. Schroeder has a more liberal view of policy transfer, while not as cavalier as policy makers looking for a "quick fix," more optimistic than the literature in Chapter 5 would suggest.

7 National Character

The extensive discussion of context throughout this book necessitates an exploration into the notion of national character. Does national character exist? Some may argue that it does not, even for small countries. However, some feel that a national character does exist. Kandel believed that it does exist, and that it influences a country's education system as well. Mallinson also published literature on this matter. The writings of both authors suggest that the concept of national character has complex roots:

> The concept of nationality does not, however, lend itself readily to such a simple definition as loyalty to a common ideal; there are other factors and explanations that cut across it. There are those who would insist that a nation is or should be a racial unit with common ancestors, common kin, common language, common culture, a common homeland, and certain common characteristics. (Kandel, 1933, p. 6)

Eventually, Kandel states, "Nationality implies a spiritual tie which binds together a group of individuals that feels itself as one." He also writes, "A nation is then a group of individuals sharing a common culture [...] Nationalism, then, implies a common language, common customs, and a common culture" (ibid., pp. 7–8). Nationalism, therefore, also has influences in education:

> The history of education can point to numerous examples of changes in the development of educational theories and practices which have been consequent upon changes and crises in political, economic, and social conditions, but never before has education been so sensitive to the problems with which society is confronted. Always intimately bound up with the fabric of life, education has never been looked upon as it is today not only as an important instrument of social control but as one of the most valuable aids for social reconstruction. (Ibid., pp. 1–2)

Mallinson agrees: "Education, then, is a social force in the sense that any educational system must reflect closely the ethos of people it is called upon to serve" (Mallinson, 1957, p. 2). Nations can use education in order to strengthen the citizens' ties as a nation: "The national characteristics of any given nation will find their expression in the nation's schools, and those schools are constantly used to strengthen and perpetuate the national characteristics and outlook" (ibid., p. 8). As nations evolve, so do their education systems: "Obviously the schools must closely reflect the social pattern holding in any particular country as do reforms in education the changing tone and temper of the people" (ibid., p. 48).

According to Kandel and Mallinson, national character does exist, and even influences the education system of a country. Therefore, one can better justify many of the discussions that took place throughout this book. For example, the concept of national character and education helps explain the difficulty in educational policy borrowing and the many strengths of Finnish education, including the factors such as equality, the National Curriculum, literacy, the popularity of teaching, and the like as factors behind Finland's PISA performance. Kandel and Mallinson's descriptions of national character and education clarify the significance of national factors in the education system. National character also must take into account the Finnish concept of *sisu*.

The delicately intricate web of features influencing the Finnish education system and its success in PISA can boil down to one underlying factor: *sisu*. While one can explain the Finnish educational successes due to interlocking, interwoven reasons such as Finnish politics, the Nordic egalitarian ideal, the wars and recovery, or the recession of the 1990s, the one concept of *sisu* encompasses all of these intertwined factors.

To reiterate the definition of this word, Chapter 2 described *sisu* as this:

> *Sisu* is a key word in Finnish. It means dogged determination, strength of character or just plain guts. Few nations have battled against such a harsh climate and, at times, against such overwhelming odds as successfully as the Finns; they have pulled themselves up by their own bootstraps, and today, their average income per head [...] is among the world's 10 highest. (Chislett, 1996, p. 17)

This strong will and internal strength in the face of adversity provide an overarching explanation for the reasons behind Finnish success in PISA. For example, many of the interviewees credited the high value and regard for education in Finland as contributing to its top PISA ranking. The history of Finland, its struggles for independence, civil war, World War II battles, and deep recession, all contribute to the value of education in Finnish society. Overcoming these setbacks as successfully as the Finns have done required *sisu*. The highly literate society and pride in the Finnish language stem from the struggle of Finnish speakers for rights in the Finnish language. One can explain this struggle, and triumph, with *sisu*.

8 Summary

This chapter discussed the views of Finnish education ministers, head teachers, teachers, and professors on the immense cross-national attraction directed towards Finland recently, as well as views of OECD officials. The chapter also delved into the notion of national character.

The Finnish education ministers addressed the difficulty of education policy transfer and the presence and importance of cultural heritage within an education system. Context and external factors highly influence a system of education. A survey like PISA, they felt, highlighted the need for deeper investigation into education systems. The head teachers had a different view, as most had direct experience with the vast amounts of PISA tourists visiting Finnish schools. They stated how PISA tourism took a toll on the schools and their roles as head teachers. However, the steady influx of PISA tourists aided the heads in looking inward and finding weaknesses within their own education system. Related to this, some thought that Finns should investigate other systems of education in a similar manner, in order to improve their education as well. Some of the head teachers felt this immense cross-national attraction was just one trend in a longer history of such attraction.

The teachers possessed sceptical views of the possibility of policy transfer. They also experienced PISA tourism, but believed that these visitors came looking for easy answers, the "secret weapons" and the "big secret." However, the teachers acknowledged the fact that all education systems, including the Finnish one, had too many complexities to easily transfer successful features. They believed that the PISA tourists kept looking for things that did not exist, as Finnish education "is just plain education." Furthermore, a difficulty in comparison exists, due to the varying contexts of each country. The teachers felt Finnish education had many cultural ties.

The Finnish professors of education also felt the effects of the immense cross-national attraction directed toward Finland. The PISA tourism, they believed, helped them learn about themselves and their own system of education. They, much like the teachers, viewed the possibility of policy transfer with scepticism. They also stressed the importance of an education system's context, and highlighted the need for deeper, qualitative investigation behind the quantitative results of PISA. They stated that Finland was simply "the best in that test." In terms of policy transfer, they believed that no easy "quick fix" solutions existed. In the opinions of the professors, education has many cultural ties, and transplantation of education does not yield the same results in another context. One professor attributed the Finnish educational success to *sisu*, Finnish tenacity or "guts." This very context-related concept illustrates the need to look beyond PISA's quantitative results and the immense importance of context in education systems.

The OECD officials, in terms of cross-national attraction, acknowledged that the immense interest in Finland and subsequent PISA tourism must be difficult for the country. They even recounted how they needed to council the Finnish education officials before the release of the PISA scores due to the cross-national attraction that would ensue. Similarly, they needed to counsel countries from trying to implement "quick fix" solutions due to their disappointing PISA outcomes. One OECD official believed that PISA would begin a new era of policy borrowing, and he felt that borrowing should be encouraged in order to make improvements. However, others thought that culture played an important role. While not all elements of an education system could transfer, some "policy malleable" elements, the "ingredients for success," could provide improvements for other countries.

With the literature stressing the importance of a country's context in education, the topic of national character comes up. National character, a spiritual tie of common culture, uses education to strengthen citizens' ties with a nation. Thus, national character can influence an education system, as seen through *sisu's* influence on the Finnish people and education system.

CHAPTER 10

The Temptation of Uncritical International Transfer: The Politics of Finland's Success in PISA

1   Introduction

Finland's overwhelming success in PISA has drawn much attention to the country and its education system; however, it has also added to the temptation of the aforementioned "quick fix" and "phony" policy solutions. While it has created a dialogue for education and has increased the visibility of education internationally, PISA has also essentially created an international "league table," with countries eager to perform in the survey. While the OECD created PISA in response to the wishes of member countries, PISA has made education much more political. The scramble to perform well in international achievement studies such as PISA has led to pressure to make "quick fix" decisions for political pull. Comparativists have urged throughout time that a country's context is intertwined with its education system. Nevertheless, PISA and Finland's success in the survey have led to even more temptation for uncritical policy transfer.

2   Policy Transfer

As discussed in Chapter 5, policy transfer has many pitfalls, and must be undertaken in a manner which properly "indigenises" the borrowed policy into the new context. The temptation of policy transfer becomes more acute with perceived educational inferiority, as, "The more urgent and intractable our educational problems seem to be, the more tempting becomes the notion of a 'quick fix'" (Noah, 1984, p. 550). This echoes Phillips and Ochs' cycle of policy borrowing, where politicians implement "quick fix" and "phony" solutions in times of political necessity or for "immediate political impact." The league tables, so to speak, generated by surveys such as PISA add to this feeling of urgency and of "intractable" educational problems.

The worrying trend of emphasising large-scale, quantitative measurement over the "high ecological validity of qualitative research," and this importance within recent education policy making has resulted in the adoption of large-scale policies, which do not consider the difficulty of implementation and the role culture plays within each educational context (Vulliamy, 2004, p. 266). Separating education from its historical, political, and cultural contexts can have "devastating unintended consequences that need to be understood by policy makers if they are to break the cycle of policy failure" (ibid., p. 267). What works in one culture has little chance of surviving in another, unless policy makers seriously consider the role of context in education. Policies are often implemented, "uncritically," into a new context: "Countries import educational policies from other countries, with high hopes fuelled by widespread discussion of such policies in the literature, despite the lack of evidence of the effective practice of such policies" (Crossley & Vulliamy, 1984, p. 198). Similarly, Noah states:

> [...] international borrowing of educational ideas and practices has more failures to record than success. Transplantation is a difficult art, and those who wish to benefit from the experience of other nations will find in comparative studies a most useful set of cautions, as well as some modest encouragement. (1984, p. 556)

In other words, a borrowed educational policy often does not reap the same benefits for the borrowing country as it did in the original context. This potential for "abuse" of the comparative education field for political clout calls for careful consideration and borrowing in order to successfully implement foreign practices, avoiding "wholesale" transfer but with consideration of context and adaptation (1984, pp. 558–559). However, the "modest encouragement" that Noah speaks of again echoes those of other comparativists, suggesting that informed borrowing and careful "indigenisation" into the borrowing context could lead to successful policy transfer.

Successful implementation and internalisation of foreign educational practices do occur and have been documented, as the London borough of Barking and Dagenham successfully reformed its schools to implement education practices from Switzerland and Germany (Ochs, 2006). The borrowed policy passed through the stages and filters of policy borrowing, as stated previously by Phillips and Ochs (2003), which distorted and converted the original practice into the one implemented. The foreign education policies went through interpretation, continued with transmission, followed by reception, and finally, implementation. In the end, the London borough did successfully implement a foreign education policy, but by carefully following five goals:

1. A strong commitment to improving the school system
2. Strong key partnerships to provide support in the process
3. Awareness of the challenges at hand when implementing a foreign system into one's own
4. Recognising that the process would require continuous commitment and repetition

5. Considering the contexts of both countries throughout the policy borrowing stages (Ochs, 2006, p. 616).

This example illustrates the possibility, whether at the macro or micro level, of adopting aspects of the Finnish model for educational improvement.

Therefore, with "responsible scholarship," "knowledge of what is being proposed and tried in cognate situations abroad is indispensable for reasoned judgement about what we need to do at home" (Noah, 1984, pp. 559, 552). Among other things, comparative education can aid successful education policy. With sensitive and careful implementation, comparative education *can* draw upon good examples of education, such as Finland, as indicated by the OECD's PISA. However, the next section of this chapter discusses the potential "abuse" (Noah, 1984) of comparative education data in the form of PISA.

3 Examples of the Politicisation of PISA

PISA has caused a large impact in the educational world, the political world, and the media. The survey's influence has increased since the release of its first scores in 2001, and politicians now examine PISA results in order to fuel political and educational debate, or to reinforce education policy reform (Baird et al., 2011). However, what is overlooked, or not mentioned, is the lack of statistical significance of changes between surveys and ranked countries, or the change, usually a decrease, in rankings due to the increase in participating countries. For example, Germany's reaction to its performance in PISA, known as PISA-Shock, had political and education policy implications. This, discussed at length in Chapter 5, illustrates the impact that PISA has already had on education policy. German PISA-Shock, along with other countries' reactions to the survey, illustrates the increasing politicisation of the PISA results. This section touches upon some responses to the survey, many of which add to the "sabre-rattling political rhetoric to drive through educational reforms" (Baird et al., 2011, p. 2) and the "'edu-political' chess match" (Rappleye, 2006, p. 238), that now are associated with PISA results, even though the connection between education policy content and PISA results is not always correlated (Baird et al., 2011).

Various countries have used PISA results in order to fuel political debate and justify educational reform. France's reaction to its PISA results, which hover around the OECD average, influenced political debate around grade repetition among French students. Furthermore, the government received criticism for over-exaggerating the PISA results in a negative light to justify recent education policy reform (Baird et al., 2011). Canada, a high-performing country, largely faced praise for its PISA outcomes; however, lower-performing provinces have instilled targets and testing in order to improve outcome. While the sentiment in the country is avoid educational complacency due to the high results, international achievement studies and their results have also increased a standardisation culture in Canada, traditionally with a devolved structure due to the autonomy of the provinces. The highly devolved system of Switzerland also underwent changes after the first PISA results. As the nation-state, which consists of cantons, does not assess nationally, PISA provided educational data for the nation-state as a whole. The impact of international achievement surveys such as PISA and the IEA's TIMSS and PIRLS has led Switzerland to coordinate education, including curricula, within the entire nation-state, and begin the process of evaluating and assessing the country as a whole. Here we see PISA's influence on education policy, politics, and education reform, in both high-performing and low-performing countries.

German delegates, along with representatives from other countries, visited Finland after its initial success in PISA. The main newspaper in Finland, *Helsingin Sanomat,* announced in 2002: "Germans Join Queue Examining Finnish School System." Germany's performance heavily contrasted with that of Finland. "Germany [...] came out of the OECD report with its reputation as an old cultural pillar in ruins, with results that put it at or near the bottom of the pile in all categories" (Helsingin Sanomat, 22 May 2002). The German Education Minister admitted that the PISA scores came as a "shock," triggering a proposal by the German federal government to spend 4 billion Euros on educational improvement (ibid.). The "negative external evaluation" that characterises many countries' PISA performances, especially in the first round of PISA, seems to have hit Germany the hardest.

As stated previously, Germany's PISA-Shock has been well documented in academic literature (e.g. Ertl, 2006; Gruber, 2006); thus, in Germany, PISA had a very strong influence on education policy, instigating major educational reform. Before PISA, the highly-regarded German system concentrated on fostering *Bildung;* while often translated into "education" in English, *Bildung* actually means the wider, holistic development of an individual (Neumann et al., 2010). The education system also formerly stressed educational input rather than output. However, following the initial PISA-Shock, it became apparent that the German notion of *Bildung* did not align with PISA's form of measurement. Thus, PISA led to fundamental educational reform, moving away from policies of educational input to policies of educational output. The humanistic view of *Bildung* shifted to an economic- and PISA-influenced concept of "literacy." This led to national education standards in Germany, and a standardisation of the curricula, curiously close to PISA measurements. These standards were created by PISA and Germany's underperformance in the survey.

Norway experienced its own PISA-Shock, due to the low performance, especially in comparison with the other Nordic countries. The media often plays a role in policy change (Baird et al., 2011; Elstad, 2012; Takayama, 2008). For example, Norway's PISA-Shock, sparked by a decline in PISA results over the years, fuelled educational debate, especially when placing blame and responsibility for the decline (Elstad, 2012). Thus, PISA had a major impact on Norwegian education policymaking, as it allowed for the "political shaping of policy content," moulded by the "political spin" of the media (ibid., p. 18). The Norwegian PISA-Shock resulted in the legitimisation of education policy based on accountability, measurement, and targets with reforms for both curriculum and assessment (ibid.; Baird et al., 2011).

Japan, traditionally a high-scoring country in cross-national achievement studies, also falls prey to PISA pressure on policy reform. Takayama (2008) documented the influence of PISA in Japanese education reform debates. As the Japanese fear that their once-admired education system has been declining, educational actors have suggested that Japan's educational reforms should align themselves with those praised by the OECD. PISA's rankings permeated local Japanese political debate, heavily influenced by the media. Takayama argues that "political necessity" fuelled these educational debates, not careful interpretation of the PISA data (ibid., p. 389). He discusses the relationship between economic competition and international education standings:

> It is in this human capitalist discourse of globalisation and knowledge economy that the mega economic competition is directly translated into the international educational horserace. The standing in the international league tables has become the virtual prophecy of the nation's future survival or decline, thus generating unprecedented global fever over the results. (Takayama, 2008, p. 389)

Externalisation justifies the politicisation of international surveys such as PISA and its influence on major policy reform (Takayama, 2008). Politicians can, and do, use the misreading and misinterpretation of data, such as the PISA tables, as a catalyst for immediate political action. Surveys such as PISA give policy makers a "powerful ideological tool" which helps justify otherwise controversial education reform (ibid., p. 391). PISA helped ignite education reform debate in Japan, and the media helped fuel the debate. In fact, the Ministry of Education even became involved with the reporting of the PISA 2003 scores in the media, hoping to mould public opinion on the matter (ibid.). The media published misleading interpretations of the Japanese PISA data, for example, not taking into account statistical significance of the data, or providing enough background information (ibid.). This exploitation of the PISA data by the Japanese Ministry of Education was used to set some controversial policy reform. This example illustrates the political impact PISA possesses, even so soon after its birth.

Japan, like Germany, experienced its own PISA-Shock (Takayama, 2009). The perceived decline in PISA performance between the 2000 and 2003 surveys led many Japanese to flock to Finland for educational inspiration. This cross-national attraction to Finland, due to PISA, has led to much Finnish influence in Japanese education. For example, the aforementioned "Finnish Method Promotion Association" took Finnish textbooks and translated them into Japanese (ibid., p. 51). Furthermore, the "Finnish method" of teaching gained so much attention and popularity that Japanese "experts" of Finnish education published books on the matter (ibid., p. 52). The Finnish teaching methodology gathered so much respect that even the Japanese Ministry of Education promoted Finnish reading strategies in national reading plans. This cross-national attraction and policy transfer is otherwise known as the "Finlandisation phenomenon" (ibid.).

Takayama (2009) argues that this policy borrowing was conducted uncritically. Methodological weaknesses characterise the data collected by these Japanese "experts" on Finnish education. These "experts" have constructed an image of Finnish educational success and Japanese educational decline. Furthermore, none of the "experts" have bothered to look at the Finnish education system with a critical eye. This uncritical acceptance of Finnish education's merits has made this uncontested truth a basis for Japanese educational reform. Finland and its education system, therefore, were used to suit political agendas. In Japan, Finnish education became a "cultural construct" used for reform in a supposed educational crisis (ibid., p. 67), developed into a symbol with different meanings to different parties, and was used to promote different agendas. When examples of education are made into these symbols or constructs, the initial attraction to these places leads to borrowing of educational policy, as with the case of Japan. Finland and its education system have continued to hold this authority over Japanese educational reform and the related debates.

The example of Finnish education and Japanese PISA-Shock illustrates the "cultural politics" of Finnish education within Japanese educational reforms (Takayama, 2009, p. 67). The Finnish education system possesses a "hero" image within the Japanese perspective (ibid., p. 68). Globalisation destabilises identities, causing people, localities, and nations to look elsewhere to reinvent a new identity. In an educational view, this new global view of education, as illustrated by PISA, has caused countries to question their systems and philosophies and look to other countries for guidance. This tendency gives a false sense of security when anticipating the success of educational reform. This idealisation of Finland has been used by political actors to criticise current policies and generate changes. Local and national influences within globalisation need to be taken into account when conducting comparative study, but were overlooked. In this case, Japanese politicians and the media interpreted, perhaps on purpose, the PISA data into a binary comparison of "us" versus "them," but, in reality, those wishing to learn from elsewhere must question the certainty of successful policy borrowing in educational reform.

When juxtaposing Takayama's arguments with the Phillips and Ochs policy borrowing models, one could claim that Japan's cross-national attraction to Finland began with "negative external evaluation" due to less than satisfactory PISA results in both 2000 and 2003 (Phillips & Ochs, 2004, p. 778). The Finnish "hero" image (Takayama, 2009, p. 68) and the symbol of Finnish education were used by politicians, uncritically, to promote reforms based on political agendas. This would-be "phony" policy borrowing, as the borrowing on the micro and macro levels, for example of textbooks, teaching techniques, and policy was conducted for immediate impact (Phillips and Ochs, 2004, p. 780). Japan's own PISA-Shock shows the temptation for "quick fix" borrowing, uncritical policy transfer, and "phony" political solutions. The Japanese reaction to PISA and its subsequent attraction to Finland illustrate the politicisation of PISA and international achievement studies, along with the temptation for uncritical transfer.

Here we see how even countries commonly credited with enviable education systems can and have fallen prey to the politicisation of education and education policy due to the influence of international achievement studies. These surveys, and namely PISA, now steer education reform, even with tenuous connections between the policies and PISA results. The following sections discuss the impact of PISA within the UK context.

4   Major Policy Borrowing from Finland: The Case of the MTL

The most salient factor behind Finland's PISA success, the teachers, has already had implications for English education policy, in the rapid development, launch, and withdrawal, of the first national, government-funded professional Master's degree for teachers. The Master's in Teaching and Learning (MTL) was introduced in April 2010 in England, piloted mainly to Newly Qualified Teachers (NQTs) in the Northwest of the country. The programme had its funding withdrawn only one year after its introduction. The MTL had been intended to be "a key lever for schools in England, helping to further raise the status of the teaching profession, and align us with the highest performing education systems in

THE TEMPTATION OF UNCRITICAL INTERNATIONAL TRANSFER   201

the world" (TDA, 2010b, p. 4), implying that the MTL was created in response to Finland's top performance in PISA and the quality of the teachers. The introduction of the MTL in England therefore may be one of the first instances of major policy borrowing from the Finnish context.

England, although with a respectable, well above average outcome in PISA in 2000, for example (OECD, 2004a), has, as illustrated by the initiation of the MTL, succumbed to "negative external evaluation" (Phillips & Ochs, 2004, p. 778). Therefore, the introduction of this type of Master's degree in England falls under the "phony" type of decision-making, for the decision to introduce the MTL came right before the UK general elections of 2010 (ibid.; TDA, 2010a). As mentioned previously, "phony" decision-making refers to interest in external education systems by politicians for immediate political impact.

As the MTL was essentially a pilot study, the Master's policy with its original Finnish influences did not achieve full implementation into the English system. The astute Finnish attitude of "continuity and change" acknowledges the importance of time before assessing the efficacy of an education policy. For example, many Finns credit the comprehensive school reforms of the 1970s for Finland's top performance in PISA. In other words, they believe the students taking PISA were the children of these reforms, benefiting from an egalitarian view of education. Unfortunately, the withdrawal of funding for the MTL with its original intentions will not allow anyone to see whether this Master's degree would have improved teacher quality, and ultimately, education in England.

One could argue strongly that the MTL was borrowed uncritically. The borrowing of Finland's system, especially by England, has curious policy implications. Webb et al. (1998) point out that the education policies in England and Finland have been moving in opposite directions for some time. For example, the 1988 Education Reform Act in England introduced for the first time a "detailed and prescriptive" National Curriculum (Webb et al., 1998, p. 540). This Act came from a New Right ideology from a Conservative government. However, in 1994, Finland decided to "dismantle" its National Curriculum which had been in place for over twenty years, and instead encouraged school-based curricula. This constructivist approach has encouraged Finland to move away from national agendas and towards school-based curricula and active learning. Nevertheless, a 2004 Act reinstated some standardisation with a strengthening of the National Core Curriculum, which replaced the more prescribed National Curriculum in 1985 (Webb et al., 2009; Chung, 2009). In England, a 1992 Act created the Office for Standards in Education (OFSTED). OFSTED, has along with the government, increased its influence on the teaching and curriculum in England. In contrast, Finland dissolved its national system of inspection in the 1970s, moving to local inspection until 1991, and finally, school self-inspection (Chung, 2009; Webb et al., 1998, 2004). While Finland has no national testing until the end of upper-secondary education, England has high-stakes standardised testing (Webb & Vulliamy, 1999, p. 230).

These divergences affect teaching philosophies and practices. English teachers feel the pressure to move from progressive education back to traditional pedagogy. Conversely, Finnish teachers have been encouraged to move towards progressive teaching styles and away from traditional teaching practice (Webb & Vulliamy, 1999). The Finnish national comprehensive school curriculum, established in the 1970s, and the reforms of the 1990s have been "filtered through a particularly Nordic welfare state tradition" which has emphasised egalitarian values and equality (Webb et al., 2004, p. 84). These filters mentioned by Webb, et al. echo the Phillips and Ochs (2003) model of filters in the policy borrowing process. In addition to their cycle of policy borrowing, Phillips and Ochs (2004) discuss the filters involved in the policy borrowing process, which distort and alter the original educational policy. The borrowed policy goes through various stages before the policy becomes properly "lent." The implementation of a borrowed policy distorts the original "image." In the end, the borrowing country can have a very different educational practice from that originally borrowed. It could be argued that Finland's own education system has been borrowed, or "filtered," from other contexts. This illustrates the cyclical nature of policy borrowing, as Phillips and Ochs (2004) theorised.

The previous paragraph suggests that both policy and practice in Finland have gone through proper implementation into the Finnish and Nordic context. Even concepts of teacher professionalism differ between Finland and England. The English concept leans towards the definition showing that professional teachers follow government directives of standards, while the Finnish definition of professionalism refers to teacher empowerment and autonomy (Webb et al., 2004). There are also differences in levels of trust in teachers, as in England low levels of trust between society and teachers exist, perhaps due to performance data such as league tables and standards, while in Finland teachers enjoy high levels of trust from the national and local governments, as well as at the school level. All of this suggests that the MTL's implementation into the English education policy overlooked the importance of context, and even the trends within the two education systems, thus indicating that the MTL's original premise was borrowed uncritically.

Thus, inherent differences in the English and Finnish education systems would inevitably have made it difficult to successfully borrow aspects of policy. The withdrawal of MTL funding now makes it difficult to gauge the success, or lack thereof, of the MTL programme as originally intended. However, the MTL still exists in 52 universities, as one choice in many Master's degrees offered to teachers in England. While none of these Master's degrees are compulsory, they are encouraged. The wide variety of Master's degrees offered suggests that education policy, especially with the Master's degrees for teachers within the English context, has a passive approach to teacher education. It could be argued that this lack of commitment is due to the lack of political consensus in education within the UK context, and the use of education within the aforementioned "'edu-political' chess match" (Rappleye, 2006, p. 238) and the "sabre-rattling political rhetoric to drive through educational reforms" (Baird et al., 2011, p. 2). The shortage of unified opinion in education policy, and in this case, teacher education policy, illustrates this *laissez-faire* attitude to postgraduate education for England's teachers.

English and Finnish education policy, as discussed in this chapter, have been diverging since the late twentieth century, adhere to different philosophies and values, and even approach teacher education in a disparate manner. As Noah stated, "transplantation is a difficult art," meaning external policies have difficulty in succeeding in other environments (1984, p. 556). One can infer that the UK government has implemented the MTL in England as a "quick fix" policy, following the success of Finland in PISA, even though some research shows that a Master's degree will not improve teaching practice (e.g. Noah, 1984, p. 550; Ochs & Phillips, 2002a, pp. 7–8; Goldhaber & Brewer, 2000; Whitehurst, 2002). Furthermore, one could also argue that the MTL falls under the category of "phony" decision-making, expressing interest in foreign systems of education in order to make political impact (Phillips & Ochs, 2004, p. 780). The explicit comparison with "highest performing education systems in the world" (DCSF, 2008, p. 12) and "international competitors" (DCSF, 2008, p. 6) is a clear-cut example of such a strategy. Interestingly, despite initiatives such as the MTL, England has not succeeded in cultivating teaching as a respected occupation, much less a profession, and despite the initiative behind the MTL, no requirement for higher degrees, namely Master's degrees, exists for teachers (Baird et al., 2011).

5   Major Policy Borrowing from Finland: The Case of the White Paper

The 2010 White Paper, *The Importance of Teaching,* highlighted the importance of high-quality teachers and the role they play in high-performing education systems. This book has previously discussed how much of Finnish PISA success is attributed to the high quality of the teachers, as only top students enter the teaching profession, thus achieving and maintaining high educational attainment. Unlike the MTL, which never explicitly ascribed its policy initiation to Finnish influences, the White Paper clearly pinpointed PISA as a key measure of educational success.

The White Paper called for more practically based teacher education within the classrooms by expanding school-based routes into teaching; however, the Paper also calls for "University Training Schools," modelled after Finland's university-affiliated teacher training schools, or *normaalikoulu*. This *normaalikoulu* differs from Finnish state schools, or municipality schools, as it receives its funding through the university. The head teachers and teachers are employed as part of the university. Teachers within the *normaalikoulu* elect the head teachers from within the school, and they serve as head for six years. Teachers at the *normaalikoulu* must have a Master's degree, teaching qualification, and a minimum of two years of experience. Salaries are higher than average, in order to accommodate extra responsibility. Many have a degree higher than the minimum Master's degree, whether a PhD or a Licentiate degree. It is not unusual for teachers at the *normaalikoulu* to have served as lecturers in teacher education at the university, and vice versa. The *normaalikoulu* also serve research purposes. Both the teachers within the school and university staff carry out their personal research within these schools, as do students researching their dissertations.

These University Training Schools, as outlined in the 2010 White Paper, aim to improve education in England. The White Paper, however, more strongly focuses on moving teacher education away from the university to a school-centred approach, stressing what "is really important" (DfE, 2010, p. 22), teacher *training* at the school level. In contrast, as previously stated, Finnish teacher education emphasises university-based learning, research, and a Master's degree. Thus, it could be argued that the White Paper overlooked the underlying principles of Finnish teacher education and instead promotes "quick fix" approaches to educational reform. As stated previously, Finnish and English education policies have been moving in opposite directions for some time. The foci of the respective teacher education systems of each country further illustrate Webb et al.'s (1998, 2004) earlier arguments. One could argue that the research-based teacher *education*, with a Master's degree differs greatly from the teacher *training* suggested in the White Paper.

Understandably, teacher education comes in a variety of forms and adheres to different philosophies in different countries (Jyrhämä et al., 2008). Teacher education may emphasise personal experiences. This comes under the model of school-based teacher education, the approach used in England. However, teacher education may take a research-based approach, based on deductive methods and grounded pedagogical theory. This is the approach used in Finland. Finland and England, therefore, use two very different methods of teacher education; England's emphasises school-based learning and personal experiences, while Finland's stresses research and theory. Interestingly, the White Paper denotes synthetic phonics and the management of poor behaviour as "key skills" (DfE, 2010, pp. 22–23). This suggests the White Paper views teaching as a *vocation*, and the on-the-job training required allows trainees, like apprentices, to pick up specific skills. Conversely, the Finnish approach of research and theory implies that teaching is not a vocation, but a *profession*.

The White Paper, much like the MTL, also provides fuel for the aforementioned "'edu-political' chess match" (Rappleye, 2006, p. 238) and the "sabre-rattling political rhetoric to drive through educational reforms" (Baird et al., 2011, p. 2). The change in UK government in 2010 from the Labour party to the coalition of the Conservative and Liberal Democrat parties led to the coalition claiming to clean up the educational "mess" left by Labour. The then-Secretary for Education, Michael Gove, claimed that the White Paper was essentially a "bespoke response" to the 2009 PISA survey (Gove, 2010; Baird et al., 2011, p. 15). Interestingly, however, the policies outlined in the White Paper do not necessarily correlate to the PISA 2009 results (Baird et al., 2011). This echoes Baird et al.'s (2011) argument earlier in this chapter stating that PISA drives education reform, despite weak correlations between PISA results and the reformed policy.

The "instant and public" nature (Morris, 2012, p. 91) of international comparisons such as PISA, provides so-called evidence from which to spur policy reform. In the case of the White Paper, this has resulted in a "selective focus" on the countries, like Finland, that inspired the policy paper (ibid., p. 97). Morris (2012) cites, much as this chapter has argued already, that Finnish and English teacher education have very different foci; yet, the White Paper calls for school-based training for teachers. In fact, this illustrates how policy borrowing, or policy transfer has been used to endorse comparative evidence, one of the reasons to stimulate education policy reform. While academics caution against uninformed policy transfer due to the issue of contexts, governments and politicians encourage the use of policy borrowing to promote reform. This "highly politicised process of policy making" creates "a problem that requires a solution" (ibid., p. 90). Thus, much like in Germany, Norway, Canada, Switzerland, and Japan, England also has proposed policy changes that do not align with PISA's actual findings. In fact, Morris argues that England has not learned any lessons from PISA or Finland, and that Finland's actual educational strengths have been largely ignored by the White Paper. This "wholesale" reform in order to "select and project" policy agendas (ibid., pp. 93, 105) illustrates both the misuse of comparative data, and the tenuous connections between actual PISA results and governmental policy agendas.

Unfortunately, policy transfer seemingly cannot exist separate from political drama. As stated previously, Rappleye argues that "policy borrowing is by definition a highly *political* process" (2006, p. 238). Halpin and Troyna (1995) cite how politicians have more interest in a borrowed policy's political power than in the actual implications on the home education system. Therefore, in this view, policies have less significance than the political discourse they generate (ibid.). They state how policy borrowing "has more to do with form than content." Similarly, as stated previously in Chapter 1, myth can influence policy more than science (Yore et al., 2010), which decreases the possibility of actual academic research influencing education policy. Again, to reiterate the argument in the first chapter, instead of evidence-based policy change, it is "policy-based evidence-making" (ibid.). This dangerous reversal of policy protocol illustrates the lack of informed policy making, and the "phony" and "quick fix" decisions made by politicians. If the model of Finnish education, and in this case, Finnish teacher education in the form of the university training school, is used, or, more accurately, misused for political power rather than for potential effect on the education system, then the policy does not have a chance at indigenising and improvement. This would be classed as "inappropriate transfer," since insufficient attention was given to the context and ideologies behind the borrowed policy (Dolowitz & Marsh, 2000, p. 17).

6 Education and Education Policy in the 21st Century

This book, and especially this chapter, has shown the impact of PISA, especially in terms of politics and education policy. The paradigm shift that has occurred, as discussed throughout this book, indicates that education no longer means *paideia* (Moutsios, 2010), but a political tool by which to secure economic success within global competition. The 2013 release of PIAAC, the aforementioned survey of adult skills, and the measurement of higher education skills in AHELO, both of which are administered by the OECD, can only add to this paradigm shift. As stated earlier in the book, "What physicists realised some time ago, but educational testing people seem averse to acknowledging, is that when you measure something you change it" (Riley & Torrance, 2003, p. 424). The measurement of education, while admittedly in place before the initiation of PISA, has spawned a testing frenzy on local, national, and international levels. The addition of PIAAC and AHELO to the OECD's educational testing portfolio signals that more international surveys of achievement are likely to occur. This could indicate that the GERM movement could spread even further with more virulence.

PISA has changed Finland as well. As the focus of international attention, the Finnish education system has experienced much "PISA tourism" over the years. Finland has somehow managed to maintain an equitable, efficient, and high-performing education system while upholding immunity to GERM, by not implementing the now ubiquitous high-stakes testing, league tables, and accountability. This anomaly separates Finland from other countries, most of which have some, or many, features of GERM. Slowly, it has become apparent that education for Finland can become an "export product." Education has become a "global edu-business" in recent years (Ball, 2012, p. 2). This can occur when exploiting, or taking advantage of perceived educational misfortune. While this is not to suggest that Finland is taking advantage of its enviable position in the world educational rankings, the considerable attention that Finland has received and the advice sought have led to partnerships worldwide. EduCluster (2013), for example, is a Finnish organisation that, through collaboration and partnerships with participating countries, provides services to help achieve "educational excellence" in conjunction with "Finnish experts." This includes guidance with education reform, professional development and training, quality assurance, skills development, and insights into Finnish education. These collaborations have occurred in Asia, the Middle East, Europe, Africa, and South America. Could this mean that educational export will become Finland's next big industry? Could this also mean that these collaborations and partnerships indicate that some informed policy transfer, or policy learning can, and has, occurred?

This chapter has suggested earlier that Finnish and English education policy have been moving in opposite directions for some time. This book adds to the assertions of Webb et al. (1998) by arguing that the implementation of free schools and academies within the English education system has added to this. The differentiation of compulsory education, much like the curriculum policy, school inspections, and teacher education, also travels further from the Finnish education ethos. Finnish children have one route for school until the age of 16. All pupils must attend the compulsory school. In England, however, pupils have the option of the private system, free schools, academies, state schools, and faith schools. While faith schools, state schools, and the private school system have existed for some time, the academies and free schools are relatively new additions. Furthermore, the academies started as a policy in order to tackle "failing" secondary schools under the Labour administration as city academies in 2000, and academies in 2002 with support from sponsors. The coalition of the Liberal Democrats and the Conservative parties, beginning in 2010, transformed the academies as all publically-funded schools had the possibility to convert into an academy. Also in contrast to the previous Labour administration, the coalition government encouraged top-performing schools in OFSTED inspections to convert to academy status and mentor poorer-performing schools. Free schools, first opened in 2011, are essentially academies set up by parents, teachers, or charitable organisations. The various pathways that compulsory education in England possesses illustrate the diverse and wide-ranging options for English pupils.

Similarly, as stated previously, the 2010 White Paper outlines reforms to the teacher education system, both changing and diversifying the routes into teaching. Interestingly, though, much like compulsory education for Finnish pupils, there is only one route into teaching in Finland. One could argue that the constant changes within the English education system, whether for compulsory education or teacher training, also move in the opposite direction from the Finnish "continuity and change" mantra. While the English system has long had multiple routes for both compulsory education and teacher training, the Finnish system adheres to the egalitarian view of one pathway for all. One could also view England's multiple routes to teaching and compulsory education as part of the educational "ecosystem" (Kemmis & Heikkinen, 2012, p. 157) of the country, suggesting this approach is not necessarily detrimental to the education system overall. On the other hand, this approach could epitomise the incoherence and lack of focus that the English education system now possesses. Therefore, this adds to the argument that the compulsory education system in England follows the pattern of the MTL, along with the proposed changes to teacher education, succumbing to too much change and a lack of continuity.

The PISA 2012 results, released in December of 2013, showed a decline in the Finnish results. The main focus of this survey, mathematical literacy, showed that Finland had slipped in the rankings, although maintaining mean score higher than the OECD average (OECD, 2013b). This survey, which involved 65 countries and economies, saw Finland ranked 12th in mathematical literacy, behind Shanghai-China, Singapore, Hong Kong, Taiwan, South Korea, Macau, Japan, Lichtenstein, Switzerland, The Netherlands, and Estonia. However, in reading literacy, Finland ranked 6th out of the 65 countries, behind Shanghai-China, Hong Kong, Singapore, Japan, and South Korea. In scientific literacy, Finland ranked 5th, behind Shanghai-China, Hong Kong, Singapore, and Japan. While the press (e.g. Coughlan, 2013) largely focused on the East Asian countries' top outcomes in the 2012 survey, the Finnish decline in the survey brings up some interesting issues. While empirical research on the matter would take some time, initial reaction from Finnish academics speculate that the increase of immigration between the initial PISA survey from 2000 to the 2012 administration explains the slight decline in mean scores (Bernelius, 2013).

Thus, the PISA results from 2000 juxtaposed with the 2012 and 2015 outcomes, and any future PISA testing, such as the 2018 survey, provide an interesting and valuable case study from which to evaluate the role of immigration within Finnish society, and also educational outcome. Finnish could also provide another valuable case study from which to observe the trends in educational interest. In the 1980s, much interest circulated on the Japanese education system, and related to this, the economic success of the country (e.g. Gruber, 1989; Tobin et al., 2009). This interest, however, declined with the decline in the Japanese economy. The PISA 2012 results show an increased interest in the East Asian countries due to the high outcomes in the survey. While the press, as stated previously, demonstrated much interest in these countries after the release of the PISA 2012 scores, this illustrates the uncritical eye in which people view PISA and other test results. The East Asian education systems exist in a much different "ecosystem" (Kemmis & Heikkinen, 2012, p. 157) to the Western and European context. Even with the slight decline, interest in Finland is still valid, perhaps along with rising European performers such as Estonia and Poland, or the North American top-performer, Canada.

Education in the 21st century has been transformed by international testing, and the politicisation of education and education policy has instigated a paradigm shift. Education no longer exists for the cultivation of the individual; instead, education contributes to human capital and the labour market. The expansion of the OECD's educational testing with PIACC and AHELO only indicates this will continue throughout the rest of the century. The case of Finland, while showing a slight decline starting with the 2012 PISA survey, provides an interesting case study from which to view a high-performing country in an international achievement study, but somehow avoiding the GERM symptoms so prevalent in other education systems, especially those with high outcomes in PISA but maintaining this with particularly virulent strains of GERM. Future PISA results will, no doubt, provide fodder for educational debate and dialogue for years to come.

7   Summary

The temptation of, and interest in, policy transfer have seemingly increased since the advent of PISA. PISA also contributes to feelings of educational inferiority, which adds to this lure to borrow policy. However, as discussed previously in this book, policy transfer is a difficult process, and theorists still stress the importance of context when utilising foreign models for education reform. Limitations always exist when borrowing policy, and comparativists have long warned about the difficulty in successful policy transfer. Informed policy transfer is difficult, but can occur, such as in the London borough of Barking and

Dagenham, but with careful consideration of context and "responsible scholarship." Nevertheless, many attempts at "looking elsewhere" seems to lead to "quick fix" and "phony" policy solutions, illustrating the politicisation of education and international achievement studies.

This politicisation of PISA shows the influences the survey has on educational reform. These influences drive reforms which often base themselves, uncritically, on PISA. This chapter has highlighted examples from France, Canada, Switzerland, and Norway, in addition to Germany and Japan. German PISA-Shock, a now classic form of "negative external evaluation," saw PISA triggering a huge impact on German education policy, changing the education system's focus from inputs to outputs, and from *Bildung* to a measurable form of education. PISA also influenced reform debates in the country, stemming from political necessity, not informed analysis of the PISA data. In other words, standing in the international "league tables" now influences a nation's education policy and educational future.

This chapter also discussed a Japanese PISA-Shock as well, as both the media and politicians exploit the PISA data in order to facilitate sour feelings toward the education system and policy change. This Japanese PISA-Shock saw the uncritical transfer of Finnish education policy, with the use of textbooks based on Finnish counterparts, teaching by Finnish "methods," and by creating a Finnish "hero" image. This uncritical transfer is known as the "Finlandisation Phenomenon." The use of Finland's "methods" also indicates uncritical acceptance of the merits of the Finnish education system, now an uncontested truth. Finland fuelled these "phony" and "quick fix" changes in Japan, giving education policy makers and teachers a false sense of security.

England, also, used the Finnish example to drive education reform. The Master's of Teaching and Learning, or MTL, was to align English teacher education to that of Finland's. The funding of the government-funded MTL was withdrawn, although the MTL still exists if students wish to pay fees. This does not adhere to the "continuity and change" approach the Finns have to education reform. Furthermore, policies in the two countries have curiously moved away from each other in ideology and structure, indicating divergent policy decision-making and goals. This divergence also includes teaching philosophy and practice. Therefore, the MTL could be seen as a "quick fix" and "phony" policy solution, and borrowed in an uncritical manner.

The 2010 White Paper in England also exemplifies another case of major policy borrowing from Finland. The policy paper suggested initiating "university training schools" based on the Finnish model of teaching practice. However, it also suggested more school-based routes into teaching, drawing away from the university element of teacher preparation in England. Thus, Finland views teacher preparation as an education for a profession; in contrast, England views teacher preparation as training, getting ready for a vocation. The differing "ecosystems" of Finland and England show how the university training school may be transferred to a hostile "environment." The "pick 'n' mix" (Morris, 2012, p. 89) nature of the 2010 White Paper illustrates how PISA both drives politically-motivated education reform, and politicians use education as fodder to blame opposing parties.

The politicisation of international assessments such as PISA has suggested that a paradigm shift of education and education policy has occurred. Education has become increasingly political, and the new surveys from the OECD, PIACC and AHELO, only add to this. PISA changed Finland, not only with PISA tourism, but also because Finns now increasingly view education as an export product. Looking at the future of education, it seems that England continues to shift its education policy away from the Finnish model. England's education policy now encourages the initiation of free schools and prompts state schools to switch to academy status. Finnish pupils have one route through compulsory education. Similar to this, future teachers in England have a range of options from which to choose. Conversely, in Finland, pupils have only one route through compulsory education and through teacher education. Interestingly, however, the 2012 and 2015 PISA scores showed a slight decline in the Finnish results. What does this mean for the future of Finnish education, at least from the outside perspective? Finland still provides an interesting case study of a Western country with high educational outcome, achieving these results without the influence of GERM. Furthermore, Finland offers an interesting case study through which to observe educational trends throughout the 21st century.

The writings of comparativists over time, such as Sadler, Noah, Phillips, and Crossley, warn of education systems' deep roots within a country's context. However, Kamens and McNeely (2009) argue that if nations are perceived as truly unique, then international testing would not be viable. The birth of international achievement studies with the IEA perhaps changed this view, even though some viewed the IEA assessments as an exploration into the differences between the education systems in different countries. However, since the late 1960s, according to Kamens and McNeely, a change has occurred, and international testing "no longer seem[s] like a case of comparing apples to oranges" (2009, p. 8). This change in perspective, along with the growth in international assessments and their political use, denotes a shift in the view of education. While Sadler and subsequent comparativists warn of the importance of educational context and difficulty in policy transfer, the politicisation of cross-national assessments shows how education is widely viewed in isolation. This has led to educational reforms fuelled by political agendas and uncritical policy borrowing. This paradigm shift, therefore, holds many dangers. If education is perceived in this manner, then international assessments such as PISA will become even more politicised, and even more uncritical transfer will occur. PISA, the league tables it generates, and the potential policy borrowing from Finland could significantly contribute to "globally influential policy agendas" (Crossley & Watson, 2009, p. 643).

Conclusion

PISA has caused a paradigm shift in education, and Finland's consistent top performance in the survey has garnered much interest from education policy makers looking to improve their home education systems. Therefore, this book explored the reasons behind Finland's success in PISA, issues in policy transfer, and the new context of education policy, now very much influenced by international assessments and the global league tables they produce. While most of the strengths of Finnish education outlined in this book relate to very contextual factors, policy makers still very much want to emulate the Finnish education system, even though comparative education theory warns about the difficulty of this. The Finnish respondents who contributed to the data in this book warned against the copying and borrowing of Finnish education policy, as they also spoke of the interlinked relationship between education and Finnish context. Nevertheless, the new, global context of education policy making serves as a catalyst for uncritical policy transfer, decisions made under political pressure or for political influence. International assessments such as PISA and the league tables they generate illustrate the politicisation of education and educational testing.

The case of Finland in PISA raises many issues in different realms of education. Comparativists over the years have discussed at length the dangers of uncritical policy transfer. Nevertheless, policy borrowing has existed for centuries. Japan has borrowed its current education system from the West, and Japan has garnered "cross-national attraction" from many a country due to its success in education and industry. However, the advent of international studies of achievement, especially PISA, has magnified the appeal of policy borrowing, especially in the case of Finland. The seductive nature of Finland's PISA scores and its education system has become very alluring in terms of policy borrowing; however, we still must heed the warnings of these comparativists about the dangers of uncritical policy transfer.

One must wonder what will happen if Finland keeps up its consistently high performance in future PISA results. While Finland's recent PISA scores declined slightly, Finland still remained a top performer from a Western context, undoubtedly maintaining high interest from both Western and Eastern contexts, keeping high levels of cross-national attraction and making the Finnish model just as, or even more tempting to borrow. Will countries sensitively borrow from Finland, properly indigenised to the home context, or will the lure of Finnish PISA success supersede the warnings of these comparativists? This book has shown that global factors now affect education policy. Surveys such as PISA have created a global standardisation of education, and they have reinforced the relationship between education and economics. Global competitiveness adds to this. All of this intensifies the temptation to borrow policy in an uncritical manner.

After all of the accolades, one must wonder if Finland should really serve as a model of education for the entire world. Obviously, the findings in this book as well as the PISA data more than demonstrate the strength and success of the education system. However, is this "Finlandisation phenomenon" (Takayama, 2009, p. 52) really just? Takayama cites how, in Japan, there exists no real critical analysis of the OECD and Finnish education. While much criticism circles around the Japanese education system, this critical eye does not apply to that of Finland. This uncritical acceptance of heroic foreign examples simply ignores the literature questioning the "Finland phenomenon" (ibid., p. 64). Takayama argues that research shows a lack of confidence within Finland of the Finnish government's "uncritical conformity" to the OECD and the possibly negative effect the marketisation of Finnish education has had on their egalitarian, consistent system.

Simola et al. (2002) cite how after the Finnish economic crash of the 1990s, a shift to the right occurred within Finnish politics, with general consensus. This economic depression spurred a reconstruction of the Finnish Welfare State into one that acknowledged the globalised world and the necessity of a market economy dictated by international organisations such as the OECD and the World Bank. Simola et al. argue that education policy also shifted to the right, resulting in a "hidden education policy" based on market values and free choice (ibid., p. 249). They state how even Finland succumbed to globalisation. The connection between education and economics is also apparent to the Finns, and the importance of economic competitiveness and a productive labour market also has become an important component of Finnish education. However, these changes brought about a danger of inequality within the Finnish education system, one that valued egalitarian values very strongly. These market values stressed individualism, which Simola et al. predicted would deem some students "winners" or "losers," most probably relating to social class and parental education (ibid., p. 252).

Simola et al. (2002) cite how the decentralisation of Finnish education led to regional inequality, which contradicts OECD data and general consensus about Finnish education. Admittedly, this inequality may be on a much smaller scale than in other countries, but does bring up how observers of Finnish education do not cast a critical eye on the information given as suggested by Takayama (2009). Curiously, this managerialist view of education was encouraged by the OECD in 1995, even before the creation of PISA. They promoted decentralisation of the public sector, with stress on performance. This leads to a focus on results and targets. Simola et al. refer to "hardening competition and strengthening divisions in Finnish society in the last decade" (ibid., p. 256). They refer to a competition and divisions in Finnish society as well, which may not be apparent in other literature pertaining to Finnish education. Even the heralded Finnish teacher does not have immunity to these pressures. Simola et al. state that teachers show signs of "exhaustion, frustration and pessimism" amongst the "increasing pressure and a more hectic pace" of their profession (ibid., p. 257). They uncover how even a Finnish teacher's work has changed direction, from the teaching and learning concerned with a student's growth to a "public performance" (ibid., p. 258). Teachers also feel the pressure of top-down reforms and governance. These characteristics mentioned by Simola et al. are much more reminiscent of countries such as the UK, those with high-stakes testing and external accountability. The argument presented by these authors illustrates the lack of criticality, also mentioned by Takayama (2009), when it comes to viewing the Finnish education system.

The use of "heroic foreign examples" (Takayama, 2009, p. 63) in Japanese educational reform and the uncritical acceptance of the Finnish example also illustrate the interest in Finland even from high-performing countries in PISA. However, as we can see, the arguments of Simola et al. show that criticisms of the Finnish system do exist. These are even more poignant after the release of the PISA scores since 2012. Furthermore, Takayama states, "The shift in Finnish education discourse has had tangible consequences. For example, managerialisation of teachers' work, less regulated school choice, and quasi-market, standardised-test-based accountability are increasingly felt by Finnish students [...] and teachers" (2009, p. 65). The suggested decline in Finnish education is not taken into account when looking for educational models; for example, "Japanese progressive observers exclude these critical studies from their narrative of Finnish success" (ibid.). Therefore, an uncontested truth forms the basis for educational reform. This trend in Japanese education policy shows the possibility of a worrying trend, one that comparative education theorists have warned about. This uncritical view of education policy and risk of uncritically informed education policy borrowing indicates "quick fix" and "phony" solutions are indeed being used by politicians and education policy makers.

Takayama (2009) writes how the Japanese use Finland to suit the political agendas in the country. The Finnish model of education has become a powerful authority for Japanese education reform. This illustrates how the Japanese, and no doubt most countries in the world, have idealised Finland for its educational prowess, as indicated by PISA. Idealising a country and its education system in this way overlooks the importance of the local and national factors. This has become obscured due to globalisation and a shift of power to the international level. Takayama argues that this gives politicians and policy makers a "false sense of certainty about future reform directions fabricated through such comparison" (ibid., p. 69).

Takayama (2009) and Simola et al.'s (2002) contributions to comparative education literature illustrate the disconnect between theory, practice, and policy. This book especially highlights the need for a closer relationship between comparative education theory and policy, as comparativists have long warned about the problematic nature of and difficulty in transferring education policy. However, as Takayama shows, politicians and education policy makers have been using the Finnish model to fuel political agendas. Furthermore, this occurs without full investigation and critical analysis of the outside system, in this case that of Finland. Simola et al. illustrate that even a high-achieving, high-performing education system has its problems. Even the Finnish education system, based on egalitarian values and grounded in a Welfare State, faces similar challenges due to accountability, pressures on the teaching profession, and global influences. The connection between educational theory, policy, and practice increases due to the new global influence on education policy. PISA and the results it generates have added to the politicisation of education and of testing.

As the influence of multi-national agencies on education policy increases, will the power and authority of these agencies affect education policy and structure? The authority of the OECD and the influence of PISA have created, in essence, international high-stakes testing and international league tables. This raises the question of how countries will cope with the pressure to perform well. Will countries try to emulate, by policy transfer, the education systems of internationally successful countries? Will this eventually create an educational policy convergence, with countries having similar educational structure? Will similar educational structure produce comparable results?

While education systems can make structural changes and reforms, a country cannot implement another country's cultural, social, political, and historical context. Countries can learn from the Finnish example, but only if the policy is sensitively implemented into the context of the "borrowing" country. Since the time of Sadler, the late nineteenth and early twentieth centuries, comparativists have been calling for the sensitivity to culture and context when considering education systems and warning of the dangers of uncritical policy transfer.

These aforementioned warnings of comparativists highlight the importance of improved understanding of the nature, role, and impact of international

CONCLUSION

studies of achievement, the importance of more critical analyses of the results of such studies and the implications of the success of countries such as Finland. Furthermore, words of caution also come from educationalists and other academics about the policy and political implications of international assessments such as PISA, the role of these international league tables, and the role of multi-lateral agencies such as the OECD.

Global factors are now affecting education policy. Policy makers at a national level are under pressure to follow global prescriptions. These assessments, which are essentially experiments, are changing policy. Blindly following "successful" policies, such as in Finland, may be much more problematic than many realise. This can lead to new phenomena of uncritical international policy transfer and policy convergence.

APPENDIX

List of Participants

[Note: Identifying features have been removed. Teachers and head teachers have first names only. Ministers, professors, and OECD officials are all pseudonyms]

Teachers

Name	Sex	Subjects taught	Years of experience (at time of interview)
Linda	Female	Swedish	4
Hans	Male	Physics, Mathematics	36
Aino	Female	Biology, Geography	25
Saija	Female	Finnish	1
Jukka S.	Male	Mathematics	30
Benny	Male	Mathematics, Physics, Chemistry	5
Sanna	Female	Swedish	3
Krister	Male	Mathematics, Physics, Chemistry	25
Jukka E.	Male	Finnish	7
Maarit	Female	Mathematics, Physics, Chemistry	10
Toni	Male	Mathematics, Physics, Chemistry	3
Christer	Male	Biology, Geography	26
Pia	Female	Swedish	19
Jonny	Male	Mathematics	1
Miikka	Male	Finnish	20
Terttu	Female	Chemistry, Mathematics	17

Head Teachers

Name	Sex	Former teaching subject	Years as head teacher (at time of interview)
Magnus	Male	History, Social Studies	1
Pentti	Male	Mathematics, Physics, Chemistry, Information Technology	15
Elvi	Female	History	7
Kalevi	Male	Gym	10
Mai-Len	Female	Special Needs	5
Seppo	Male	Mathematics, Physics, Chemistry	11

Education Professors

Name	Sex	Area of Specialism
Professor Virtanen	Male	Director Emeritus, Finnish Institute for Educational Research
Professor Laukkanen	Female	Reading Literacy, Large-scale International Assessment
Professor Karpinen	Male	Mathematics, Large-scale International Assessment
Professor Rantanen	Male	Science, Large-scale International Assessment
Professor Huttunen	Male	Educational Assessment, Special Education
Professor Koivula	Female	Educational Assessment, Education Policy
Professor Sundqvist	Male	Educational Assessment, Behavioural Sciences
Professor Kallio	Male	Teacher Education

Education Ministers

Name	Sex	Tenure as Minister of Education	Field of study
Minister Jussila	Male	2001-2006	Sociology of Education
Minister Halonen	Male	1994-1999	Law

APPENDIX: LIST OF PARTICIPANTS

OECD Officers

Surname	Gender	Role at the OECD
Schroeder	Male	Head of Indicators and Analysis Division
Chadwick	Male	Manager of PISA globally
Chevalier	Male	Finance expert for Education at a Glance
Khan	Male	Head of the education training policy division at the OECD's education directorate

References

Adams, R. J. (2003). Response to 'cautions on OECD's recent educational survey (PISA).' *Oxford Review of Education, 29*(3), 377–389.

Angus, L. (1993). The sociology of school effectiveness. *British Journal of Sociology of Education, 14*(3), 333–345.

Antikainen, A. (1990). The rise and change of comprehensive planning: The Finnish experience. *European Journal of Education, 25*(1), 75–82.

Antikainen, A. (2010). The capitalist state and education: The case of restructuring the Nordic Model. *Current Sociology, 58*(4), 530–550.

Auld, E., & Morris, P. (2014). Comparative education, the 'new paradigm' and policy borrowing: Constructing knowledge for educational reform. *Comparative Education, 50*(2), 129–155.

Back to school: Some remedial lessons are needed for European leaders. (2006, March 23). *The Economist.* Retrieved September 6, 2007, from https://www.economist.com/europe/2006/03/23/back-to-school

Bacon, W. (1970). *Finland.* London: Robert Hale & Company.

Baird, J., Isaacs, T., Johnson, S., Stobart, G., Yu, G., Sprague, T., & Daugherty, P. (2011). *Policy effects of PISA.* Oxford: Oxford University Centre for Educational Assessment. Retrieved from http://oucea.education.ox.ac.uk/wordpress/wp-content/uploads/2011/10/Policy-Effects-of-PISA-OUCEA.pdf

Beech, J. (2006). The theme of educational transfer in comparative education: A view over time. *Research in Comparative and International Education, 1*(1), 2–13.

Begrem, T., Björkqvist, O., Hansén, S., Carlgren, I., & Hauge, T. E. (1997). Research on teachers and teacher education in Scandinavia: A retrospective review. *Scandinavian Journal of Educational Research, 41*(3–4), 433–458.

Bereday, G. Z. F. (1964). *Comparative method in education.* New York, NY: Holt, Reinehart and Winston, Inc.

Bernelius, V. (2013, December 3). *School and society – The relationship between learning results and social segregation.* Invited lecture at Finnish Ambassador's residence, for PISA and the Future of the Finnish Education System, London.

Binham, P. (1968). The young and their education. In S. Nickels, H. Kallas, & P. Friedman (Eds.), *Finland, an introduction* (pp. 156–167). London: George Allen & Unwin Ltd.

Bonderup Dohn, N. (2007). Knowledge and skills for PISA – Assessing the assessment. In *Journal of Philosophy of Education, 41*(1), 1–16.

Chislett, W. (1996). *Finland: A coming of age.* London: Euromoney Publications PLC.

Chung, J. (2009). *An investigation of reasons for Finland's success in PISA* (Doctoral dissertation). University of Oxford, Oxford.

Chung, J., Atkin, C., & Moore, J. (2012). The rise and fall of the MTL: An example of European policy borrowing. *European Journal of Teacher Education, 35*(3), 259–274.

Coe, R., & Fitz-Gibbon, C. T. (1998). School effectiveness research: Criticisms and recommendations. *Oxford Review of Education, 24*(4), 421–438.

Coughlan, S. (2013, December 3). *PISA tests: UK stagnates as Shanghai tops league table.* Retrieved June 4, 2014, from http://www.bbc.co.uk/news/education-25187997

Cowan, R. (2006). Acting comparatively upon the educational world: Puzzles and possibilities. *Oxford Review of Education, 32*(5), 561–573.

Crossley, M., & Vulliamy, G. (1984). Case study research methods and comparative education. *Comparative Education, 20*(2), 193–207.

Crossley, M., & Watson, K. (2009). Comparative and international education: Policy transfer, context sensitivity and professional development. *Oxford Review of Education, 35*(5), 633–649.

Cummings, W. K. (1989). The American perception of Japanese education. *Comparative Education, 25*(3), 293–302.

Dale, R. (2000). Globalization and education: Demonstrating a "common world educational culture" or locating a "globally structured educational agenda?." *Educational Theory, 50*(4), 427–448.

Department for Children, Schools and Families (DCSF). (2008). *Being the best for our children*. London: DCSF.

Department for Education. (2010). *The importance of teaching: The schools white paper 2010*. London: Crown Copyright.

Dolowitz, D. P., & Marsh, D. (2000). Learning from abroad: The role of policy transfer in contemporary policy-making. *International Journal of Policy and Administration, 31*(1), 5–24.

Duru-Bellat, M., & Suchaut, B. (2005). Organisation and context, efficiency and equity of educational systems: What PISA tells us. *European Educational Research Journal, 4*(3), 181–194.

Edmonds, R. (1979). Effective schools for the urban poor. *Educational Leadership, 37*(1), 15–34.

Education System in Finland. (n.d.). Retrieved October 19, 2005, from http://www.minedu.fi/minedu/education/general_education.html

Educational standards compared: Britain scores. *The Economist,* 6 December 2001, Retrieved April 24, 2012, from economist.com

EduCluster. (2013). *EduCluster Finland.* Retrieved December 8, 2013, from http://www.educlusterfinland.fi/en

Elstad, E. (2012). PISA debates and blame management among the Norwegian educational authorities: Press coverage and debate intensity in the newspapers. *Problems of Education in the 21st Century, 48,* 10–22.

Entorf, H., & Mioiu, N. (2004). What a difference immigration policy makes: PISA results, migration background and social mobility in europe and traditional countries of immigration. *German Economic Review, 6*(3), 355–376.

Ertl, H. (2006). Educational standards and the changing discourse on education: The reception and consequences of the PISA study in Germany. *Oxford Review of Education, 32*(5), 619–634.

Eskelinen, H. (1968). Independence and after. In S. Nickels, H. Kallas, & P. Friedman (Eds.), *Finland, an introduction* (pp. 41–60). London: George Allen & Unwin Ltd.

Esping-Andersen, G. (1990). *The three worlds of welfare capitalism*. Cambridge, MA: Polity Press.

Fagerholm, K. A. (1960). Finland in the nordic family circle. In U. Toivola (Ed.), *Introduction to Finland 1960* (pp. 69–78). Helsinki: Werner Söderström Osakeythiö.

Finnish National Board of Education. (2001). *The development of education*. Retrieved 6 November 2008, http://www.ibe.unesco.org/International/ICE/natrap/Finland.pdf#search=%22International%20bureau%20o%20of%20education%20the%20development%20of%20education%20national%20report%20of%20Finland%22

Finnish National Board of Education. (2004). *National core curriculum for basic education 2004*. Helsinki: Finnish National Board of Education.

Finnish National Board of Education. (2006). *General upper secondary education*. Retrieved November 6, 2008, from http://www.oph.fi/english/pageLast.asp?path=447,4699,4840,4845

Finnish National Board of Education. (2007). *LUMA*. Retrieved June 11, 2008, from http://www.oph.fi/english/pageLast.asp?path=447;65535;77331;77333;77340

Finnish National Board of Education. (2008). *Basic education*. Retrieved November 6, 2008, from http://www.oph.fi/english/page.asp?path=447,4699,4847; http://www.oph.fi/english/curricula_and_qualifications/basic_education

Finnish National Board of Education. (n.d.). *Education in Finland*. Helsinki, Finland.

Finnish National Board of Education. (n.d.-a). *Basic education*. Retrieved January 23, 2014.

Finnish National Board of Education. (n.d.-b). *Finnish education in a nutshell*. Retrieved January 24, 2014, from http://www.oph.fi/download/146428_Finnish_Education_in_a_Nutshell.pdf

Finnish National Board of Education. (n.d.-c). *Quality assurance in general education: Steering Instead of control*. Retrieved March 27, 2014, from http://www.oph.fi/download/148966_Quality_assurance_in_general_education.pdf

Fox, F. (1926). *Finland today*. London: A. & C. Black Ltd.

Gilmour, K. (1931). *Finland*. London: Methuem & Co. Ltd.

Goldhaber, D. D., & Brewer, D. J. (2000). Does teacher certification matter? High school teacher certification status and student achievement. *Educational Evaluation and Policy Analysis, 22*(2), 129–145.

REFERENCES

Goldstein, H. (2004a). Education for all: The globalization of learning targets. *Comparative Education, 40*(1), 7–14.

Goldstein, H. (2004b). International comparisons of student attainment: Some issues arising from the PISA study. *Assessment in Education, 11*(3), 319–330.

Gorard, S., & Smith, E. (2004). An international comparison of equity in education systems. *Comparative Education, 40*(1), 15–28.

Gove, M. (2010, December 17). Pisa slip should put a rocket under our world-class ambitions and drive us to win the education space race. *Times Education Supplement.* Retrieved June 4, 2014, from http://www.tes.co.uk/article.aspx?storycode=6066185

Grek, S., Lawn, M., Lingard, B., Ozga, J., Rinne, R., Segerholm, C., & Simola, H. (2009). National policy brokering and the construction of the European education space in England, Sweden, Finland and Scotland. *Comparative Education, 45*(1), 5–21.

Grisay, A., & Monseur, C. (2007). Measuring the equivalence of item difficulty in the various versions of an international test. *Studies in Educational Evaluation, 33*, 69–86.

Gruber, K. H. (1989). Note of failure to appreciate British primary education in Germany and Austria. *Comparative Education, 25*(3), 363–364.

Gruber, K. H. (2006). The impact of PISA on the German education system. In H. Ertl (Ed.), *Cross-national attraction in education: Accounts from England and Germany* (pp. 195–208). Oxford: Symposium Books.

Hall, W. (1967). *The finns and their country.* London: Max Parrish & Co.

Halls, W. D. (1970). Present difficulties in educational reform: Some points of comparision. In C. Fuhr (Ed.), *Educational reform in the federal republic of Germany.* Paris: UNESCO.

Halpin, D., & Troyna, B. (1995). The politics of education policy borrowing. *Comparative Education, 31*(3), 303–310.

Helsingin Sanomat. (2002, May 22). *Germans join queue examining Finnish schools system.* Retrieved September 20, 2007, from http://www2.hs.fi/english/archive/news.asp?id=20020522IE7

Herranen, M. (1995). Finland. In T. N. Postlethwaite (Ed.), *International encyclopedia of National systems of education.* Cambridge: Pergamon Press.

Higginson, J. H. (1979). *Selections from Michael Sadler.* Liverpool: Dejall & Meyorre.

Hiilamo, H. (2012). Rethinking the role of church in a socio-democratic welfare state. *International Journal of Sociology and Social Policy, 32*(7–8), 401–414.

Ichikawa, S. (1989). Japanese education in American eyes: A response to William K. Cummings. *Comparative Education, 25*(3), 303–307.

In Praise of Finland: What the European Union should learn from its New President. (2006, July 6). *The Economist.* Retrieved September 6, 2007, from https://www.economist.com/europe/2006/07/06/in-praise-of-finland

International Association for the Evaluation of Educational Achievement. (n.d.). Retrieved February 12, 2008, from http://www.iea.nl/

Jacobson, M. (1987). *Finland, myth and reality*. Helsinki: Otava.

Jakobi, A. P. (2009). Global education policy in the making: International organisations and lifelong learning. *Globalisation, Societies and Education, 7*(4), 473–487.

Jensen, C. (2011). Determinants of welfare service provision after the golden age. *International Journal of Social Welfare, 20*(2), 125–134.

Juva, M. (1968). A thousand years in Finland. In S. Nickels, H. Kallas, & P. Friedman (Eds.), *Finland, an introduction* (pp. 17–36). London: George Allen & Unwin Ltd.

Jyrhämä, R., Kynäslahti, H., Krokfors, L., Byman, R., Maaranen, K., Toom, A., & Kansanen, P. (2008). The appreciation and realization of research-based teacher education: Finnish students' experiences of teacher education. *European Journal of Teacher Education, 31*(1), 1–16.

Kamens, D. H., & McNeely, C. L. (2009). Globalization and the growth of international educational testing and National assessment. *Comparative Education Review, 54*(1), 5–25.

Kandel, I. (1933). *Studies in comparative education*. London: George G. Harrap and Company Ltd.

Kemmis, S., & Heikkinen, H. L. T. (2012). Future perspectives: Peer-group mentoring and international practices for teacher development. In H. L. T. Heikkinen, H. Jokinen, & P. Tynjälä (Eds.), *Peer-group mentoring for teacher development* (pp. 144–170). London: Routledge.

King, K. (2007). Multilateral agencies in the construction of the global agenda on education. *Comparative Education, 43*(3), 377–392.

Kirby, D. (2006). *A concise history of Finland*. Cambridge: Cambridge University Press.

Kivinen, O., & Rinne, R. (1994). The thirst for learning, or protecting one's Niche? The shaping of teacher training in Finland during the 19th and 20th centuries. *British Journal of Sociology of Education, 15*(4), 515–527.

Krokfors, L., Jyrhämä, R., Kynäslahti, H., Toom, A., Maaranen, K., & Kansanen, P. (2006). Working while teaching, learning while working: Students teaching in their own class. *Journal of Education for Teaching, 32*(1), 21–36.

Kuisma, M. (2007). Social democratic internationalism and the welfare state after the 'golden age.' *Cooperation and Conflict, 42*(1), 9–26.

Laine, J. (2011). *Parliamentarism*. Retrieved March 20, 2014, from http://finland.fi/Public/default.aspx?contentid=160051&nodeid=41805&culture=en-US

Lie, S., & Linnakylä, P. (2004). Nordic PISA 2000 in a sociocultural perspective. *Scandinavian Journal of Educational Research, 48*(3), 227–230.

Liiten, M. (2004, February 11). Ykkössuosikki: Opettajan Ammatti. *Helsingin Sanomat*. Retrieved February 15, 2008, from http://www.hs.fi/artikkeli/Ykkössuosikki+opettajan+ammatti/1076151893860

REFERENCES   227

Lehtonen, M. (2016). 'What's going on?' in Finland: Employing stuart hall for a conjunctural analysis. *International Journal of Cultural Studies, 19*(1), 71–84.

Louhivouri, J. (1968). The church and education. In H. Kallas & S. Nickels (Eds.), *Finland: Creation and construction* (pp. 176–177). London: George Allen and Unwin Ltd.

Lundahl, L. (2016). Equality, inclusion and marketization of Nordic education: Introductory notes. *Research in Comparative and International Education, 11*(1), 3–12.

Lyne, J. (2001). *Who's No. 1? Finland, Japan, and Korea, says an OECD education study.* Retrieved from October 24, 2005, from http://www.conway.com/ssinsider/snapshot/sf011210.htm

Mallinson, V. (1957). *An introduction to the study of comparative education.* London: William Heinemann Ltd.

Meuret, D. (2006). Equity and efficiency of compulsory schooling: Is it necessary to choose and if so on what grounds? *Prospects, XXXVI*(4), 389–410.

Ministry of Education, Finland. (2005). Retrieved October 24, 2005, from http://www.minedu.fi/minedu/

Ministry of Education. (n.d.-a). *Administration in education.* Retrieved November 6, 2008, from http://www.minedu.fi/OPM/Koulutus/koulutusjaerjestelmae/koulutuksen_hallinto_ja_paeaetoeksenteko/?lang=en

Ministry of Education. (n.d.-b). *Administration and finance.* Retrieved 6 November 6, 2008, from http://www.minedu.fi/OPM/Koulutus/ammattikorkeakoulutus/hallinto_ohjaus_ja_rahoitus/?lang=en

Ministry of Education. (n.d.-c). *Studies and degrees.* Retrieved November 6, 2008, http://www.minedu.fi/OPM/Koulutus/ammattikorkeakoulutus/opiskelu_ja_tutkinnot/?lang=en

Morris, P. (2012). Pick 'n' mix, select and project; Policy borrowing and the quest for 'world class' schooling: An analysis of the 2010 schools white paper. *Journal of Education Policy, 27*(1), 89–107.

Moutsios, S. (2009). International organisations and transnational education policy. In *Compare, 39*(4), 467–478.

Moutsios, S. (2010). Power, politics and transnational policy-making in education. *Globalisation, Societies and Education, 8*(1), 121–141.

National LUMA Centre. (2005). Retrieved June 12, 2008, from http://www.helsinki.fi/luma/english/

Neumann, K., Fischer, H. E., & Kauertz, A. (2010). From PISA to educational standards: The impact of large-scale assessments on science education in Germany. *International Journal of Science and Mathematics Education, 8*, 545–563.

Niiniluoto, Y. (1960). Finland – An introduction. In U. Toivola (Ed.), *Introduction to Finland 1960* (pp. 11–16). Helsinki: Werner Söderström Osakeythiö.

Noah, H. J. (1984). The use and abuse of comparative education. *Comparative Education Review, 28*(4), 550–562.

Nordenskiöld, E. (1919). Finland: The land and people. *Geographical Review, 7*(6), 361–376.

Nurmi, V. (1990). Education in Finland. *International Journal of Educational Management, 4*(2), 27–32.

Ochs, K. (2006). Cross-national policy borrowing and educational innovation: Improving achievement in the London Borough of Barking and Dagenham. *Oxford Review of Education, 32*(5), 599–618.

Ochs, K., & Phillilps, D. (2002a). *Towards a structural typology of cross-national attraction in education* (pp. 1–43). Lisbon: Educa.

Ochs, K., & Phillips, D. (2002b). Comparative studies and 'cross-national attraction' in education: A typology for the analysis of English interest in educational policy and provision in Germany. *Educational Studies, 28*(4), 325–339.

Ochs, K., & Phillips, D. (2004). Processes of educational borrowing in a historical context. In K. Ochs & D. Phillips (Eds.), *Educational policy borrowing: Historical perspectives* (pp. 7–23). Oxford: Symposium Books.

OECD. (2001). *Knowledge and skills for life: First results from the OECD Programme for International Student Assessment (PISA)*. Paris: OECD.

OECD. (2004a). *Messages from PISA 2000*. Paris: OECD.

OECD. (2004b). *Problem solving for tomorrow's world: First measures of cross-curricular competencies from PISA 2003*. Paris: OECD.

OECD. (2007). *PISA 2006: Science competencies for tomorrow's world: Executive summary*. Paris: OECD.

OECD. (2010). *PISA 2009 results: What students know and can do – Student performance in reading, mathematics and science* (Vol. 1). Paris: OECD.

OECD. (2013a). *OECD skills outlook 2013: First results from the survey of adult skills*. Paris: OECD.

OECD. (2013b). *PISA 2012 results in focus: What 15-year-olds know and what they can do with what they know*. Paris: OECD.

OECD. (2014). *Testing student and university performance globally: OECD's AHELO*. Retrieved March 20, 2014, from http://www.oecd.org/ahelo

OECD. (n.d.-a). *PISA – The OECD programme for international student assessment*. Paris: OECD. Retrieved June 17, 2007, from http://www.oecd.org/dataoecd/51/27/37474503.pdf

OECD. (n.d.-b). *About OECD*. Retrieved November 7, 2005, from http://www.oecd.org/about/0,2337,en_2649_201185_1_1_1_1_1,00.html

OECD. (n.d.-c). *FAQ: OECD PISA*. Retrieved August 9, 2007, from http://www.oecd.org/document/53/0,3343,en_32252351_32235731_38262901_1_1_1_1,00.html

OECD: Finnish education highly efficient. 18 September 2007, Retrieved September 20, 20007, from http://www.yle.fi/news/id70076.html

OECD study: Finnish school system efficient. (2002, October 30). *Helsingin Sanomat*. Retrieved September 20, 2007, from http://www2.hs.fi/english/archive/news.asp?id=20021030IE5

REFERENCES

Palaiologou, I. (2010). Policy context in England in the implementation of the early years foundation stage. In I. Palaiologou (Ed.), *The early years foundation stage: Theory and practice* (pp. 3–18). London: Sage Publications.

Paulston, R. G. (1977). Separate education as an ethnic survival strategy: The Finlandssvenska case. *Anthropology & Education Quarterly, 8*(3), 181–188.

Phillips, D. (1989). Neither a borrower nor a lender be? The problems of cross-national attraction in education. *Comparative Education, 25*(3), 267–274.

Phillips, D. (2000a). Beyond travellers' tales: Some nineteenth-century british commentators on education in Germany. *Oxford Review of Education, 26*(1), 49–62.

Phillips, D. (2000b). Learning from elsewhere in education: Some perennial problems revisited with reference to British interest in Germany. *Comparative Education, 36*(3), 297–307.

Phillips, D. (2006). Investigating policy attraction in education. *Oxford Review of Education, 32*(5), 551–559.

Phillips, D., & Ochs, K. (2003). Processes of policy borrowing in education: Some explanatory and analytical devices. *Comparative Education, 39*(4), 1–14.

Phillips, D., & Ochs, K. (2004). Researching policy borrowing: Some methodological challenges in comparative education. *British Educational Research Journal, 30*(6), 773–784.

Phillips, D., & Schweisfurth, M. (2006). *Comparative and international education: An introduction to theory, method and practice.* Trowbridge: The Cromwell Press.

Pollard, A. (1989). British primary education: Response to Karl Heinz Gruber. *Comparative Education, 25*(3), 365–367.

Pongratz, L. A. (2006). Voluntary self-control: Education reform as a governmental strategy. *Education Philosophy and Theory, 38*(4), 471–482.

Prais, S. J. (2003). Cautions on OECD's recent educational survey (PISA). *Oxford Review of Education, 29*(2), 139–163.

Prais, S. J. (2004). Cautions on OECD's recent educational survey (PISA): Rejoinder to OECD's response. *Oxford Review of Education, 30*(4), 569–573.

Raiker, A. (2011). *Finnish university training schools: Principles and pedagogy.* Retrieved from http://www.beds.ac.uk/__data/assets/pdf_file/0003/83433/finnishmodel-110713-finland-v2.pdf

Rappleye, J. (2006). Theorizing educational transfer: Toward a conceptual map of the context of cross-national attraction. *Research in Comparative and International Education, 1,* 223–240.

Riley, K., & Torrance, H. (2003). Big change question: As national policy-makers seek to find solutions to National education issues, do international comparisons such as TIMSS and PISA create a wider understanding, or do they serve to promote the orthodoxies of international agencies? *Journal of Educational Change, 4*(4), 419–425.

Rinne, R., Kivirauma, J., & Simola, H. (2002). Shoots of revisionist education policy or just slow readjustment? The Finnish case of educational reconstruction. *Journal of Education Policy, 17*(6), 634–658.

Rizvi, F., & Lingard, B. (2000). Globalization and education: Complexities and contingencies. *Educational Theory, 50*(4), 419–426.

Rowan, B., Bossert, S. T., & Dwyer, D. C. (1983). Research on effective schools: A cautionary note. *Educational Researcher, 12*(4), 24–31.

Rutter, M., & Maughan, B. (2002). School effectiveness findings 1979–2002. *Journal of School Psychology, 40*(6), 451–475.

Saari, J. (1944). Finnish nationalism justifying independence. *Annals of the American Academy of Political and Social Science, 232*, 33–38.

Sahlberg, P. (2007). Education policies for raising student learning: The Finnish approach. *Journal of Education Policy, 22*(2), 147–171.

Sahlberg, P. (2011). The fourth way of Finland. *Journal of Educational Change, 12*, 173–185.

Sammons, P. (2006). The contribution of international educational effectiveness: Current and future directions. *Educational Research and Evaluation, 12*(6), 583–593.

Sammons, P., Hillman, J., & Mortimore, P. (1995). *Key characteristics of effective schools: A review of school effectiveness research.* London: Institute of Education, University of London.

Schagen, I., & Hutchinson, D. (2007). Comparisons between PISA and TIMSS – We could be the man with two watches. *Education Journal, 101*, 34–35.

Seppänen, P. (2003). Patterns of 'public-school markets' in the Finnish comprehensive school from a comparative perspective. *Journal of Education Policy, 18*(5), 513–531.

Siikala, J. (2006). The ethnography of Finland. *Annual Review of Anthropology, 35*, 153–170.

Simola, H. (2005). The Finnish miracle of PISA: Historical and sociological remarks on teaching and teacher eduaction. *Comparative Education, 41*(4), 455–470.

Simola, H., Rinne, R., & Kivirauma, J. (2002). Abdication of the education state or just shifting responsibilities? The appearance of a new system of reason in constructing educational governance and social exclusion/inclusion in Finland. *Scandinavian Journal for Educational Research, 46*(3), 247–264.

Simola, H., Rinne, R., Varjo, J., Pitkänen, H., & Kauko, J. (2009). Quality Assurance and Evaluation (QAE) in Finnish compulslry schooling: A national model or just unintended effects of radical decentralisation? *Journal of Education Policy, 24*(2), 163–178.

Singleton, F. (1989). *A short history of Finland.* Cambridge: Cambridge University Press.

Sisu Group. (n.d.). *What is Sisu? Sisu is a unique Finnish concept.* Retrieved February 8, 2008, from http://www.sisugrp.com/sisuis.htm

Suolahti, E. E. (1960). Cultural relations. In U. Toivola (Ed.), *Introduction to Finland 1960* (pp. 196–202). Helsinki: Werner Söderström Osakeythiö.

REFERENCES

Takayama, K. (2008). The politics of international league tables: PISA in Japan's achievement crisis debate. *Comparative Education, 44*(4), 387–407.

Takayama, K. (2009). Politics of externalization in reflexive times: Reinventing Japanese education reform discourses through "Finnish PISA success." *Comparative Education Review, 54*(1), 51–75.

Tani, S. (2004). Curriculum reform and primary geography in Finland: A gap between theory and practice. *International Research in Geographical and Environmental Education, 13*(1), 6–20.

The race is not always to the richest. (2007, December 6). *The Economist.* Retrieved January 16, 2008, from http://www.economist.com/world/international/displaystory.cfm?story_id=10251324

The war in Lapland. (n.d.). Retrieved November 5, 2008, from http://www.rajajoki.com/lapland.htm

Thomas, B. (2006, March 26). *The Finnish line.* Retrieved November 5, 2008, from http://www.washingtonpost.com/wp-dyn/content/article/2006/03/22/AR2006032201943.html

TIMSS and PIRLS International Study Center. (n.d.). Retrieved November 5, 2008, from http://www.timss.org/

Tobin, J., Hsueh, Y., & Karasawa, M. (2009). *Preschool in three cultures revisited: China, Japan, and the United States.* London: University of Chicago Press.

Training and Development Agency for Schools (TDA). (2010a). *Annual report and accounts 2009–10.* London: TSO.

Training and Development Agency for Schools (TDA). (2010b). *The master's in teaching and learning participant handbook.* London: TSO.

Välijärvi, J., Linnakylä, P., Kupari, P., Renikainen, P., Arffman, I. (2002). *The Finnish success in PISA – And some reasons behind it: PISA 2000.* Jyväskylä: Jyväskylä University Institution for Educational Research.

Välijärvi, J., Linnakylä, P., Kupari, P., Renikainen, P., Sulkunen, S., Törnroos, J., & Arffman, I. (2007). *The Finnish success in PISA – And some reasons behind it 2: PISA 2003.* Jyväskylä: Jyväskylä University Institution for Educational Research.

Viltanen, N., & Peltonen, M. (2008, February 15). *Children with immigrant backgrounds do not explain PISA success.* Retrieved February 22, 2008, from http://www.helsinki.fi/news/archive/2-2008/15-16-16-06.html

Vulliamy, G. (2004). The impact of globalisation on qualitative research in comparative and international education. *Compare, 34*(3), 261–284.

Waldow, F. (2008). Economic cycles or international reform models? Explaining transformations of the educational policy-making discourse in Sweden, 1930–2000. *Scandinavian Journal of Educational Research, 52*(3), 243–258.

Webb, R., & Vulliamy, G. (1999). Changing times, changing demands: A comparative analysis of classroom practice in primary schools in England and Finland. *Research Papers in Education, 14*(3), 229–255.

Webb, R., Vulliamy, G., Häkkinen, K., & Hämäläinen, S. (1998). External inspection of school self-evaluation? A comparative analysis of policy and practice in primary schools in England and Finland. *British Educational Research Journal, 24*(5), 539–556.

Webb, R., Vulliamy, G., Hämäläinen, S., Sarja, A., Kimonen, E., & Nevalainen, R. (2004). A comparative analysis of primary teacher professionalism in England and Finland. *Comparative Education, 40*(1), 83–107.

Webb, R., Vulliamy, G., Sarja, A., Hämäläinen, S., & Poikonen, P. (2009). Professional learning communities and teacher well-being? A comparative analysis of primary schools in England and Finland. *Oxford Review of Education, 35*(3), 405–422.

West, A., & Ylönen, A. (2010). Market-oriented school reform in England and Finland: School choice, Finance and governance. *Educational Studies, 36*(1), 1–12.

Whitehurst, G. J. (2002, March 5). *Scientifically based research on teacher quality: Research on teacher preparation and professional development*. White House Conference on Preparing Tomorrow's Teachers. Retrieved January 30, 2016 from http://www.stcloudstate.edu/tpi/initiative/documents/assesment/Scientifically%20 Based%20Research%20on%20Teacher%20Quality.pdf

Whittaker, D. J. (1983). Ten years on: Progress and problems in Finland's school reform. *Comparative Education, 19*(1), 31–41.

Willms, J. D. (2003). *Student engagement at school: A sense of belonging and participation. Results from PISA 2002*. Paris: OECD.

Yore, L. D., Anderson, J. O., & Chiu, M.-H. (2010). Moving PISA results into the policy arena: Perspectives on knowledge transfer for future considerations and preparations. *International Journal of Science and Mathematics Education, 8*, 593–609.

Index

assessment   xi, 1–3, 5, 6, 9–12, 14, 15, 22, 25, 59, 61–63, 68, 73, 75–90, 100, 104, 105, 124, 126, 129, 141, 147, 148, 157–159, 161, 163, 166–176, 183, 189, 198, 211–213, 217, 220

comprehensive school   2, 35, 54, 56, 58, 60, 67, 70, 71, 73, 99, 101, 112, 118, 133, 141, 149, 161, 170, 201, 202
context   xi, 1, 3–49, 56, 59, 67, 74–76, 78, 80, 86–97, 102–106, 118, 129, 134, 135, 146, 148, 175, 178, 182, 185, 189, 190, 192–196, 200–203, 205, 206, 209–211, 213, 216
cross-national attraction   3, 90, 92, 95, 96–105, 177–193, 199, 200, 213

education minister   2, 4, 14, 80, 107, 115, 139, 148, 156, 177–178, 190, 192, 197, 220,
education policy   xi, 1, 3–23, 88, 91, 93–96, 100, 104, 106, 119, 148, 153, 164, 174, 177–198, 200–211, 213–217, 220

Finland   xi, 1–5, 11, 18, 24–75, 85, 87, 89–92, 99–103, 105–145, 147–155, 156, 158–170, 173, 175–194, 196, 197, 199–217
Finnish   xi, 1–5, 24–44, 46–74, 85, 88, 90, 97, 99, 100, 102, 103, 105–189, 191–193, 196, 197, 199–211, 213–216

global   xi, 1, 3, 4, 6–23, 35, 75, 77, 90, 99, 102, 106, 129, 147, 171, 174, 177, 198, 199, 206, 207, 212–214, 216, 217, 221
globalisation   xi, 7, 9–17, 19, 20, 22, 46, 80, 96, 104, 105, 156, 198–200, 214, 216

head teacher   5, 70, 71, 73, 81, 83, 106, 112, 118–121, 130, 131, 135–137, 140, 145, 147–151, 153, 158, 159, 164, 173–175, 177–181, 184, 190, 192, 204, 220
history   3–5, 24–29, 36, 38, 42–44, 46, 47, 49, 54, 65, 67, 93, 101, 115–118, 120, 128, 129, 188, 191, 192, 220

international achievement studies, 1, 4, 6, 7, 10–11, 16, 18, 19, 20, 22, 23, 90, 96, 102, 104, 106, 153, 163, 194, 197, 200, 209–211

International Association for the Evaluation of Educational Achievement (IEA)   1, 6, 75, 76, 79, 85, 90, 147, 152, 153, 168–172, 176, 197, 211

league table   xi, 2, 5, 8, 14, 16, 23, 63, 84, 86, 88, 100, 124, 129, 194, 198, 202, 207, 210, 212, 213, 216, 217

Master's in Teaching and Learning (MTL)   12, 103, 200–203, 205, 208, 210
measurement   9, 11, 15–18, 76, 84, 87, 101, 126–127, 129, 147–150, 161, 163, 164, 168, 175, 194, 197, 198, 206
mixed-ability   130–137, 145, 146

national character   91, 92, 177, 190–193
national core curriculum   57, 59–62, 64, 162, 201
national curriculum   55, 57, 59–61, 63, 64, 98, 113, 120, 126–127, 129, 167, 175, 191, 201
negative external evaluation   94, 95, 97, 100–102, 105, 166, 176, 186, 187, 197, 200, 201, 210
Nordic   4, 32, 33, 36, 39, 40, 43–47, 51, 54, 56, 68, 74, 75, 111, 116, 128, 129, 133, 155, 160, 161, 170, 171, 182, 186, 188, 191, 198, 202

Organisation for Economic Cooperation and Development (OECD)   xi, 1, 4–6, 8, 9, 12–18, 22, 23, 32, 34–36, 40, 41, 56, 58, 75–84, 87–90, 93, 94, 96, 100, 101, 106, 111, 114, 122, 123, 127–130, 147, 150, 152, 154–158, 160, 161, 163, 165, 171, 172, 174–177, 186–190, 192–194, 196–198, 206, 208, 209, 211, 214, 216, 217, 221
outcome   2–4, 10, 14, 16, 18, 24, 46, 49, 56, 73, 74, 76, 79, 83, 85, 86, 88, 101, 102, 106–108, 113, 114, 116, 118, 124, 127, 135, 141, 150, 152, 155, 156, 159, 161, 163–167, 176, 180, 186, 187, 193, 196, 197, 201, 208, 209, 211

policy   xi, 2–4, 6–23, 28, 30–32, 39, 40, 43, 44, 49, 65, 79–81, 84, 88, 89, 91–106, 119, 148, 153, 164, 174, 177–198, 200–211, 213–217, 220, 221

policy borrowing   4, 11, 19, 20, 21, 23, 79, 91–96, 99, 102–106, 177, 181, 184, 185, 188, 191, 193–196, 199, 200–206, 209, 210, 212, 213, 215
policy maker   xi, 7, 11, 12, 16, 18, 21, 81, 88, 93, 94, 99, 102, 104, 110, 145, 149, 153, 154, 158, 164, 169, 172, 179, 184, 190, 195, 198, 210, 213, 215–217
policy transfer   xi, 1, 3–5, 8, 9, 11, 12, 23, 91–105, 123, 155, 177–196, 199, 200, 205–207, 209, 211, 213, 216, 217
politicisation   3–5, 11–17, 19, 21, 23, 88, 104, 196–200, 209–211, 213, 216
Programme for International Student Assessment (PISA)   xi, 1–6, 8–18, 21–24, 46–48, 52, 53, 58, 62, 67, 72–91, 95, 96, 99–103, 105–108, 111, 113–121, 123–131, 135, 136, 138–141, 144–189, 191–217, 221

teacher   4–7, 38, 51, 56, 58, 59, 61–64, 67–74, 81, 83, 98, 99, 100, 103, 106–125, 127–143, 145–153, 158–161, 164, 165, 167, 168, 171, 173–175, 177–184, 188, 190, 192, 193, 200–208, 210, 211, 215, 219, 220
teacher education   4, 51, 63, 67–74, 107–110, 123, 127, 130, 140, 148, 151–153, 203–208, 210, 211, 220
teacher training   64, 68–71, 73, 107–109, 111, 115, 123, 152, 153, 204, 208

uncritical   xi, 3, 11, 18, 194–217

vocational school   61, 64, 112, 141, 161

white paper   203–206, 208, 210, 211

Printed in the United States
By Bookmasters